REPORT

UPON THE

CENSUS OF RHODE ISLAND,

1865;

WITH THE STATISTICS OF THE POPULATION, AGRICULTURE, FISHERIES AND MANUFACTURES OF THE STATE.

Prepared under the Direction of the Secretary of State,

BY

EDWIN M. SNOW, M. D.,
SUPERINTENDENT OF THE CENSUS.

PROVIDENCE:
PROVIDENCE PRESS COMPANY, STATE PRINTERS.
1867.

Office of the Secretary of State,
Providence, February 20, 1867.

To the Honorable the General Assembly of the State of Rhode Island:

Gentlemen: — At the session of the General Assembly in January, 1865, an act was passed providing for the taking of a decennial census of the inhabitants of the State; and at the May session following, an additional act was passed, requiring the statistics of the manufactures, business and agriculture of the State to be taken at the same time.

The acts alluded to, direct the Secretary of State, with the advice of the Governor, to provide such blanks for the returns of the census and statistics as they may deem necessary, and to employ the requisite agents to perform the several duties required by the acts in question.

No time was lost in making the preliminary arrangements for this important work, and the State was fortunate in securing the services of Dr. Edwin M. Snow, of Providence, a gentleman whose experience and high reputation as a statistician is not surpassed, if equalled, by that of any one in the United States. This gentleman was therefore made Superintendent of the Census, with full power to prepare such printed blanks and to adopt such plans as would ensure the careful collection of the facts contemplated by the act; to condense and tabulate them; to accompany them with such remarks, in the form of a report, as would elucidate and render them most useful, and to superintend their publication.

All this work has been performed in the most satisfactory manner, and the printed abstract will be found to contain many more particulars relating to the population of the State, the statistics of its manufactures, business, and agriculture, than have ever before been brought together, in relation to this State, and upon some subjects, more than have ever been collected by any State in the Union.

The report of Dr. Snow is herewith respectfully submitted.

JOHN R. BARTLETT,
Secretary of State.

CONTENTS.

PART I.

REPORT ---- ix—cxii

Introductory ---- ix

State bureau of statistics ---- xi

Plan of this report ---- xiii

I. THE STATE OF RHODE ISLAND AS IT IS ---- xv—xxiv

Natural features of the State ---- xv

Density of population in each town, (TABLE) ---- xvi

Density compared with other States ---- xvii

Villages and post offices in Rhode Island, (TABLE) ---- xix

II. POLITICAL DIVISIONS AND PREVIOUS CENSUSES ---- xxiv—xlvii

County divisions, History of ---- xxv

Counties and towns, with date of incorporation, from what taken, original names, changes of boundaries, &c., (TABLE) ---- xxvii

PREVIOUS censuses, with population of each town, (TABLE) ---- xxxii

Notes upon table of previous censuses ---- xxxiv

Rate per cent. of increase or decrease of population of each town in Rhode Island, 1748 to 1865, (TABLE) ---- xxxvi

Remarks upon changes of population at different periods ---- xxxviii

Censuses of Providence ---- xlii

COLORED population of Rhode Island ---- xlii

Colored persons and Indians in each town in the State, at different dates, 1730 to 1865, (TABLE) ---- xliv

Percentage of colored persons at different periods ---- xlvi

The colored race not self sustaining in New England ---- xlvii

III. COMMENTS UPON THE TABLES ---- xlviii—cxii

1. COMMENTS UPON THE TABLES OF POPULATION ---- xlviii

Dwelling houses and families ---- xlviii

Sex and color of the population ---- l

NATIVITY ---- l

Migration of population within the State ---- lii

Natives of other States living in Rhode Island ---- liii

Natives of Rhode Island in other States ---- liv

FOREIGNERS by birth, in Rhode Island ---- liv

Percentage of foreigners at different dates ---- lv

Remarks on the subject of nativity of the population ---- lv

Serious defect in censuses in this country ---- lvii

Nativity alone, in censuses, worse than useless ---- lvii

Parentage of population important ---- lix
NATIVITY and parentage of population of Rhode Island ---- lix
Persons of mixed parentage ---- lix
Percentages by nativity and by parentage, in Providence ---- lx
Remarks on decrease of native American population in New England ---- lxi
Sex, by nativity and parentage in Providence ---- lxii
AGE and sex ---- lxiii
Proportions of the sexes at different ages in Rhode Island, (TABLE) ---- lxv
Proportions of total population at different ages in different countries, (TABLE) ---- lxvi
DEPENDENT and productive classes, (COMPARATIVE TABLE) ---- lxvii
Age and parentage in Providence ---- lxviii
List of persons in each town, ninety years of age and over, (TABLE) ---- lxix
Education, and absence from school ---- lxxii
Improvement in Providence ---- lxxiii
IGNORANCE, cannot read and write ---- lxxiv
Proportion of ignorance in classes of the population ---- lxxvi
Relative proportions in different classes ---- lxxviii
Want of education in Providence, 1855 and 1865 ---- lxxix
Number who sign marriage certificates with a mark ---- lxxx
Conclusions in relation to ignorance ---- lxxxi
DEAF and dumb, blind, insane, &c ---- lxxxi
NATURALIZED voters in Rhode Island ---- lxxxii
MILITARY and naval service ---- lxxxiii
Proportions furnished the army and navy in the several counties ---- lxxxiv
OCCUPATIONS of the population, 1860 and 1865, (TABLE) ---- lxxxiv
2 COMMENTS UPON THE TABLES OF AGRICULTURAL STATISTICS ---- lxxxvi
Products of agriculture in Rhode Island, 1850, 1860 and 1865, (TABLE) ---- lxxxvii
General results obtained, valuable ---- lxxxix
Total value of agricultural investments and products, for the year ---- xc
Average yield per acre in Rhode Island, of several crops ---- xc
Average yield per acre greater in Rhode Island than at the West ---- xci
3. COMMENTS UPON THE TABLES OF FISHERIES AND SHORE STATISTICS ---- xcii
Statistics of fisheries, &c., in the State, 1860 and 1865, (TABLE) ---- xciii
Importance of the fisheries in Rhode Island ---- xciv
4. COMMENTS UPON THE TABLES OF MANUFACTURES ---- xcv
Manufactures in Rhode Island for the year ending June 1, 1865, (TABLE) ---- xcvii
Cotton manufactures in Rhode Island, (TABLE) ---- xcix
Woolen manufactures, (TABLE) ---- c
Iron manufactures, (TABLE) ---- ci
Statistics of manufactures, by counties, 1860 and 1865, (TABLE) ---- cii
PRODUCTS of manufactures in the State, one year, (TABLE) ---- ciii
Substances used in manufactures, (TABLE) ---- cv
DAILY products in Rhode Island, (TABLE) ---- cv
Spindles and looms in use ---- cvi
POWER used in manufactures ---- cvii
Kind of power used in each town, (TABLE) ---- cviii
Importance of manufactures in Rhode Island ---- cix
Importance of full and correct statistics ---- cx
Conclusion, recapitulatory ---- cxi

PART II.

TABULAR STATISTICS .... 1—98

1. TABLES OF POPULATION .... 1—52

TABLE I. Showing the population, number of dwelling houses, number of families to each dwelling, and number of persons to each dwelling and each family, in each town of the State 2

TABLE II.—SEX AND COLOR. Showing the sex and color of the population in each town, and division of the State 3

TABLE III. Showing the particulars of tables I and II, in the cities of Providence and Newport, by wards 4

TABLE IV.—NATIVITY. Showing in general terms the birth places of the population 5

TABLE V.—NATIVITY. Showing how many of the inhabitants of each town were born in each town and county in Rhode Island .... 6—9

TABLE VI.—NATIVITY. Showing how many of the inhabitants of each town and county of the State were born in each of the United States .... 10—12

TABLE VII.—NATIVITY. Showing how many of the inhabitants of each town in the State were born in each foreign country .... 13—15

TABLE VIII.—NATIVITY. Showing the particulars of table IV in the cities of Providence and Newport, by wards 16

TABLE IX.—NATIVITY. Being table V for the city of Providence, by wards; showing how many of the inhabitants of each ward, in the city of Providence, were born in each town and county in Rhode Island 17

TABLE X.—NATIVITY. Being table V for the city of Newport, by wards; showing how many of the inhabitants of each ward in the city of Newport, were born in each town and county in Rhode Island 18

TABLE XI.—NATIVITY. Being table VI for the city of Providence, by wards; showing how many of the inhabitants of each ward in the city of Providence, were born in each of the United States 19

TABLE XII.—NATIVITY. Being table VI for the city of Newport, by wards; showing how many of the inhabitants of each ward in the city of Newport, were born in each of the United States 20

TABLE XIII.—NATIVITY. Showing the particulars of table VII in the city of Providence, by wards; showing how many of the inhabitants of each ward in the city of Providence were born in each foreign country 21

TABLE XIV.—NATIVITY. Showing the particulars of table VII in the city of Newport, by wards; showing how many of the inhabitants in each ward of the city of Newport were born in each foreign country 22

TABLE XV.—PARENTAGE. Showing the parentage of the population in each town and county in the State .... 23—24

TABLE XVI.—PARENTAGE. Being table XV for Providence and Newport, by wards; showing the parentage of the population in each ward 25

TABLE XVII.—NATIVITY AND PARENTAGE COMPARED. Showing the number and proportions of the population by nativity and by parentage in each town in the State. Mixed parentage given according to the birth-place of the fathers 26

TABLE XVIII.—NATIVITY AND PARENTAGE COMPARED. Being table XVII for for the cities of Providence and Newport, by wards. Those of mixed parentage according to birth-place of their fathers 27

TABLE XIX.—SEX OF FOREIGN BORN. Showing the sex of the population of foreign birth in each ward of the city of Providence 28

TABLE XX.—SEX AND PARENTAGE. Showing the parentage and sex of the whole population in each ward of the city of Providence 28

TABLE XXI.—AGE AND SEX. Showing the number of each sex, in each division of ages, in each town and county in Rhode Island, and in Providence and Newport, by wards .... 29—37

TABLE XXII.—AGE AND PARENTAGE. Showing the number of American, and of foreign parentage, in each division of ages, in each ward of the city of Providence; those of mixed parentage being placed according to the birth-place of their fathers 38

TABLE XXIII.—ATTENDING SCHOOL. Showing the population in each town between the ages of 5 and 15, and the number of all ages who attended public, select, or catholic schools, in each town, during the year ending June 1, 1865 39

TABLE XXIV.—ATTENDING SCHOOL. Being table XXIII for the cities of Providence and Newport, by wards 40

TABLE XXV. Showing the number of deaf and dumb, blind, insane, idiotic, paupers, and convicts, in each town in the State 41

TABLE XXVI.—WANT OF EDUCATION. Showing how many persons in each town in the State, of the age of 15 years and over, can neither read nor write, and how many can read but cannot write; the statistics according to parentage ..... 42—43

TABLE XXVII.—WANT OF EDUCATION. Being table XXVI, for the cities of Providence and Newport, by wards 44

TABLE XXVIII.—NATURALIZED VOTERS. Showing how many natives of foreign countries have become voters under the laws of Rhode Island, in each town and county in the State 45

TABLE XXIX.—NATURALIZED VOTERS. Being table XXVIII for the cities of Providence and Newport, by wards 46

TABLE XXX. MILITARY AND NAVAL SERVICE. Showing how many of the inhabitants of each town in the State, who were living on the first day of June, 1865, were at that time, or had been since 1860, in the military or naval service of the United States 47

TABLE XXXI.—MILITARY AND NAVAL SERVICE. Showing how many of the inhabitants of each county in Rhode Island, who were living June 1, 1865, were at that time, or had been since 1860, in the military or naval service of the United States: and also showing the States in which they enlisted 48

TABLE XXXII.—OCCUPATIONS. Showing the occupations of persons of 15 years and over, as reported in the census of the population in the whole State ..... 49—51

2. TABLES OF AGRICULTURAL STATISTICS ..... 53—64

TABLE XXXIII.—AGRICULTURAL STATISTICS of the State of Rhode Island, census of June 1, 1865 54

TABLE XXXIV.—AGRICULTURAL STATISTICS. Showing the number and size of the farms in each town and county of Rhode Island 61

Additional agricultural statistics, (TABLES) 62

3. TABLES OF FISHERIES AND SHORE STATISTICS ..... 65—70

TABLE XXXV.—FISHERIES AND SHORE STATISTICS. Showing the statistics in Rhode Island for the year ending June 1, 1865 66

4. TABLES OF STATISTICS OF MANUFACTURES ..... 71—98

Statistics of manufactures in the State, alphabetically arranged ..... 72—95

Additional manufactures 96

TABLE XXXVI.—MANUFACTURES. Showing the statistics of manufactures in each town and city in Rhode Island, for the year ending June 1, 1865 97

APPENDIX ..... 99—112

Census acts of the General Assembly in 1865 100

Blank used for statistics of population 103

Blank used for agricultural statistics 104

Blank used for fisheries and shore statistics 105

Blank used for statistics of manufactures 106

Instructions issued for census of 1865 107

CENSUS

OF

RHODE ISLAND.

JUNE 1, 1865.

REPORT.

THE present volume contains the results obtained by the Census of Rhode Island; the statistics of population being for the first day of June, 1865, and those of agriculture, fisheries, and manufactures, for the year ending at that date.

The census was taken in pursuance of an Act of the General Assembly passed March 17, 1865, and of an "Act in Amendment of and in Addition" thereto, passed on the 10th of June of the same year. These Acts, copies of which are given in the Appendix, provide for taking a census of the inhabitants, and also the statistics of the manufactures, business, and agriculture of the State, on the 1st day of June, 1865, and every tenth year thereafter.

The late period at which these Acts of the General Assembly were passed, and the amendments and additions provided in the second Act, caused much delay in the preparation of the blanks, and also in obtaining the statistics, and in preparing the tables from them, which rendered it impossible to complete the final report at the time required by law. The delay has, however, given an opportunity to make the tables much more full and complete than they would otherwise have been.

At the January session, (1866,) of the General Assembly, a partial report was presented, containing the statistics of the population, agriculture, and fisheries of the State. Since that time, the statistics of manufactures have been prepared and printed, and are given in the present volume, together with the statistics already presented in the partial report. A copy of the returns of the census of the population of each town and city, has been deposited in the office of the Secretary of State, and has been bound in suitable volumes. These volumes contain the name and other particulars, of every man, woman, and child living in the State on the 1st day of June, 1865; and also the names of those belonging in the State, who were absent at that date, in the Army or in the Navy of the United States, or elsewhere. The original returns of the census of population are deposited in the clerks' offices of the several towns and cities, and it is presumed that each town will have them suitably bound for preservation and for reference.

As the preparation of the blanks for the census was not commenced until nearly the date at which the statistics were to be obtained, it was impossible to give them as much thought and study as was desirable. An examination of the tables given in this volume, in connection with the explanations and comments upon them, will show, however, that an immense amount of information was obtained by the census, and that, in many important particulars, it was more full and complete than any United States census ever taken in this State. A description of the blanks used, and a copy of the "Instructions" accompanying them will be found in the Appendix to this volume.*

The Acts of the General Assembly under which the present census was taken, make provision for collecting many other facts which it was impossible to obtain on account of the late date at which the work was commenced. It is obvious that a complete statement of all the resources and capabilities of the State would be extremely interesting to our citizens, and of great value and constant utility to the legislative, as well as other departments of the government. Such a statement would contain a multitude of facts which will not be found in this volume. Among them would be the statistics of commerce and trade; the value of real and personal estate, and rate of

---

* In this connection, I wish to acknowledge my indebtedness to the Superintendent of the Census of the State of New York, Dr. Franklin B. Hough of Albany, for many valuable hints. His report on the census of that State, in 1855, was probably the most complete work of the kind ever published in this country, and that upon the census of 1865, judging from the blanks used, and from the plan proposed, will be still more complete and perfect.

taxation in each town; the statistics of education; the religious statistics; the statistics of pauperism, insanity, &c., &c.; all of which, and many more, are not only desirable, but are, in a measure, absolutely necessary for a full understanding of the interests of the State, and for intelligent legislation in relation to them.

As the Census Acts of the General Assembly provide for a census of the State in 1875, and every tenth year thereafter, there will be abundant time and opportunity in future, to make arrangements for obtaining all the information that is desired, and for its prompt publication.

BUREAU OF STATISTICS.

But the question arises, and is worthy the consideration of the General Assembly, whether a decennial census is sufficient to meet the wants of the State. A census taken only once in ten years, must from necessity be taken under the direction of inexperienced persons, and of persons who have no opportunity to investigate the subject, and devise the best plan for the blanks, or the best system of doing the work. Everything will be done without plan or system, and in the most disadvantageous manner. No two censuses will correspond with each other in the kind, or amount, or completeness, of the information obtained.

Besides this, a decennial census may, from accidental circumstances, fail entirely to give any correct idea of very many of the statistics desired to be obtained. For example; the statistics of no single year can show truly the facts for a series of years, in relation to manufactures, agriculture, trade, commerce, and many other subjects. It is desirable and necessary for the interests of the State, that these statistics and many others, should be obtained and published as often as every year.

Again, a census taken in the manner it is usually taken, and at such long intervals, is not the best method of obtaining the facts desired. I have no doubt that all the facts obtained by a decennial census and many more, excepting those relating to the population, could be obtained far more correctly every year, and with slightly if any additional expense, by other methods. Experience, in this State as well as in other States, in connection with vital statistics, has shown the great value of establishing the habit among the people of giving and collecting statistical information. The vital statistics of the State are constantly improving, from year to year, and now, tens of thousands of our people feel an interest in the subject, and are desirous that the facts relating to their families should be fully recorded. The importance and value of these records have been fully shown, particularly during the last five years. The information they have furnished, in connection with claims against the general government, has saved the people of the State, many times more than the expense of making the records.

Similar results would follow from the frequent collection and publication of other statistical information. The people would soon understand the subject better; doubts would be removed; an interest in such information would be created; and our citizens, being convinced that no improper use would be made of the facts, would become desirous that full particulars should be obtained.

I conceive it, then, to be a necessity, and a necessity which will soon be acknowledged and acted upon, that in this State, as well as in other States, and in the General Government, Bureaus of Statistics should be established, which should have the charge of the collection, collation, and publication of all kinds of statistical information.

The limited extent, and internal geographical and political divisions of our State are extremely favorable for the easy collection of this information. A suitable person, authorized by the State, would be able, through the authorities of the several towns, by correspondence, and otherwise, to collect a great amount of valuable information, annually, at a comparatively slight expense. The same person might have the charge of the preparation and publication of the Registration Reports, and of the decennial census. By his acquired knowledge and experience, and by correspondence with other States, and with the officers of the general government, he would soon be able to introduce order, system, and economy in the collection of the statistics of the State, and to produce reports which would be of great value to its legislators, to its citizens, and to the country. The subject is commended to the consideration of the General Assembly.*

---

*Since the preceding remarks were written, I have noticed the following, from the Report on the United States Census for 1850, which is specially pertinent to the subject, and confirmatory of what I have written:

"The present Census system of the United States is, in many respects, defective. It is very difficult to obtain, upon short notice, and for a brief period, able statistical talent in Washington. By the time an office has acquired experience, it is disbanded.

PLAN OF THIS REPORT.

In preparing the blanks for taking the census of 1865, I have not copied those of any other census ever taken; but have provided for obtaining all the information usually obtained by the national censuses of the State, and have added other items which seemed to be important. A reference to the tables will show in some particulars, a more complete analysis of the population of the State than was ever before obtained, and in relation to some points, information will be found which is not given in any census of any State, ever published.

This being the case, a complete comparison on all points of this census with any other, is impossible. I have, therefore, thought it best not to attempt a comparison of particulars obtained, with those of the previous national censuses of the State.

As this is the first complete census ever taken and published by the State, it seemed to be better to adopt a plan more with reference to the future than the past.

I propose, then, in this Report, to omit any extended comparisons of the facts obtained with those of past dates, and to confine myself, as briefly as possible, to general remarks and explanations of the census of 1865; to give as clear a view as possible of the present

---

The persons selected as enumerators are often proved, by the returns, to be entirely incompetent, for which, perhaps, the low rate of compensation or the mode of appointment may be assigned as reasons. The districts embraced by each enumerator are too large; if practicable for accuracy, they should be as small as the districts in Great Britain. In this case, the permanent State and county officers ought to form a part of the machinery. It would be well for Congress to recommend the establishment of State Bureaus of Statistics, and rely upon them for all other information than the decennial enumerations of the people. These State Institutions, adopting the machinery at present in operation for assessment purposes, might greatly economize the expense; and, upon condition of their collecting information according to certain forms to be prescribed by the Federal Government, be aided in some shape from the treasury, or at least their reports, annually or biennially, might be condensed and published with those of the Departments at Washington. The reports of foreign consuls could be embraced in the same volume. Information of this sort is indispensable to the National Legislature, and is every day called for in its deliberations. The States would very soon adopt the suggestion, and a beginning is recommended with such as first adopt it."

I may add that in taking the census of Providence, in 1865, I divided the city into small districts, and employed twenty-eight enumerators, all that could be obtained upon short notice. The result was in the highest degree satisfactory. The whole enumeration of the population of the city was completed in about two weeks, and in a much better manner than it is usually done.

condition of the State, and to explain the nature and importance of the facts obtained by the census, and which are given in the tabular portion of the present volume.

This report will be divided into three parts as follows:

I. THE STATE OF RHODE ISLAND AS IT IS. Its natural physical characteristics, area, density of population, and villages.

II. POLITICAL DIVISIONS AND PREVIOUS CENSUSES OF THE STATE.

III. COMMENTS UPON THE TABLES.

1. *Remarks on Tables of Population.*
2. *Agricultural Statistics.*
3. *Fisheries.*
4. *Manufactures.*

In the first part, a table will begin, showing the population, area, and density of population of each town and county in the State; and also a list of the villages in the State, with their population.

In the second part, a table will be given, showing the date of incorporation or settlement of each town, with other information relating to their history; also tables showing the total population, the number of blacks and Indians, and the percentage of increase or decrease of the total population of each town, according to the previous censuses of the State, from 1708 to 1865, inclusive. The past and present condition, and future prospects of the colored population in Rhode Island, are discussed in this part of the report.

In the third part, the sex, ages, birthplaces, parentage, and other classifications of the population are considered; and various tables illustrating the subject are given. Tables and comparisons are also given to illustrate and explain the value of the statistics of agriculture, fisheries, and manufactures in Rhode Island.

I. THE STATE OF RHODE ISLAND.

NATURAL FEATURES.

Rhode Island is the smallest State in the Union, being only about 50 miles in length, and 35 in width. Though its area is limited, it has a great diversity of soil and even of climate. In some parts it is quite hilly, though not mountainous, in others it is level; in some parts the soil is heavy and wet, in others it is sandy and dry. The winters are tempered by the abundance of salt water, and are milder than in the same latitude farther inland.

The State is divided into two unequal parts by Narragansett Bay, which extends inland about 30 miles from the ocean. Five of the thirty-three towns in the State are situated on islands. Though the coast line of the State is only about 45 miles, the Narragansett Bay, with its numerous arms and islands, gives about 350 miles of shore washed by tide water, to the State.

There are numerous fresh water ponds in the State, and in the southern part there are many extensive ponds of salt water.

The State is divided into five counties, and these contain thirty-three towns. The towns are extremely irregular in shape, and there is a great difference in their size. The smallest town in area, is Warren, which has only 4.7 square miles. The largest town, South Kingstown, is more than sixteen times larger than Warren, and has 77.9 square miles. The average for the whole State is about 32 square miles to each town.

The whole area of the State is 1054.6 square miles. This is obtained from Walling's map of the State, and is undoubtedly very nearly correct. The area usually given in geographies and gazetteers is 250 to 300 miles greater, and probably includes the waters of Narragansett Bay.

The total population of the State, in 1865, was 184,965, which gives 175.4 inhabitants to each square mile, a density of population considerably greater than that of any other of the United States.

A table on the next page shows the population of each town, by the census of 1865, the area in square miles of each town, and the number of persons living to each square mile of area in each town and county, and in the whole State.

TABLE.—*Density of population in Rhode Island*, 1865.

TOWNS AND DIVISIONS OF THE STATE.	Population in 1865.	Area in Square Miles.	Persons to each Square Mile.
Barrington	1,028	9.3	110.5
Bristol	4,649	10.3	451.3
Warren	2,792	4.7	594.0
BRISTOL COUNTY	8,469	24.3	348.5
Coventry	3,995	58.6	68.2
East Greenwich	2,400	17.1	140.3
West Greenwich	1,228	49.1	25.0
Warwick	7,696	44.2	174.1
KENT COUNTY	15,319	169.0	90 6
Jamestown	349	9.5	36.7
Little Compton	1,197	21.4	55.9
Middletown	1,019	12.5	81.5
Newport	12,688	7.0	1812.6
New Shoreham	1,308	10.5	124.5
Portsmouth	2,153	23.4	92.0
Tiverton	1,973	31.8	62.0
NEWPORT COUNTY	20,687	116.1	178.2
Burrillville	4,861	53.2	91.3
Cranston	9,177	33.7	272.3
Cumberland	8,216	33.6	244.5
East Providence	2,172	12.5	173.7
Foster	1,873	48.8	38.3
Glocester	2,286	53.2	42.9
Johnston	3,436	24.1	142.5
North Providence	14,553	15.0	970.2
Pawtucket	5,000	6.9	724.6
Scituate	3,538	52.3	67.6
Smithfield	12,315	73.3	168.0
TOWNS PROVIDENCE COUNTY	67,427	406.6	165.8
PROVIDENCE CITY	54,595	6.7	8148.5
Charlestown	1,134	39.8	28.5
Exeter	1,498	58.0	25.8
Hopkinton	2,512	43.6	57.6
North Kingstown	3,166	42.6	74.3
South Kingstown	4,513	77.9	57.9
Richmond	1,830	38.9	47.0
Westerly	3,815	31.1	122.8
WASHINGTON COUNTY	18,468	331.9	55.6
WHOLE STATE	184,965	1054.6	175.4

By the settlement of the boundary question with Massachusetts, in 1862, Rhode Island gained some territory and population, as follows:

In Pawtucket,	Gain	6.9 square miles	4,200 population.
In East Providence,	Gain	12.5 "	1,700 "
Total gain,		19.4 square miles.	5,900 population.
In Fall River	Loss	11.2 square miles	3,377 population.

This leaves a net gain to Rhode Island of 8.2 square miles of territory, and 2,523 inhabitants.

The density of population in Rhode Island, 175.4 to each square mile, is nearly the same as that of France, (176,) and is greater than that of Prussia, Bavaria, Austria, Denmark, Scotland, Sweden, or Norway.

The following shows the number of square miles of territory, the total population, and the number of persons to a square mile in each of the New England States, by the national census of 1860:

States.	Square Miles.	Population.	Persons to each square mile.
Maine	30,000	628,279	20.9
New Hampshire	9,280	326,073	35.1
Vermont	9,056	315,098	34.8
Massachusetts	7,800	1,231,066	157.8
Rhode Island	1,046	174,620	166.9
Connecticut	4674	460,147	98.4
Total	61,856	3,135,283	50.6

By the State census of Massachusetts, in 1865, the population was 1,267,239, which gives 162.4 persons to each square mile.

The census of 1860 was taken before the settlement of the boundary question between Rhode Island and Massachusetts; consequently the area of Rhode Island, as given above, is slightly less than that of the present time.

The report on the United States census of 1860 gives the area of Rhode Island as 1,306 square miles, which, as we have already shown, is a mistake.

After Rhode Island, Massachusetts and Connecticut, the greatest density of population in any State, in 1860, was in New York, 84.3 persons to each square mile; next, New Jersey, 80.7; Maryland, 73.4; Pennsylvania, 63.2, &c., as may be seen on page 121 of "The Preliminary Report on the Eighth United States Census."

The greater density of population in Rhode Island as compared with other States, is owing to its limited territory, and to the large proportion of its inhabitants who are engaged in manufactures which have tended to concentrate the population in cities and villages. A very large percentage of the population is living in villages and in the two cities of Providence and Newport; and almost the whole increase of population in the State, for years past, has been in the cities and villages, while the population of the farming districts has remained stationary, or has declined.

Referring to the census of 1865, in connection with density of population, and leaving out the cities of Providence and Newport, we find the least density in West Greenwich, 25 persons to the square mile, and the greatest in North Providence, 970.

Deducting the two cities, and a few towns in which a large portion of the territory is occupied by villages, the density of population will be greatly reduced. For example: the cities of Providence and Newport, and the six towns, Bristol, Warren, Cranston, Cumberland, North Providence and Pawtucket, contain, in the aggregate, 117.9 square miles of territory, and a population of 111,670. This is only 11 per cent. of the area of the State; but is more than 60 per cent. of the population.

If we deduct these from the area and population of the State, we have in the rest of the State, 936.7 square miles, with a population of 73,295, which gives only 78 persons to each square mile.

VILLAGES.

I have referred to the concentration of population in villages in Rhode Island. In order to show this more fully, directions were given in taking the census to mark on the returns the exact boundaries of all the villages in the State. From these returns the following list is made. The instructions were not fully carried out in all cases, and considerable correspondence and inquiry have been necessary to complete the list, and it is still very imperfect as will be evident on slight examination. I think, however, that in the aggregate, the population of the villages as given, is less than the actual number.

The table gives the name of each village, the town or towns and the county in which it is situated, and the population of the village living in each town. The population given is for the first day of June, 1865. Some of the villages have increased largely since that date.

For reference, I have marked the villages in which post offices are established, and have also added all the post offices in the State which are not located in villages:

VILLAGES AND CITIES IN RHODE ISLAND.

NAME.	TOWN.	COUNTY.	Population.
Adamsville, P. O	Little Compton	Newport	106
Albion, P. O	Smithfield	Providence	169
Allendale	North Providence	"	238
Allenton, P. O	North Kingstown	Washington	37
Allenville	Smithfield	Providence	243
Anthony	Coventry	Kent	422
Apponaug	Warwick	"	370
Arcadia, P. O	Exeter ..61 Richmond ..49	Washington "	110
Arctic	Warwick	Kent	350
Arkwright	Coventry ..128 Cranston .. 76	" Providence	204
Arnold's Mills	Cumberland	"	30
Ashaway, P. O	Hopkinton	Washington	251
Ashland	Scituate	Providence	59
Ashton, P. O	Smithfield	"	60
Barberville	Hopkinton	Washington	48
Barrington, P. O	Barrington	Bristol	No Village.
Barrington Center, P.O.	"	"	"
*Bellville	North Kingstown	Washington	53
Bethel	Hopkinton	"	34
Branch Bridge	North Providence	Providence	299
Brick Yard	Barrington	Bristol	149
Bristol, P. O	Bristol	"	3,669
Browning Mill	Richmond ..21 Exeter ..30	Washington "	51
Burdickville	Hopkinton	"	52
Burrillville, P. O	Burrillville	Providence	No Village.
Canonchet	Hopkinton	Washington	59
Carolina Mills, P. O	Richmond ..286 Charlestown ..188	" "	474
Centerdale, P. O	North Providence	Providence	238
Centerville	Hopkinton	Washington	67
Centerville, P. O	Warwick	Kent	499
Central Falls	Smithfield	Providence	2,098
Cæsarville	Johnston	"	35
Chepachet, P. O	Glocester	"	657
Clark's Mill	Richmond ..62 Charlestown ..38	Washington "	100
Clayville	Scituate ..235 Foster .. 36	Providence "	271
Clyde Works	Warwick	Kent	117
Coal Mines	Portsmouth	Newport	348
Commons' Village	Little Compton	"	100
Coventry Center, P. O	Coventry	Kent	198
Crompton	Warwick	"	929
Cumberland Hill, P. O	Cumberland	Providence	126
Cowesett	Warwick	Kent	228
Charlestown, P. O	Charlestown	Washington	No Village.
Davisville, P. O	North Kingstown	Washington	105
Diamond Hill, P. O	Cumberland	Providence	105
Dorrville, P. O	Westerly ..368 Hopkinton .. 11	Washington "	379
Dry Brook	Johnston	Providence	144
Dyerville	North Providence	"	136

* Has greatly increased in population since the census was taken.

VILLAGES AND CITIES IN RHODE ISLAND.

NAME.	TOWN.	COUNTY.	Population.
Elmdale	Scituate	Providence	55
Elmwood	Cranston	"	1,655
East Providence, P. O.	East Providence	"	339
Escoheag, P. O	West Greenwich	Kent	No Village.
Exeter, P. O	Exeter	Washington	No Village.
Exeter Hollow	Exeter	"	40
Fisherville	Exeter	Washington	68
Fiskeville, P. O	Cranston 115 Scituate 16	Providence "	131
Forestdale	Smithfield	"	342
Foster Center, P. O	Foster	"	30
Foster, P. O	"	"	No Village.
Glendale	Burrillville	Providence	279
Glenford	Scituate	"	205
Gray Stone	North Providence	"	119
Georgiaville, P. O	Smithfield	"	497
Graniteville	Burrillville	"	367
Graniteville	Johnston	"	175
Greene, P. O	Coventry	Kent	No Village.
Greenwich, P. O	East Greenwich 1,765 Warwick 110	" "	1,875
Greenville, P. O	Smithfield	Providence	622
Geneva	North Providence	"	153
Hall's Mill	Exeter	Washington	32
Hamilton	North Kingstown	"	181
Harrisville	Burrillville	Providence	621
Harmony, P. O	Glocester	"	40
Harris' Mills	Coventry	Kent	458
Hillsdale	Richmond	Washington	56
Hope Valley	Hopkinton 158 Richmond 59	" "	217
Hope Village	Scituate	Providence	342
Hopkinton City, P. O	Hopkinton	Washington	78
Hopkins' Mills	Foster	Providence	79
Huntsville	Burrillville	"	89
Ingrahamville	Pawtucket	Providence	49
Jackson	Scituate	Providence	19
Jamestown, P. O	Jamestown	Newport	No Village.
Kenyon's Mill	Richmond 66 Charlestown 3	Washington "	69
Kingston, P. O	South Kingstown	"	191
Knightsville, P. O	Cranston	Providence	140
Lafayette, P. O	North Kingstown	Washington	150
Laurel Ridge	Burrillville	Providence	407
Lebanon	Pawtucket	"	99
Lime Rock	Smithfield	"	153
Lippitt	Warwick	Kent	347
Locustville	Hopkinton	Washington	206
Lonsdale, P. O	Smithfield	Providence	1,048

VILLAGES AND CITIES IN RHODE ISLAND.

NAME.	TOWN.	COUNTY.	Population.
Lonsdale, (New Village.)	Cumberland	Providence	374
Lottery Village	Westerly	Washington	137
Lyman's Mill	North Providence	Providence	125
Leonard's Corner, P. O.	East Providence	"	No Village.
Little Compton, P. O.	Tiverton	Newport	No Village.
Manchester Print Works	Smithfield	Providence	174
Manton, P. O.	North Providence...260 Johnston...105	" "	365
Manville, P. O.	Smithfield...223 Cumberland... 35	" "	258
Mapleville, P. O.	Burrillville	"	355
Merino	Johnston	"	269
Mohegan, P. O.	Burrillville	"	219
Munrotown	Bristol	Bristol	87
Moscow	Hopkinton	Washington	24
Mt. Vernon, P. O.	Foster	Providence	No Village.
Newport, P. O.	Newport City	Newport	12,688
Nayatt, P. O.	Barrington	Bristol	No Village.
Narragansett Ferry, P. O.	South Kingstown	Washington	43
Narragansett Mills	North Kingstown	"	93
Narragansett Pier, P. O.	South Kingstown	"	92
Nasonville	Burrillville	Providence	84
Natick, P. O.	Warwick	Kent	1,202
Nausocket	"	"	70
Newtown	Portsmouth	Newport	367
Nooseneck Hill, P. O.	West Greenwich	Kent	No Village.
North Scituate, P. O.	Scituate	Providence	"
New Shoreham, P. O.	New Shoreham	Newport	"
Oakland	Burrillville	Providence	104
Old Pond Factory	Scituate	"	96
Old Warwick	Warwick	Kent	525
Olneyville, P. O.	Johnston...1,036 North Providence..2,273	Providence "	3,309
Omega	East Providence	"	147
Pascoag, P. O.	Burrillville	Providence	722
Pawtucket, P. O.	Pawtucket... 4,572 North Providence. 4,983	" "	9,555
Pawtuxet, P. O.	Cranston... 372 Warwick... 305	" Kent	677
Peacedale, P. O.	South Kingstown	Washington	741
Perryville, P. O.	"	"	58
Phenix, P. O.	Warwick...590 Coventry... 25	Kent "	615
Pine Hill, P. O.	Exeter	Washington	No Village.
Plainville	Richmond	"	98
Plainville	Burrillville	Providence	139
Pontiac	Warwick	Kent	180
Potter Hill, P. O.	Hopkinton...148 Westerly...145	Washington "	293
Pottowomut	Warwick	Kent	106
Ponagansett	Scituate	Providence	96
Portsmouth, P. O.	Portsmouth	Newport	No Village.

VILLAGES AND CITIES IN RHODE ISLAND.

NAME.	TOWN.	COUNTY.	Population.
Providence, P. O	Providence City	Providence	54,595
Quidnick, P. O	Coventry	Kent	746
Quonocontaug, P. O	Charlestown	Washington	No Village.
Rice City, P. O	Coventry	Kent	No Village.
Richmond Village	Scituate	Providence	52
River Point	Warwick	Kent	540
Rockland, P. O	Scituate	Providence	254
Rockville, P. O	Hopkinton	Washington	170
Rocky Brook, P. O	South Kingstown	"	496
Saundersville	Scituate	Providence	72
Saxonville	Burrillville	"	88
Sayles' Bleachery	Smithfield	"	175
Simmons' Lower Village	Johnston	"	131
Simmonsville	"	"	180
Silver Spring	North Kingstown	Washington	140
Shady Lea	"	"	90
Shannock, P. O	{ Richmond 55 { Charlestown 22	" "	} 77
Slatersville, P. O	Smithfield	Providence	687
Smithville	Scituate	"	257
Slocumville, P. O	North Kingstown	Washington	40
Somerville	Warwick	Kent	65
South Scituate, P. O	Scituate	Providence	No Village.
South Providence	Cranston	"	3,491
Spragueville	"	"	1,389
Spragueville	Smithfield	"	137
Summit, P. O	Coventry	Kent	No Village.
Stone Bridge	Tiverton	Newport	243
South Foster, P. O	Foster	Providence	No Village.
Smithfield, P. O	Smithfield	"	"
South Portsmouth, P. O	Portsmouth	Newport	"
Smith's Hill	North Providence	Providence	2,413
Tower Hill	Cumberland	Providence	35
Tower Hill, P. O	South Kingstown	Washington	45
Tiverton Four Cor.'s, P. O	Tiverton	Newport	130
Tiverton, P. O	"	"	No Village.
Tooleville	North Providence	Providence	125
Union Village	Smithfield	Providence	74
Usquepaug, P. O	{ Richmond 86 { South Kingstown 76	Washington "	} 162
Valley Falls, P. O	{ Cumberland 812 { Smithfield 558	Providence "	} 1,370
Vue de L'Eau	East Providence	"	42
Wakefield, P. O	South Kingstown	Washington	596
Wanskuck	North Providence	Providence	492
Washington	Coventry	Kent	379
Warren, P. O	Warren	Bristol	2,344
Watchemoket	East Providence	Providence	791
W. Greenwich Center, P. O	West Greenwich	Kent	No Village.

VILLAGES AND CITIES IN RHODE ISLAND.

NAME.	TOWN.	COUNTY.	Population.
West River Village	North Providence	Providence	1,168
Westerly P. O.	Westerly	Washington	2,465
White Rock	Westerly	Washington	280
Whitman	Coventry	Kent	72
Wickford, P. O.	North Kingstown	Washington	707
Willettville	"	"	67
Woodville, P. O.	Hopkinton 129 Richmond 20	" "	149
Woodville	North Providence	Providence	295
Wyoming, P. O.	Richmond 208 Hopkinton 143	Washington "	351
W. Glocester, P. O.	Glocester	Providence	No Village.
Warwick, P. O.	Warwick	Kent	"
Warwick Neck, P. O.	"	"	"
Woonsocket, P. O.: Woonsocket 4,325	Cumberland	Providence	7,512
Social 438	"	"	
Clinton 189	"	"	
Unionville 181	"	"	
Smith's Village 112	"	"	
Jencksville 76	"	"	
5,321	5,321		
Bernon 1,211	Smithfield	"	
Globe 746	"	"	
Hamlet 234	"	"	
2,191	2,191		
Yawker	Exeter	Washington	75

It is evident that, in some cases, the places named do not deserve the title of villages; but they are given as marked in the returns of the census.

It is probable that very few persons will examine the preceding list of villages without finding, or thinking that they find, errors in it. I can only say that every exertion has been made to make it correct, and that it has caused a great amount of trouble to complete it.

Two things should be remembered in connection with it:

First. That the boundaries of villages are in most cases almost entirely arbitrary, and in very many instances there would naturally be a difference of opinion as to the exact limits which should be included in a village.

Second. It should be remembered that the population given is for the first day of June, 1865, and that in some cases there have been great changes in the population since that date.

The foregoing list includes two cities with a population of 67,283; 165 villages with a population of 80,042; 30 post offices not located in villages. The whole number of post offices in the State, is 93.

The aggregate population of the two cities, and 165 villages is 147,325, which is 79.65 per cent. of the whole population of the State. The cities contain 36.37 per cent., and the villages 43.28 per cent. of the whole population, leaving only 37,640, or 20.35 per cent. of the population of the State living outside of the cities and villages. We have no data for comparing these figures with those of any other State; but presume that if such comparison could be made, it would show that the proportion of the population, living in villages and cities, is considerably greater in Rhode Island than in any other State.

Neither can we make any comparison of the population living in villages in 1865, with any previous date, as no previous census of the State has ever given this information. An examination of a table of the population of each town at different periods, to be given hereafter, will show that nearly all the increase in the population of the State, for many years, has been in the cities and in those towns which are largely interested in manufactures, while the strictly farming portions of the State have remained stationary with respect to population, or have declined.

II. POLITICAL DIVISIONS AND PREVIOUS CENSUSES OF RHODE ISLAND.

It is fortunate, for statistical purposes, that the changes in the territorial limits of cities and towns in Rhode Island have been very few as compared with some of our neighboring States. In the earlier history of the State, towns were divided, and new towns were incorporated as the convenience of the population required; but from the year 1781, when Scituate was divided and the town of Foster was incorporated, to the year 1856, a period of 75 years, only one new town, (Burrillville in 1806,) was created, and no changes of any importance were made in the limits of towns. In 1856, Tiverton was divided and the town of Fall River was created, and in 1862, Pawtucket and East Providence were admitted from Massachusetts, and Fall River was ceded to that State. These comprise all the important changes made in the boundaries of towns, in Rhode Island, during the last eighty-five years.

The history of the County divisions of the State is as follows:

During the first sixty-seven years after the settlement at Providence, in 1636, nine towns were formed; but no county organizations were created. These towns were Providence, Portsmouth, Newport, Warwick, Westerly, New Shoreham, North Kingstown, East Greenwich, and Jamestown.

On the twenty-second day of June, 1703, the Colony was divided into two counties, called Newport county, and the county of Providence Plantations.

Newport county included the towns on the islands, namely, Portsmouth, Newport, Jamestown, and New Shoreham, with Newport as the shiretown.

The county of Providence Plantations included all the towns on the main land of the Colony, and it was provided that the courts should be held at Providence and Warwick the first year, and at Kingston and Westerly the next year.

Again, June 16, 1729, the Colony was divided into three counties. Newport county remained as before. The portion of the State which had been called King's Province was organized into a county and called King's county. It included the towns of Westerly, North Kingstown, and South Kingstown, or all the main land of the State south of East Greenwich.

The remainder of the State, including East Greenwich, Warwick, and Providence, was called Providence county, with Providence as the shiretown.

Again, January 27, 1746–47, five towns were admitted to the Colony from Massachusetts. Of these, Little Compton and Tiverton were added to Newport county; Cumberland was added to Providence county; and a new county, called Bristol, was created February 17, 1746–47, which included the towns of Warren and Bristol, with the latter as the shiretown.

Again, June 11, 1750, East Greenwich, West Greenwich, Warwick, and Coventry were taken from Providence county and incorporated as Kent county, with East Greenwich as the capital.

In the year 1765, an Act was passed, dividing the State into five counties. This Act was merely a reënactment and confirmation of the Acts already referred to, and made no changes in the organization of the counties.

Since June, 1750, a period of 116 years, no changes have been made in the territorial limits of the five counties in the State, except that Fall River in Newport county has been ceded to Massachusetts, and Pawtucket and East Providence have been added to Providence county.

The name of King's county was changed to Washington county, October 29, 1781, after the surrender of Cornwallis. The preamble of the Act by which the change was made, is as follows:

> "Whereas, since the declaration of the independence of the United States of America, it becomes the wisdom of the rising republic to obliterate, as far as may be, every trace and idea of that government which threatened our destruction——."

And yet, at the present time, more than half the towns in the State are named after persons or places connected with English history. It is somewhat remarkable that notwithstanding the great abundance of Indian names connected with the history of Rhode Island, and with localities in the State, not a single town in the State has a name of Indian origin, except Pawtucket which has recently been received from Massachusetts.

We cannot help thinking that, to this generation at least, Conanicut, Potowomut, Shawomet, Seaconnet, Pocasset, and Misquamicut would sound more pleasantly than Jamestown, East Greenwich, Warwick, Little Compton, Portsmouth, and Westerly; and similar changes might have been made, with advantage, in other towns. But these remarks are beyond the province of statistics.

INCORPORATION OF TOWNS.

In connection with the previous censuses of Rhode Island, it seemed important to know the date of incorporation of the several towns, in order to understand the effects of the changes of territorial limits upon the population of each town at the different periods when the censuses were taken. I have, therefore, with considerable trouble, prepared the following table which shows the date of the incorporation of each town and county, with explanatory remarks in regard to the names, changes of boundaries, and other particulars of each town. The table will be found convenient for reference as it condenses and arranges information from many sources, some of which it has been difficult to obtain. The dates given previous to 1790, are mostly obtained from Arnold's History of Rhode Island. After considerable examination, I have been unable to find any mistake in the dates as given in that History:

Towns in Rhode Island, *with date of Incorporation, &c.*

COUNTIES AND TOWNS.	DATE OF INCORPORATION.	From what taken, original names, changes of boundaries, &c.
BRISTOL COUNTY.	February 17, 1746–47..	Incorporated with same county limits as at present. Originally the county consisted of two towns, Bristol and Warren. Afterwards, June, 1770, Warren was divided, and the town of Barrington was incorporated.
Barrington...........	June 11, 1770.........	Taken from Warren, which see.
Bristol..............	January 27, 1746–47...	Five towns received from Massachusetts this date.
Warren.............	January 27, 1746–47...	See Bristol. The territory of the town of Warren when admitted to the State, included the town of Barrington, and a portion of the towns of Swanzey and Rehoboth, in Massachusetts. In 1770, Warren was divided, and one of the original names, (Barrington,) was given to the new town.
KENT COUNTY....	June 11, 1750.........	Taken from Providence county. Incorporated with same county limits as at present; and same towns.
Coventry............	August 18, 1741.......	Taken from Warwick.
East Greenwich.......	October 31, 1677......	Incorporated as the town of *East* Greenwich. Name changed to Dedford, June 23, 1686. The original name restored in 1689. Town divided in 1741.
West Greenwich......	April 1, 1741..........	Taken from East Greenwich, which see.
Warwick.............	Original town.........	First settled January, 1642–43. Named from Earl of Warwick, who signed the Patent of Providence Plantations, March 14, 1643. The first action of the inhabitants as a town was August 8, 1647. Indian name Shawomet.
NEWPORT COUNTY	June 22, 1703.........	Originally included Newport, Portsmouth, Jamestown, and New Shoreham.
Fall River............	October 6, 1856.......	Taken from Tiverton. Ceded to Massachusetts in the settlement of the Boundary question, March 1st, 1862. See Pawtucket and East Providence.

TOWNS IN RHODE ISLAND, *with date of Incorporation, &c.—Continued.*

COUNTIES AND TOWNS.	DATE OF INCORPORATION.	From what taken, original names, changes of boundaries, &c.
Jamestown..........	November 4, 1678.....	Named in honor of King James. Indian name Quononoqutt. (Conanicut.)
Little Compton........	January 27, 1746-47...	One of five towns received from Massachusetts. Indian name, Seaconnet.
Middletown	June 13, 1743.........	Town in the "middle" of the island. Taken from Newport.
Newport.............	Original town.........	Settled, 1639. Line between Newport and Portsmouth established September 14, 1640. Incorporated as a City June 1, 1784. City charter given up March 27, 1787. City incorporated the second time at the May session, 1853, and the charter accepted May 20, 1853.
New Shoreham.......	November 6, 1672.....	Admitted to Colony as Block Island, May 4, 1664. When incorporated in 1672, name changed to New Shoreham "as signes of our unity and likeness to many parts of our native country." Indian name, Manasses or Manisses.
Portsmouth	Original town.........	Settled, 1638. Indian name Pocasset. "At a quarter meeting of the first of ye 5th month, 1639, it is agreed upon, to call this town Portsmouth." At the "Generall Courte" at "Nieuport," twelfth of first month, 1640, the name of Portsmouth was confirmed.
Tiverton.............	January 27, 1746-47...	One of five towns received this date. See Bristol, Warren, &c. Indian name, Pocasset.
PROVIDENCE CO...	June 22, 1703.........	Originally incorporated as the County of Providence Plantations, and included the present territory of Providence, Kent, and Washington counties, excepting the present towns of Cumberland, Pawtucket and East Providence. See Kent and Washington counties.
Burrillville...........	November 17, 1806....	Taken from Glocester. The date given is the time when the town was first authorized to meet to elect town officers. Named from Hon. James Burrill.

TOWNS IN RHODE ISLAND, *with date of Incorporation. &c.—Continued.*

COUNTIES AND TOWNS.	DATE OF INCORPORATION.	From what taken, original names, changes of boundaries, &c,
Cranston	June 10, 1754	Taken from Providence. Probably named from Samuel Cranston, who was Governor of Rhode Island from March, 1698, to April 26, 1727, when he died.
Cumberland	January 27, 1746–47	One of five towns received this date. See Tiverton, Bristol, &c. Until incorporated in Rhode Island, was known as Attleboro' Gore. Named from Cumberland in England.
East Providence	March 1, 1862	The westerly part of Rehoboth, Massachusetts, was incorporated as Seekonk, February 26, 1812. The westerly part of Seekonk was annexed to Rhode Island, incorporated as a town, and named East Providence, in the settlement of the Boundary question in 1862. See Pawtucket and Fall River.
Foster	August 20, 1781	Taken from Scituate. Named probably from Hon. Theodore Foster.
Glocester	February 20, 1730–31	Taken from Providence. At this date an Act was passed "for erecting and incorporating the out-lands of the town of Providence, into three towns." These towns were Scituate, Glocester, and Smithfield.
Johnston	February 26, 1759	Taken from Providence. Named in honor of Augustus Johnston, Esq., the Attorney General of the Colony at that time.
North Providence	June 10, 1765	Taken from Providence. A small portion re-united to Providence June 29, 1767.
Pawtucket	March 1, 1862	Name of Indian origin. Part of Seekonk, Mass., was incorporated as the town of Pawtucket, March 1, 1828. The whole town of Pawtucket, except a small portion lying easterly of Seven Mile river, was annexed to Rhode Island with East Providence, which see.
Providence	Original town	Settled, 1636. Named Providence by Roger Williams, "in gratitude to his supreme deliverer." Originally comprised the whole county. City incorporated, 1832.

TOWNS IN RHODE ISLAND, *with date of Incorporation, &c.—Concluded.*

COUNTIES AND TOWNS.	DATE OF INCORPORATION.	From what taken, original names, changes of boundaries, &c.
Scituate..............	February 20, 1730–31..	Taken from Providence. See Glocester.
Smithfield............	February 20, 1730–31..	Taken from Providence. See Glocester.
WASHINGTON CO..	June 16, 1729.........	Originally called the Narragansett country. Named King's Province March 20, 1654. Boundaries established May 21, 1669. Incorporated June 1729, as King's county, with three towns and same territory as at present. Name changed to Washington county, October 29, 1781.
Charlestown..........	August 22, 1738.......	Taken from Westerly.
Exeter..............	March 8, 1742–43.....	Taken from North Kingstown.
Hopkinton...........	March 14, 1757.	Taken from Westerly.
North Kingstown.....	October 28, 1674......	First settlement, 1641. Incorporated, 1674, under the name of King's Towne, as the seventh town in the Colony. Incorporation re-affirmed 1679. Name changed to Rochester, June 23, 1686. Name restored 1689; see East Greenwich. Kingstown divided into North and South Kingstown in February, 1722. Act provided that North Kingstown should be the eldest town.
South Kingstown......	February 26, 1722–23..	See North Kingstown. Pettiquamscut, settled January 20, 1657–58.
Richmond............	August 18, 1747.......	Taken from Charlestown.
Westerly.............	May 14, 1669.........	Original name Misquamicut. Incorporated May 1669, under the name of Westerly, as the fifth town in the Colony. Name of Westerly changed to Haversham June 23, 1686, but soon restored. See East Greenwich.

In several cases the exact date of the passage of the Act of Incorporation of towns could not be ascertained. In such cases, the date of the meeting of the General Assembly, at which the Act was passed, is given.

PREVIOUS CENSUSES OF RHODE ISLAND.

The notes given in connection with each town in the preceding list, render any further explanations unnecessary. We, therefore, proceed to give the following table which shows the population of each town in Rhode Island, at sixteen different dates, from 1708 to 1865 inclusive. For convenient reference, in regard to the changes indicated in the population of each town, I have prefixed the date of incorporation or settlement.

The table gives the total population at each date, which until the census of 1800, included whites, blacks, and Indians.

In the United States censuses, from 1800 to 1860 inclusive, "Indians not taxed," were not enumerated, and are not included in the population. All classes are included in the census of 1865.

A table will be given hereafter, showing the number of blacks and Indians, at different dates, and explanations will also be given in relation to the censuses at the several dates given in the following table :

TABLE, *Showing the total population of each town in Rhode Island at different dates from 1708 to 1865, inclusive.*

TOWNS AND DIVISIONS OF THE STATE.	Date of Incorporation or Settlement.	1708.	1730.	1748.	1755.	1774.	1776.	1782.	1790.
Barrington	1770	....	....	....	....	601	538	534	683
Bristol	1747	....	....	1,069	1,080	1,209	1,067	1,032	1,406
Warren	1747	....	....	680	925	979	1,005	905	1,122
BRISTOL COUNTY	1747	....	....	1,749	2,005	2,789	2,610	2,471	3,211
Coventry	1741	....	....	792	1,178	2,023	2,300	2,107	2,477
East Greenwich	1677	240	1,223	1,044	1,167	1,663	1,664	1,609	1,824
West Greenwich	1741	....	....	766	1,246	1,764	1,653	1,698	2,054
Warwick	1643	480	1,178	1,782	1,911	2,438	2,376	2,112	2,493
KENT COUNTY	1750	720	2,401	4,384	5,502	7,888	7,993	7,526	8,848
Fall River	1856	....	....	....	....	....	....	....	....
Jamestown	1678	206	321	420	517	563	322	345	507
Little Compton	1747	....	....	1,152	1,170	1,232	1,302	1,341	1,542
Middletown	1743	....	....	680	778	881	860	674	840
Newport	1639	2,203	4,640	6,508	6,753	9,209	5,299	5,530	6,716
New Shoreham	1672	208	290	300	378	575	478	478	682
Portsmouth	1638	628	813	992	1,363	1,512	1,347	1,350	1,560
Tiverton	1747	....	....	1,040	1,325	1,956	2,091	1,959	2,453
NEWPORT COUNTY	1703	3,245	6,064	11,092	12,284	15,928	11,699	11,677	14,300
Burrillville	1806	....	....	....	....	....	....	....	....
Cranston	1754	....	....	....	1,460	1,861	1,701	1,589	1,877
Cumberland	1747	....	....	806	1,083	1,756	1,686	1,548	1,964
East Providence	1862	....	....	....	....	....	....	....	....
Foster	1781	....	....	....	....	....	....	1,763	2,268
Glocester	1731	....	....	1,202	1,511	2,945	2,832	2,791	4,025
Johnston	1759	....	....	....	....	1,031	1,022	996	1,320
North Providence	1765	....	....	....	....	830	813	698	1,071
Pawtucket	1862	....	....	....	....	....	....	....	....
Scituate	1731	....	....	1,232	1,813	3,601	3,289	1,628	2,315
Smithfield	1731	....	....	450	1,921	2,888	2,781	2,217	3,171
TOWNS, PROV. COUNTY	1703	....	....	3,690	7,788	14,912	14,124	13,230	18,011
PROVIDENCE CITY	1636	1,446	3,916	3,452	3,159	4,321	4,355	4,310	6,380
Charlestown	1738	....	....	1,002	1,130	1,821	1,835	1,523	2,022
Exeter	1743	....	....	1,174	1,404	1,864	1,982	2,058	2,495
Hopkinton	1757	....	....	....	....	1,808	1,845	1,735	2,462
North Kingstown	1674	1,200	2,105	1,935	2,109	2,472	2,761	2,328	2,907
South Kingstown	1723	....	1,523	1,978	1,913	2,835	2,779	2,675	4,131
Richmond	1747	....	....	508	829	1,257	1,204	1,094	1,760
Westerly	1669	570	1,926	1,809	2,291	1,812	1,824	1,720	2,298
WASHINGTON COUNTY	1729	1,770	5,554	8,406	9,676	13,869	14,230	13,133	18,075
WHOLE STATE	1636	7,181	17,935	32,773	40,414	59,707	55,011	52,347	68,825

TABLE, CONTINUED, *Showing the total population of each town in Rhode Island, at different dates, from* 1708 *to* 1865, *inclusive.*

TOWNS AND DIVISIONS OF THE STATE.	1800.	1810.	1820.	1830.	1840.	1850.	1860.	1865.
Barrington..........	650	604	634	612	549	795	1,000	1,028
Bristol	1,678	2,693	3,197	3,034	3,490	4,616	5,271	4,649
Warren..............	1,473	1,775	1,806	1,800	2,437	3,103	2,636	2,792
BRISTOL COUNTY.	3,801	5,072	5,637	5,446	6,476	8,514	8,907	8,469
Coventry..............	2,423	2,928	3,139	3,851	3,433	3,620	4,247	3,995
East Greenwich........	1,775	1,530	1,519	1,591	1,509	2,358	2,882	2,400
West Greenwich... ...	1,757	1,619	1,927	1,817	1,415	1,350	1,258	1,228
Warwick......	2,532	3,757	3,643	5,529	6,726	7,740	8,916	7,696
KENT COUNTY	8,487	9,834	10,228	12,788	13,083	15,068	17,303	15,319
Fall River..............	......	......	......	......	......	......	3,377	......
Jamestown............	501	504	448	415	365	358	400	349
Little Compton........	1,577	1,553	1,580	1,378	1,327	1,462	1,304	1,197
Middletown	913	976	949	915	891	830	1,012	1,019
Newport..............	6,739	7,907	7,319	8,010	8,333	9,563	10,508	12,688
New Shoreham........	714	722	955	1,185	1,069	1,262	1,320	1,308
Portsmouth	1,684	1,795	1,645	1,727	1,706	1,833	2,048	2,153
Tiverton	2,717	2,837	2,875	2,905	3,183	4,699	1,927	1,973
NEWPORT COUNTY.....	14,845	16,294	15,771	16,535	16,874	20,007	21,896	20,687
Burrillville........ ...	......	1,834	2,164	2,196	1,982	3,538	4,140	4,861
Cranston..............	1,644	2,161	2,274	2,652	2,901	4,311	7,500	9,177
Cumberland..........	2,056	2,210	2,653	3,675	5,225	6,661	8,339	8,216
East Providence.......	......	......	......	......	......	......	......	2,172
Foster	2,457	2,613	2,900	2,672	2,181	1,932	1,935	1,873
Glocester............	4,009	2,310	2,504	2,521	2,304	2,872	2,427	2,286
Johnston	1,364	1,516	1,542	2,115	2,477	2,937	3,440	3,436
North Providence......	1,067	1,758	2,420	3,503	4,207	7,680	11,818	14,553
Pawtucket............	......	......	......	......	......	......	......	5,000
Scituate..............	2,523	2,568	2,834	3,993	4,090	4,582	4,251	3,538
Smithfield............	3,120	3,828	4,678	6,857	9,534	11,500	13,283	12,315
TOWNS PROV. CO......	18,240	20,798	23,969	30,184	34,901	46,013	57,133	67,427
PROVIDENCE CITY.....	7,614	10,071	11,767	16,836	23,172	41,513	50,666	54,595
Charlestown..........	1,454	1,174	1,160	1,284	923	994	981	1,134
Exeter	2,476	2,256	2,581	2,383	1,776	1,634	1,741	1,498
Hopkinton............	2,276	1,774	1,821	1,777	1,726	2,477	2,738	2,512
North Kingstown......	2,794	2,957	3,007	3,036	2,909	2,971	3,104	3,166
South Kingstown......	3,438	3,560	3,723	3,663	3,717	3,807	4,717	4,513
Richmond........	1,368	1,330	1,423	1,363	1,361	1,784	1,964	1,830
Westerly.......... ...	2,329	1,911	1,972	1,915	1,912	2,763	3,470	3,815
WASHINGTON CO......	16,135	14,962	15,687	15,421	14,324	16,430	18,715	18,468
WHOLE STATE	69,122	77,031	83,059	97,210	108,830	147,545	174,620	184,965

NOTES ON THE TABLE.

I think the preceding table is complete and correct for every census of the State that was ever taken. A census of the City of Providence has been taken every tenth year from the year 1825 to the present time, the particulars of which will be given hereafter.

Referring to the preceding table, the following notes in relation to the different censuses, may be of interest:

The first four censuses, in 1708, 1730, 1748, and 1755, were ordered by the General Assembly, in answer to Queries sent by the Board of Trade in England.

1708. The report of this census was sent to the Board of Trade, in a communication from Governor Samuel Cranston, dated December 5, 1708. The returns showed the number of "black servants," and "white servants;" but did not give the number of Indians. There were nine towns in the colony at this date. The returns are taken from the Colonial Records of Rhode Island, volume IV., page 59.

1730. At the June Session of the General Assembly, in this year, each town was ordered to take a census, "of the inhabitants of each town, whites and others, in such way and manner as they shall think best, and pay the charges of doing thereof; and a return thereof to be made to the Governor, by the town clerk, as soon as may be." The returns show the number of whites, blacks, and Indians, in each of the ten towns then composing the colony. Since the census of 1708, the town of Kingstown had been divided into North and South Kingstown. The returns of this census, in the table, are taken from "Callender's Historical Discourse."

1748. Again, in answer to "Queries of the Board of Trade," a census of the colony was ordered by the General Assembly. This census shows the number of whites, negroes, and Indians in each town. The figures in the table are taken from "A Summary, Historical, Political, &c., by William Douglass, M. D." London: 1760. There is a mistake of nearly one thousand, in the book referred to, in the number of negroes in Newport. The number should be 1,105, as I have given it, instead of 110. At this date there were 24 towns in the colony. Five towns had been received from Massachusetts, and other towns had been incorporated since 1730, as will be seen by reference to the table.

1755. This was the last census ordered by the General Assembly in answer to Queries of the Board of Trade. The report of it was sent by Governor Stephen Hopkins, in a communication dated December 24, 1755. The only returns of this census that I have been able to find, are in "The Early History of Narragansett," by Elisha R. Potter, Jr.; R. I. Historical Collections, page 174. This only gives the total population of each town, and does not show the number of whites, blacks, and Indians. At this date there were 25 towns in the colony, Cranston having been incorporated in 1754.

1774. This was the first census taken by the sole authority of the General Assembly, and it was also the first census in which any reference was had to the ages of the population. The returns show, for each town, the number of families, the number of white, males and females "above and under" 16 years of age; the number of blacks, the number of Indians, and the total population. The whole census, giving the particulars of all the families, and the names of all the heads of families in each town in the colony, in 1774, was printed by order of the General Assembly, in 1858. At this date, 1774, there were 29 towns the in colony, Barrington, Johnston, North Providence and Hopkinton having been incorporated since 1755.

1776. This census was taken by order of the General Assembly, June Session, 1776, on "recommendation of the Most Honorable the Continental Congress." It was ordered that "the account be taken in the same manner as the inhabitants of this colony were last numbered." I have been able to find no particulars except the total number of inhabitants of each town. See R. I. Colonial Records, volume VII., page 616. The number of the towns in the colony (29,) was the same as in 1774. Arnold's History of Rhode Island, volume 2, page 333, says that seamen and other temporary absentees were not counted in this census.

1782. At the January Session this year, a census of the State was ordered by the General Assembly, and persons were appointed to take it, in each town. It was ordered that the number of families of whites, Indians, and blacks be taken, the number of males and females of each class, and the number under 16 years of age, from 16 to 21, from 21 to 50, and 50 and over. The complete returns are given in volume IX., page 653, of the Colonial Records, recently published. The town of New Shoreham was omitted from necessity, as it was in the possession of the British at that time. In the table, I have inserted the population of that town, the same as in 1776.

The three censuses of 1774, 1776, and 1782, enable us to show the effects of the Revolutionary War on the population of each town in the State. It will be noticed that nearly all the towns declined in population during the war.

The number of towns, in 1782, was 30, Foster having been incorporated in 1781. According to this census, there were 48,566 whites, 525 Indians, 464 mulattoes, and 2,342 blacks in the State, not including New Shoreham. This was the last census taken by authority of the State, until the year 1865.

1790. This was the first census taken under the authority of the National Government. William Peck was the marshal for Rhode Island. It was not as full or minute in the particulars as the State census of 1782. The particulars of this census, for all the States. are given in "Duane's Collection of Select Pamphlets," printed in Philadelphia in 1813 and 1814.

1800 to 1860. A statement of the changes made in the schedules of the several United States censuses, may be found in the introduction to the quarto volume of the Report on the Census of 1850.

It has been quite difficult to find the particulars for each town, of several of the earlier censuses. The population of each town, as given in the table, for 1790 and 1800, is taken from Duane's Select Pamphlets; the population for 1810, is from the Rhode Island American, of February 12, 1811.

In several instances the population of the State, as well as of some towns, as given in the table, differs slightly from some published statements. I have, in all cases, so far as possible, given the official figures, and think the table will generally be found to be correct.

INCREASE OF POPULATION.

The preceding table shows the actual increase or decrease of population in the several towns in Rhode Island, at different periods. But the relative increase or decrease of population, at different periods, will be shown more plainly by the percentages than by the actual numbers.

The following table shows the rate of increase or decrease, per cent., in the total population of each town and county, between the several dates as given. The minus sign (—) indicates a decrease :

TABLE, *Showing the rate per cent. of increase or decrease in the total population of each town and county in Rhode Island, in several periods, from* 1748 *to* 1865.

TOWNS AND DIVISIONS OF THE STATE.	1748 TO 1774.	1774 TO 1782.	1782 TO 1790.	1790 TO 1800.	1800 TO 1810.	1810 TO 1820.
Barrington	....	—11.1	27.9	—4.8	—7.1	5.0
Bristol	13.1	—14.6	36.2	19.3	60.5	18.7
Warren	44.0	—7.5	24.0	31.2	20.5	1.7
BRISTOL COUNTY	59.4	—11.4	29.9	18.4	33.4	11,1
Coventry	155.4	4.1	17.5	—2.2	20.8	7.2
East Greenwich	59.3	—3.2	13.4	—2.6	—13.8	—0.7
West Greenwich	130.3	—3.7	21.0	—1.4	—7.8	19.0
Warwick	36.8	—13.4	18.0	1.6	48.4	—3.0
KENT COUNTY	79.9	—4.6	17.5	—4.1	15.8	4.0
Jamestown	34.0	—38.7	47.0	—1.2	0.6	—11.1
Little Compton	6.9	8.9	15.0	2.3	—1.5	1.7
Middletown	29.5	—23.5	24.6	8.7	6.9	—2.8
Newport	41.5	—39.9	21.4	0.3	17.3	—7.4
New Shoreham	91.7	—16.9	42.7	4.7	1.1	32.3
Portsmouth	52.4	—10.7	15.6	8.0	6.6	—8.3
Tiverton	88.1	0.1	25.2	10.7	4.4	1.3
NEWPORT COUNTY	43.6	—26.7	22.4	3.8	9.8	—3.2
Burrillville	....	....	....	....	....	18.0
Cranston	....	—14.6	18.1	—12.4	31.4	5.2
Cumberland	117.9	—11.8	26.9	4.7	7.5	20.4
Foster	....	....	28.6	8.3	6.3	11.0
Glocester	145.0	—5.2	44.2	—0.4	—42.4	8.4
Johnston	....	—3.4	32.5	3.3	11.1	1.7
North Providence	....	—15.9	53.4	—0.4	64.8	37.6
Scituate	192.3	—54.8	41.6	9.0	1.8	10.4
Smithfield	541.8	—23.2	43.0	—1.6	22.7	22.2
TOWNS PROV. COUNTY	304.1	—11.3	36.1	1.3	14.0	15.2
PROVIDENCE CITY	25.2	—0.3	48.0	19.3	32.3	16.8
Charlestown	81.7	—16.3	32.7	—28.1	—19.3	—1.2
Exeter	58.8	10.4	21.2	—0.8	—8.9	14.4
Hopkinton	....	—4.0	41.9	—7.5	—22.1	2.6
North Kingstown	27.7	—5.8	24.9	—3.9	5.8	1.7
South Kingstown	43.3	—5.6	54.4	—16.8	3.5	4.6
Richmond	147.4	—13.0	60.9	—22.3	—2 8	7.0
Westerly	0.2	—5.1	33.6	1.3	—17.9	3.2
WASHINGTON COUNTY	65.0	—5.3	37.6	—10.7	—7.3	4.8
WHOLE STATE	82.2	—12.3	31.5	0.4	11.4	7.8

TABLE, CONTINUED, *Showing the rate per cent. of increase or decrease in the total population of each town and county in Rhode Island, in several periods, from* 1748 *to* 1865.

TOWNS AND DIVISIONS OF THE STATE.	1820 TO 1830.	1830 TO 1840.	1840 TO 1850.	1850 TO 1860.	1860 TO 1865.	1790 TO 1865.
Barrington	—3.5	—10.3	44.8	25.8	2.8	50.5
Bristol	—5.1	15.0	32.3	14.2	— 11.8	230.7
Warren	—0.3	35.4	27.3	—15.0	5.9	148.8
BRISTOL COUNTY	—3.4	18.9	31.5	4.6	—4.9	163.7
Coventry	22.7	—10.8	5.4	17.3	—5.9	61.3
East Greenwich	4.7	—5.1	56.3	22.2	—16.7	31.6
West Greenwich	—5.7	—22.1	—4.6	—6.8	—2.4	—40.2
Warwick	51.8	21.6	15.1	15.2	—13.7	208.7
KENT COUNTY	25.0	2.3	15.2	14.8	—11.5	73.1
Jamestown	—7.4	—12.0	—1.9	11.7	—12.7	—31.2
Little Compton	—12.8	—3.7	10.2	—10.8	—8.2	—22.4
Middletown	—3.6	—2.6	—6.8	22.0	0.7	21.3
Newport	9.4	4.0	14.8	9.9	20.7	88.9
New Shoreham	24.1	—9.8	18.0	4.6	—0.9	91.8
Portsmouth	5.0	—1.2	7.4	11.7	5.1	38.0
Tiverton	1.0	9.6	47.6	—59.0	2.4	—19.6
NEWPORT COUNTY	4.8	2.0	18.6	9.4	—5.5	44.7
Burrillville	1.5	—9.7	78.5	17.0	17.4	165.1
Cranston	16.6	9.4	48.6	74.0	22.4	388.9
Cumberland	38.5	42.2	27.5	25.2	—1.5	318.3
Foster	—7.9	—18.4	—11.4	0.2	—3.2	—17.4
Glocester	0.7	—8.6	24.7	—15.5	—5.8	—43.2
Johnston	37.2	17.1	18.6	17.1	—0.1	160.3
North Providence	44.8	20.1	82.5	53.9	23.1	1258.8
Scituate	40.9	2.4	12.0	—7.2	—16.8	52.8
Smithfield	46.6	39.0	20.6	15.5	—7.3	288.4
TOWNS PROV. COUNTY	25.9	15.6	31.8	24.2	18.0	274.4
PROVIDENCE CITY	43.1	37.6	70.1	22.0	7.8	755.7
Charlestown	10.7	—28.1	7.7	—1.3	15.6	—43.9
Exeter	—7.7	—25.5	—8.0	6.5	—14.0	—40.0
Hopkinton	—2.4	—2.9	43.5	10.5	—8.3	2.0
North Kingstown	1.0	—4.2	2.1	4.5	2.0	8.9
South Kingstown	—1.6	1.5	2.4	23.9	—4.3	9.2
Richmond	—4.2	—0.1	31.1	10.1	—6.8	4.0
Westerly	—2.9	—0.1	44.5	25.6	9.9	66.0
WASHINGTON COUNTY	—1.7	—7.1	14.7	13.9	—1.3	2.2
WHOLE STATE	17.0	12.0	35.6	18.3	5.9	168.7

It will be noticed that every town in the State shows a decrease in population, at some period of its history. This decrease is often the result of causes which are apparent. Thus, nearly every town, and the whole State, show a decrease in population between 1774 and 1782, the period of the war of the revolution. Newport, in particular, suffered largely at this period, and did not regain until 1850 the numbers it had in 1774. During the same period, 1774 to 1782, Providence remained nearly stationary, with a loss of only eleven.

At some periods the decrease shown in the table, in different towns, does not indicate an actual decrease in the population of a given territory, but is caused by the division of towns and the incorporation of new towns. Thus, from 1730 to 1748, Providence shows a decrease of 464; but during this time, four towns with a population of 3,690, were taken from Providence. A similar example, of recent date, is seen in the town of Tiverton. That town had a population of 4,699 in 1850, and only 1,927 in 1860; but during this period, Fall River, with a population of 3,377, was taken from Tiverton. Those interested in the history of each town, will find much in the table which will reward an examination of it.

Referring more particularly to the last table, we find that, during the first period, 1748 to 1774, every town in the State increased in population, and in most towns the percentage of increase was quite large.

During the war of the revolution, 1774 to 1782, every town in the State decreased in population, except Coventry, Little Compton, Tiverton, and Exeter. During this period the whole State lost 12.3 per cent. of its population. The greatest proportional loss was in Scituate, Newport, Jamestown, Middletown, and Smithfield. The large percentage of decrease in Scituate at this period, was, however, owing to the division of the town, and the incorporation of Foster.

During the eight years following the close of the war, from 1782 to 1790, every town in the State increased largely in population, the rate for the whole State being 31.5 per cent.

In the next period of ten years, 1790 to 1800, the increase of population in the State was checked, and for the whole State, the increase was only four-tenths of one per cent. In 15 towns there was a decrease. It is probable that this was owing to a considerable emigration from the State at that period.

From 1800 to 1810, there was a decrease of population in 11 towns; but in the whole State, the increase was 11.4 per cent. North

Providence and Bristol showed the greatest proportional increase. Glocester lost 42.4 per cent., all of which was owing to the division of the town, and the incorporation of Burrillville. During the period, 1810 to 1820, the State gained 7.8 per cent. in population; but 7 towns showed a loss, From 1820 to 1830, the gain in the whole State was 17 per cent.; but 13 towns showed a loss, the greatest proportional loss being 12.8 per cent. in Little Compton.

About this period a change commenced in the rate of progress of different portions of the State, which has continued to the present time, and is shown by the rapid increase of the manufacturing towns and villages, and the stationary condition, or decline of the farming sections.

From 1830 to 1840, the whole State gained only 12 per cent., and there was an actual decrease of population in 18 towns. The financial crisis of 1837, by causing the suspension of many manufactories, and the emigration of many persons to the West, affected seriously the results of the census of 1840.

The period from 1840 to 1850, was a time of general prosperity in the manufacturing interests of the State, and there was an increase of 35.6 per cent. in the population. Many towns gained largely, thus, Providence, 79.1 per cent.; Westerly, 44.5 per cent.; North Providence, 82.5 per cent.; Cranston, 48.6; Burrillville, 78.5; East Greenwich, 56.3, &c. Every town in the State gained in population, from 1840 to 1850, except West Greenwich, Jamestown, Middletown, Foster, and Exeter.

From 1850 to 1860, the increase in the population of the State was 18.3 per cent., much less than during the ten years previous. Seven towns declined in population during this period, namely, Warren, West Greenwich, Little Compton, Tiverton, Glocester, Scituate, and Charlestown. The greatest proportional gain, from 1850 to 1860, was in North Providence and Cranston.

During the five years, 1860 to 1865, including the period of the War of the Rebellion, the increase of population in the State was only 5.9 per cent. Eighteen towns in the State declined in population during this period. The largest percentage of increase was in the city of Newport, and in the towns of Cranston and North Providence. The loss in Newport county, during this period, was wholly owing to the cession of Fall River to Massachusetts. Including Fall River, the county gained considerably.

The addition of East Providence and Pawtucket to Providence county, in 1862, increased largely the percentage of gain in that county, between 1860 and 1865; and also the percentage of gain from 1790 to 1865.

The last column in the table shows the percentage of increase or decrease in each town, during the whole period of 75 years, from 1790 to 1865.

It will be seen that 8 towns in Rhode Island have less population in 1865, than they had in 1790. Four of them show a decrease of more than 40 per cent. The eight towns are West Greenwich, loss 40.2 per cent.; Jamestown, loss 31.2 per cent.; Little Compton, loss 22.4 per cent.; Tiverton, loss 19.6 per cent.; Foster, loss 17.4 per cent.; Glocester, loss 43.2 per cent.; Charlestown, loss 43.9 per cent.; Exeter, loss 40 per cent.

In relation to two of these towns, Glocester and Tiverton, the loss in population is easily accounted for. Glocester lost 1,834 of her population by the incorporation of Burrillville, in 1806. But Glocester not only lost this number of persons; she also lost the territory, which the manufacturing enterprise of later periods, has developed to such an extent, that in 1865, Burrillville contained 4,861 inhabitants, and Glocester only 2,286.

Tiverton also shows a loss of 19.6 per cent. of her population in 75 years, 1790 to 1865. This loss is wholly caused by the incorporation of the town of Fall River, in 1856. If we include the same territory that Tiverton had in 1748, that town would show a gain in every period included in the table, and Tiverton is the only town in the State that would show an actual gain of population, at every period.

But there are six towns, West Greenwich, Jamestown, Little Compton, Foster, Charlestown, and Exeter, which show an actual decrease in population, in 75 years, without any loss of territory. How shall we explain this?

If we examine the characteristics of these towns, we find that they have, almost exclusively, a farming population, without any large villages. The population is almost entirely native American. No manufacturing interests have brought in large numbers of foreigners. The whole foreign born population of all the six towns is only 144. The average number of persons to a family and to each dwelling, is considerably less in these towns than the average in the whole State.

There is nothing in these towns especially calculated to induce immigration to them; and not sufficient inducements in them to keep their young people at home.

The result is, as in all portions of New England where the prosperity and progress depend exclusively upon the farming interests, the young people emigrate, many dwellings are left for many years without children in them, a larger proportion than natural of the population is composed of persons not in the child-bearing period of life, very few children are born, and the population remains stationary, or declines.

Without giving many reasons which might be stated, or extending the discussion farther, the conclusion seems to be justified: That in the climate of New England; with the present, to a great extent, impoverished condition of its soil; and in the present state of knowledge of the art of farming; a community or town, which depends exclusively for its progress upon agriculture, cannot be expected, as a general rule, to sustain itself as to numbers, or at least, cannot increase to any great extent.

It will be noticed that the increase of population in the whole State, from 1790 to 1865, was 168.7 per cent. The extremes of loss and gain in different portions of the State, are a loss of 43.9 per cent. in Charlestown, and a gain of 1,258.8 per cent. in North Providence.

Only 7 towns, Bristol, Warwick, Cranston, Cumberland, North Providence, Smithfield, and Providence, show a greater percentage of gain than the State as a whole.

Nineteen towns either show a loss, or a gain of less than half that of the whole State; and in none of these nineteen towns does the gain equal one per cent. annually.

Providence city gained 755.7 per cent., from 1790 to 1865, or a fraction over ten per cent. annually. North Providence gained 1258.8 per cent., and Cranston, 388.9 per cent. Both of these towns are indebted for their gain, not only to the manufacturing interests within their limits; but also to their proximity to the City of Providence.

In Washington county, the greatest gain is in Westerly, 66 per cent., in 75 years; but in the whole county the gain is only 2.2 per cent. in that time. There are, comparatively, few manufactories in that county; and we are informed that that county has lost more from emigration to other States, than other portions of Rhode Island.

It is not necessary to continue the subject farther. Those interested in it will find, on examination of the table, many other points which will be instructive.

It will be evident to all, that the growth and prosperity of the State, so far at least as relates to population, has for many years depended chiefly upon its manufacturing interests.

CENSUSES OF PROVIDENCE.

In 1825, and every tenth year since that date, a census of Providence has been taken, the particulars of which are not given in the table on pages xxxii and xxxiii. The total population of Providence, by these city censuses, was as follows:

1825	15,941	1845	31,747
1835	19,277	1855	47,785

The full particulars of these censuses were published in 1856, in the appendix to a report upon the "Census of the City of Providence, taken in July, 1855; with a brief account of the Manufactures, Trade, Commerce, and other Statistics of the city; by Edwin M. Snow, M. D."

COLORED POPULATION OF RHODE ISLAND.

The subject of the condition and prospects of the negro race in this country, has acquired a new interest by the events of the last few years. At the present time, a concerted and formidable effort is making to bring large numbers of the colored population of the Southern States to New England, and to other Northern States.

It, therefore, becomes interesting and important to know the past history of the colored race in New England, that we may judge of its prospects in the future.

I do not propose to discuss the question of the policy of promoting the immigration of the blacks to New England; except so far as to give the facts in relation to their number in Rhode Island, as shown by past censuses of the State.

The blacks have existed in Rhode Island, in considerable numbers, about 170 years. In 1708 the census gave no particulars in relation to them; but stated that there were "426 black servants" in the colony. This was nearly six per cent. (5.93) of the whole population at that date. In 1748, they comprised 12.8 per cent. of the whole population.

The social position and standing of the blacks, and their facilities for progress and elevation have probably been better, at all times, in this State, than in any other portion of the country where they have comprised so large a proportion of the population.

Though slavery existed in the State for a long period, it was in a mild form, and the principles of the people in opposition to it, were shown by legislative enactments ameliorating the condition of the slaves, from the earliest periods in the history of the State.

During the war of the Revolution, the negroes were permitted to enlist in a Rhode Island regiment, and to assist in maintaining the liberties of their country. A considerable number of them enlisted, and received their freedom for so doing.

At the close of the war, February 23, 1784, an Act was passed providing that all children born after the first of March following, of slave mothers, should be free. This Act, with others encouraging the manumission of slaves, speedily removed all hindrances to their progress, which slavery might have been supposed to make.

By the present, the first constitution of Rhode Island, which went into operation on the first Tuesday of May, 1843, the negroes were allowed to vote upon the same conditions as the native American white population, and since that date they have enjoyed all the facilities for progress which the right of voting could give them.

Let us see, then, what has been the progress of the colored population in Rhode Island, with respect to numbers.

The following table shows the number of the colored population (blacks and mulattoes,) in each town in Rhode Island, at different periods, from 1730 to 1865, inclusive.

I have also added the number of Indians, in each town, at several dates.

TABLE, *Showing the number of colored persons and Indians, in each town in Rhode Island, at different periods.*

TOWNS AND DIVISIONS OF THE STATE.	BLACKS.								
	1730.	1748.	1774.	1782.	1790.	1800.	1810	1820.	1830.
Barrington	....	....	41	46	44	26	22	25	26
Bristol	....	128	114	76	108	113	177	213	171
Warren	....	50	44	35	38	52	59	66	67
BRISTOL COUNTY	....	178	199	157	190	191	258	304	264
Coventry	....	16	20	12	40	51	33	23	13
East Greenwich	40	61	69	70	85	90	67	58	55
West Greenwich	...	8	19	21	38	15	27	3	12
Warwick	77	176	189	136	259	271	231	255	221
KENT COUNTY	117	261	297	239	422	427	358	339	301
Fall River	....	....	....	....	....	....	....	....	....
Jamestown	80	110	131	65	84	80	80	51	21
Little Compton	....	62	47	34	45	32	17	11	9
Middletown	....	76	64	33	41	37	29	15	8
Newport	649	1,105	1,246	600	640	615	630	556	449
New Shoreham	20	20	55	55	104	93	32	108	128
Portsmouth	100	134	122	78	64	37	43	18	14
Tiverton	....	99	95	137	202	193	117	121	85
NEWPORT COUNTY	849	1,606	1,760	1,002	1,180	1,087	948	880	714
Burrillville	....	....	....	....	....	....	33	36	46
Cranston	....	....	60	67	83	47	110	85	78
Cumberland	....	4	17	11	8	7	8	6	5
East Providence	....	....	....	....	....	....	....	....	....
Foster	....	....	....	7	19	26	12	3	2
Glocester	....	8	19	22	23	78	13	7	6
Johnston	....	....	65	65	74	62	69	69	47
North Providence	....	....	31	17	55	17	43	69	69
Pawtucket	....	....	....	....	....	....	....	....	....
Scituate	....	16	55	22	35	36	46	34	35
Smithfield	....	30	51	47	88	47	71	83	61
TOWNS PROV. COUNTY	....	58	298	258	385	320	405	392	349
PROVIDENCE CITY	128	225	303	285	475	656	871	979	1,213
Charlestown	....	58	52	39	418	135	63	58	100
Exeter	....	63	67	94	124	94	83	66	94
Hopkinton	....	....	48	28	79	76	47	32	25
North Kingstown	165	184	211	210	295	204	196	132	122
South Kingstown	333	380	440	453	648	419	390	341	336
Richmond	.. ..	5	24	32	69	35	42	13	8
Westerly	56	59	69	64	78	50	56	66	53
WASHINGTON COUNTY	554	749	911	920	1,711	1,013	877	708	738
WHOLE STATE	1,648	3,077	3,768	2,861	4,363	3,694	3,717	3,602	3,579

TABLE, CONTINUED, *Showing the number of colored persons and Indians, in each town in Rhode Island, at different periods.*

TOWNS AND DIVISIONS OF THE STATE.	BLACKS.				INDIANS.			
	1840.	1850.	1860.	1865.	1730.	1748.	1774.	1782.
Barrington	.....	25	22	23	.....	.....	18	.....
Bristol	171	200	234	145	.....	13	16	2
Warren	55	86	52	42	.....	30	7	3
BRISTOL COUNTY	245	311	308	210	.....	43	41	5
Coventry	.....	17	1	32	.....	7	11	2
East Greenwich	.....	41	97	82	34	27	31	10
West Greenwich	.....	9	2	2	.....	1	.....	.....
Warwick	231	162	159	141	73	93	88	37
KENT COUNTY	312	229	259	257	107	128	130	49
Fall River	.....	.....	39	.....	.....	.....	.....	.....
Jamestown	.....	14	13	18	19	26	32	.....
Little Compton	.....	8	6	4	.....	86	25	13
Middletown	.....	3	11	10	.....	18	13	.....
Newport	425	628	691	705	148	68	46	17
New Shoreham	.....	44	28	30	20	20	51	51
Portsmouth	.....	5	9	6	70	51	21	7
Tiverton	60	80	25	32	.....	99	71	21
NEWPORT COUNTY	581	782	822	805	257	368	259	109
Burrillville	.....	19	30	20	.....	.....	.....	.....
Cranston	.....	125	246	241	.....	.....	19	9
Cumberland	.....	10	24	21	.....	.....	3	.....
East Providence	.....	.....	.....	23	.....	.....	.....	.....
Foster	.....	.....	.....	1	.....	.....	.....	.....
Glocester	.....	12	4	9	.....	.....	.....	.....
Johnston	.....	38	26	25	.....	.....	9	3
North Providence	64	60	67	60	.....	.....	7	5
Pawtucket	.....	.....	.....	14	.....	.....	.....	.....
Scituate	31	14	9	12	.....	6	8	.....
Smithfield	41	41	34	46	.....	20	23	12
TOWNS PROV. COUNTY	292	319	440	472	.....	26	69	29
PROVIDENCE CITY	1,302	1,499	1,537	1,711	81	50	68	6
Charlestown	.....	35	9	150	.....	303	528	280
Exeter	.....	46	43	31	.....	8	17	18
Hopkinton	.....	8	7	21	.....	.....	21	30
North Kingstown	.....	118	92	71	65	86	79	8
South Kingstown	.....	249	352	279	225	193	210	32
Richmond	.....	27	47	36	.....	3	20	1
Westerly	.....	47	36	44	250	49	37	9
WASHINGTON COUNTY	511	530	586	632	540	642	912	378
WHOLE STATE	3,243	3,670	3,952	4,087	985	1,257	1,479	576

NOTES.—In the first United States census, for the year 1790, the Indians were counted with the blacks, and the number of blacks at that date should probably be about 500 less than in the table.

In all the national censuses, since 1790, "Indians not taxed" have not been enumerated at all, and are not included in the population of the State, as given for the years, from 1800 to 1860 inclusive. In the State census of 1865, they were counted with the colored population, and this explains the great increase in the colored population of the town of Charlestown, from 1860 to 1865.

The Narragansett tribe of Indians still maintains a nominal existence in Rhode Island. They number, at the present time, 58 males, 75 females; total 133. They own about 3,000 acres of land in the town of Charlestown, the title to which has come down to them from their ancestors who occupied the State before its settlement by the whites. They are an independent nation, not taxed, and not citizens of the State or country. They are under the guardianship of the General Assembly, and cannot sell their lands. There are no Indians of pure blood among them at the present time; but the blood of the African race predominates.

I have been unable to obtain the number of the colored population, by the census of 1840, except by counties and for a few towns, which are given in the table.

I am satisfied that, in the census of 1865, and probably in all previous censuses, some colored persons are counted as whites, from the neglect of the enumerators to mark them as "colored" in the returns. The error, however, is probably similar in all censuses, and does not injure the table for purposes of comparison.

In the census of 1782, New Shoreham was not included, as it was in possession of the enemy. I have given the colored population of that town, for that year, the same as in 1774.

Previous to 1790, there is, in the census returns, no distinction in the colored population, between the slaves and the free. It is probable that until the beginning of the revolutionary war, the greater portion of the blacks were slaves, but by the effects of the war, and by manumission, the number of slaves had been reduced to 948, in 1790. The number of slaves in the State, at different dates, as shown by the United States censuses, was as follows:—1790, 948; 1800, 330; 1810, 108; 1820, 48; 1830, 14; 1840, 5.

The last slave in the State, James Howland, died in Jamestown, January 3, 1859, at the age of 100 years.

The number of colored persons in Rhode Island, (not including Indians,) and their proportion of the total population at different dates, have been as follows:

Date.	No. of Blacks.	Percentage.	Date.	No. of Blacks.	Percentage.
1708	426	5.93	1810	3,717	4.82
1730	1,648	9.18	1820	3,602	4.33
1748	3,077	12.80	1830	3,579	3.68
1774	3,768	6.31	1840	3,243	2.98
1782	2,861	5.46	1850	3,670	2.48
1790	*3,863	5.61	1860	3,952	2.26
1800	3,694	5.34	1865	4,087	2.21

* Deducting 500 for Indians.

There was a large decrease in the number, both of blacks and Indians, between the censuses of 1774 and 1782, comprising the period of the war of the revolution.

It will be noticed that the percentage of blacks, in the population of Rhode Island, has steadily decreased from the year 1748 to the present time; and that the whole number, in 1865, including the nominal Indians in Charlestown, was only 319 greater than in 1774. This is an increase of only a little more than 8 per cent. in 91 years. The white population increased more than 223 per cent. in the same period.

During this period, and particularly during the last twenty years, the immigration of blacks into Rhode Island has largely exceeded the emigration.

The results of registration in the State, since 1850, show that there are more deaths than births among the colored population. From the first day of June, 1853, to the thirty-first day of December, 1864, inclusive, the Registration Reports of Rhode Island show 929 births, and 1,025 deaths among the colored population of the State. A table in the sixth report, for the year 1858, shows that, during five years and seven months ending December 31, 1858, the percentage of deaths among the colored population, from consumption and other diseases of the respiratory organs, which depend to a great extent upon climate, was nearly double the percentage from the same diseases among the white population.

These reports also show that the proportion of deaths to the living, in Rhode Island, is more than twice as great among the colored population as among the white population.

Without pursuing the subject further, and without giving many reasons which might be stated, the conclusions are to my mind, certain, as follows:

That the colored population of New England is not self-sustaining as to numbers; that the climate and other influences are such that it would steadily decrease and, unless renewed by immigration, would, in a comparatively brief period, become extinct.

Finally, if this be true, it is not philanthropy, but positive inhumanity to the race and to individuals, to encourage their emigration from the Southern States to New England.

III. COMMENTS UPON THE TABLES.

1.—TABLES OF POPULATION.

The statistics relating to the population of Rhode Island, as obtained by the census of 1865, are given in the tabular portions of this volume, pages 1 to 52 inclusive. These statistics are given in full, for each town and county separately, and for each ward in the cities of Providence and Newport.

The information given in these tables is much more full and more minute than has ever been given in any census of the State, and on some subjects, information is given which cannot be found in any census of any State, ever published.

An examination of the tables will show to the citizens of every town in the State, a multitude of facts relating to the population of each town, which will be found interesting and important. The minute analysis of the population is especially valuable in connection with the registration of births, marriages, and deaths, and will be much used in the reports upon that subject.

It will be impossible, in this report, to dwell upon all the infinite variety of subjects that are suggested by the tables. I shall attempt only, to give such explanations as may seem to be necessary for a full understanding of the tables themselves; and to notice, briefly, such interesting, or important, or curious facts as may be suggested in the examination of them.

DWELLING HOUSES AND FAMILIES.

The first table, on page 2, shows the number of dwelling houses, and the materials of which they are built, and the number of families in each town in the State, on the first day of June, 1865.

There were 28,666 dwelling houses in the State, and 39,208 families, giving 1.4 families, and 6.45 persons to each dwelling; and 4.72 persons to each family. By the United States census of 1860, there were 27,056 dwelling houses in the State, giving 6.43 persons to each dwelling.

The average number of persons to a dwelling house, in 1860, was considerably greater in Rhode Island than in any other State of the United States; but is largely exceeded in some countries in Europe. In Scotland and in some portions of Germany, there are from 6.84 to 8.86 persons to each dwelling, and in the cities of Scotland the average is 14.11 persons to each dwelling. Some portions of New York city show a still greater average.

The greatest average number of families to each dwelling house in Rhode Island, was 1.68 in Providence, though in North Providence the number was 1.60, nearly as great.

In four towns, West Greenwich, Jamestown, Exeter, and Richmond, there were more dwelling houses than families.

The greatest average number of persons to a dwelling house was 8.06 in Providence, and 7.93 in North Providence; the smallest number was 4.38, in Richmond.

The greatest average number of persons to each family was 5.52 in Barrington; the smallest number was 4.07, in Little Compton.

To those not familiar with the subject the question may arise, why the average should be so large in Barrington? The explanation is easy. In taking the census of the families, the inmates of hotels, boarding houses, and public institutions are counted as single families. In Barrington, the whole number of families, and the total population are small, and a single very large boarding house is sufficient to increase largely the average number of persons to a family. A single family of 100 persons, deducted from the whole number in that town, would reduce the average to 5 persons to each family.

There were 926 empty dwelling houses in the State, by the census of 1865. The greatest number in any town was 120, in Newport; the least number 4, in Tiverton. In some towns, as Warwick, Cumberland, and Scituate, the large number of empty houses was mostly owing to temporary causes which have since been removed, and a census at the present time, would show a considerable increase in the number of families, and in the population.

Of the 28,666 dwelling houses in the State, 27,959 were constructed of wood, and only 432 of brick, and 275 of stone. Even in the City of Providence, 96.36 in each 100 of the dwelling houses were of wood, and only 3.64 in each 100, of brick or stone. The proportion of wooden dwelling houses is less in Cumberland than in Providence.

SEX AND COLOR.

We have already given the statistics of the colored population in Rhode Island, and have shown its rate of increase in the past. It will be noticed that, in 1865, much more than half of the whole colored population in the State, was in the cities of Providence and Newport.

In regard to sex, there were in 1865, in Rhode Island, 8,439 more females than males. The proportions of the sexes, white and colored, were as follows:

White population	47.80 males, and	52.20 females in each	100
Colored population	43.87 males, and	56.13 females in each	100
Total population	47.72 males, and	52.28 females in each	100

Though there is an excess of females in the whole State, and in most of the towns, the following towns show an excess of males, viz.: Barrington, West Greenwich, Jamestown, Middletown, New Shoreham, Portsmouth, Cranston, Glocester, Johnston, and Exeter. The same towns showed an excess of males by the census of 1860.

Generally, in New England, there is, for obvious reasons, a large excess of females in the population, while in the newer States, the opposite is true. In the whole country, in 1860, there was an excess of 730,000 males, in a population of thirty-one millions.

NATIVITY.

The subject of nativity, or birth-place of the population, is of very great interest and importance, particularly in this country, where the enormous influx of foreigners is changing the whole character of the population in some sections of the older States, and is building up immense empires in the west with a people differing in all their social characteristics from those who laid the foundations of our republic, and who have thus far exercised a controlling influence in its government.

And yet, this important subject has received but little attention, until a recent period, in the national and State censuses of this country. None of the United States censuses, until that of 1850, obtained any particulars in regard to the birth-places of the population, except that the censuses of 1820 and 1830, showed the number of "*foreigners not naturalized.*" No particulars were, however, given in relation to them.

The census of 1850 commenced a new era in this, and in other important particulars, and gives us, minutely, the birth-places of the whole population.

In the census of Rhode Island, in 1865, I have illustrated this subject very fully, giving all the particulars that can possibly be of general interest and value, and also some particulars which are of local interest only. The statistics relating to the birth-places of the population of the State, are given in tables IV to XIV inclusive, on pages 5 to 22 inclusive, of the tabular portion of this volume.

These tables show, in relation to each town and county in the State, and in relation to each ward in the cities of Providence and Newport; how many of the inhabitants were born in each town in Rhode Island, how many were born in each of the United States, and how many were born in each foreign country.

Table IV on page 5, shows in general terms the birth-places of the population of each town in the State, on the first of June, 1865. Of the 184,965 inhabitants of the State, 75,055 were born in the towns in which they resided; 37,152 had moved from the towns in which they were born, to other towns in the State, making a total of 112,207 inhabitants of the State who were born in the State; 33,055 of the inhabitants of the State were born in other of the United States; and 39,703 were born in foreign countries.

In 1860, the population of Rhode Island was: born in the State, 109,965; born in other States, 27,161; born in foreign countries, 37,394; born at sea, 14; unknown birth-place, 86; total, 174,620.

In the population of the towns of Cranston and Johnston, there were more natives of other towns in the State, than there were natives of the towns themselves.

In the towns of Cranston, Cumberland, North Providence, and Pawtucket, the number of inhabitants who were born in foreign countries was greater than the number who were born in those towns.

A word of explanation is necessary in relation to the figures in this and the following tables, for East Providence and Pawtucket. These towns were admitted from Massachusetts, in 1862. In the census of 1865, the directions, in relation to birth-place, were "if in Rhode Island, give the town; if elsewhere, give the State or country." It would seem from the figures, that in East Providence, the enumerators put down those who were born in the town, previous to 1862, as born in Massachusetts, while in Pawtucket they gave them as born in Rhode Island. Both were right, and both were wrong.

Table V, pages 6 to 9 inclusive, shows how many of the inhabitants of each town were born in each town in Rhode Island, and illustrates some curious features of the migration of the population within the limits of the State. If we look at the name of a town, at *the top* of the table, and follow the column down we see how many natives of that town are living in the State, and the towns in which they live. Thus, take the town of Warwick, and look down the column, and we find that there are 5,296 natives of Warwick living in the State; that 2,822 of them were living in Warwick; 828 in Providence; 277 in Cranston, &c. There are natives of Warwick living in every town in the State, except Jamestown; natives of West Greenwich living in every town, except Little Compton and Burrillville; natives of Providence living in every town except Tiverton, &c., &c.

If we look at the name of the town on the left of the table, and follow the line across the table, we see how many of the inhabitants of that town were born in each town in the State. Thus, take Providence city and look across the table and we find that every town in the State, except Pawtucket, is largely represented in the population of Providence. The reason that there are none in Providence who were born in Pawtucket, and but few who were born in East Providence, in the table, is because in taking the census in Providence, those who were born in those towns, previous to 1862, were put down as born in Massachusetts.

Nearly every town in the State is represented in the population of Newport, and natives of Newport are living in every town in the State except Glocester. In Newport the proportion of the whole population, who were born in the town where they reside, is larger than in most of the towns.

The table also shows how many inhabitants each town in the State has given to, and received from, each other town. Thus, Coventry has given 90 persons to Newport, and 317 to Providence; and has received 10 from Newport, and 59 from Providence. Westerly has given

37 to Providence, and received the same number from Providence. Burrillville has given 4 to Westerly, and received 2 from Westerly. New Shoreham has given 313 natives to other towns in the State, and received only 60 from other towns.

There seems to be no special law which has governed the migration of the population within the limits of the State, except the tendency of the population of the smaller towns and farming districts, to the cities and manufacturing towns.

Table VI, pages 10 to 12 inclusive, shows how many of the inhabitants of each town in Rhode Island, in 1865, were born in each of the United States.

Every State in the Union, at that time, except Oregon, was represented in the population of Rhode Island. There were natives of Connecticut, Massachusetts and New York living in every town in the State; natives of New Hampshire, in every town except Jamestown, Hopkinton, and Richmond; natives of Vermont, in every town except Jamestown, Middletown and New Shoreham; natives of Virginia, in every town except East Greenwich, Little Compton, New Shoreham, Exeter, and South Kingstown; natives of Maine, in every town except West Greenwich, Foster, Charlestown, and Exeter; natives of Pennsylvania, in every town except Jamestown, Little Compton, Tiverton, Charlestown, and Richmond.

The following shows the number of natives of other States living in Rhode Island, in 1860 and in 1865.

LIVING IN RHODE ISLAND.

Natives of	1865.	1860.
Maine	1,310	1,301
New Hampshire	1,082	1,482
Vermont	748	692
Massachusetts	17,320	13,965
Rhode Island	112,207	109,965
Connecticut	5,439	4,634
Total natives of New England	138,106	132,039
Natives of other United States	7,156	5,187
Total native born	145,262	137,226

The large increase of natives of Massachusetts living in Rhode Island in 1865, was partly owing to the annexation of Pawtucket and East Providence, in 1862.

By the United States census of 1860, the number of natives of Rhode Island living in the United States, was as follows:

NATIVES OF RHODE ISLAND, 1860.

Living in		Living in	
Maine	418	Connecticut	7,024
New Hampshire	637		
Vermont	521	Total in New England	131,891
Massachusetts	13,326	In other of the United States	23,373
Rhode Island	109,965	Total in whole country	155,264

By the census of 1860, there were 3,144,598 natives of the New England States, living in the United States. Of this number, 2,584,262 were living in the New England States, and 560,336, in other States.

During the ten years, 1850 to 1860, there was an emigration of 106,445 natives of the New England States, from New England to other States in the country; an average of 10,644 annually.

These facts are important in view of the fact, that in some towns of Rhode Island as well as in other New England States, the population is stationary as to numbers, or decreasing.

This enormous emigration of the native American population of New England shows how this population may be stationary, or even decreasing in some portions of New England, and still the same population, as a class, may be increasing in the whole country, and be fulfilling its mission in the world, to the utmost extent.

The seventh table, pages 13 to 15 inclusive, shows how many of the inhabitants of each town in Rhode Island, in 1865, were born in different foreign countries.

The following shows the number of persons of foreign birth in Rhode Island, by the censuses of 1850, 1860 and 1865:

Born in	1850.	1860.	1865.
Ireland	15,944	25,285	27,030
England	4,490	6,356	6,478
Scotland and Wales	1,000	1,536	1,403
British America	1,024	2,830	3,384
Germany	230	815	897
France	80	123	146
Portugal	58	86	75
Other countries	285	363	290
Total foreign born	23,111	37,394	39,703

There were 39,703 persons of foreign birth in Rhode Island, in 1865, or 21.46 per cent. of the whole population. Though 30 different countries were represented in this population, 39,192 of the whole number were from five countries.

The population of foreign birth, in 1850, was 15.66 per cent. of the whole population of the State; in 1860, it was 21.41 per cent., and in 1865, it was 21.46 per cent.

In the City of Providence, the number of persons of foreign birth has increased but little for the last fifteen years, while the percentage has decreased. The number and proportion of foreigners, (by birth,) in Providence, at different periods, have been as follows:

Providence.	Total Population.	Foreign born.	Percentage of Foreign.
1845	31,747	5,965	18.79
1850	41,513	10,275	24.75
1855	47,785	13,232	27.69
1860	50,666	12,570	24.80
1865	54,595	13,402	24.54

The number of natives of Ireland, living in Providence, was 378 less, in 1865, than it was in 1855.

The natives of British America show the largest proportional increase, in the foreign population of Rhode Island, during the last fifteen years. Many of these are French Canadians who are employed in our manufacturing villages. Considerable numbers of this class are found in Barrington, Coventry, Warwick, Burrillville, Cumberland and Smithfield.

In 1850, the natives of Ireland comprised 68.99 per cent. of the whole foreign population (by birth) in Rhode Island; in 1860, 67.61 per cent., and in 1865, 68.08 per cent.

REMARKS ON NATIVITY OF THE POPULATION.

It will be seen from an examination of the tables, and from the preceding comments, that I have given very minute and full information in relation to the nativity, or birth-places of the population of Rhode Island. One of the important objects of a census of population is to enable us to divide it into classes, and thus, knowing the social, political, moral, religious, or other characteristics of these classes, to study and judge of their influence upon the population and prospects of a community.

With this object in view, the subject of the nativity of a population, has many interesting and valuable features, and it is very important that the facts relating to it should be presented fully and minutely, in all censuses.

But in some classifications of the population, and in some of the most important, the nativity or birth-place of the people is of very slight importance, and if the nativity alone be given, the statistics are of little value, and will, in fact, only mislead and deceive us in all important investigations.

Take, for example, the division of the population into the two classes, American and foreign. The subject of the influence of the foreign population upon the social, moral and political prospects of this country, is one of the most important that can engage the attention of the statesman, or of any citizen.

But it is not the foreign population, by birth alone, which is exerting its influence upon our institutions, and moulding the social and other characteristics of the community;—it is the foreign population, including the children, born in this country, of foreign parents. These children, for the first generation at least, partake of all the social, moral, political, and sanitary influences of their parents, and it is through them that the chief influence of this population is exerted upon our institutions and habits, as a people.

In fact, in large portions of our country, including New England, and particularly in Rhode Island, the foreign population, by nativity, exerts very little influence upon our social or political institutions. In this State, the foreigners, by birth, comprise only about 21 per cent. of the population, very few of them are voters, their number is but very slowly increasing, and as it can increase only by immigration, the prospects of any great increase in future, are very slight. On the contrary, the prospects are, that in Rhode Island, the number of foreigners, by birth, will remain nearly stationary for the present, and in a few years will begin to decrease.

But foreigners, including their children, and through their children, are now exerting a tremendous influence, not only in Rhode Island, but also throughout the country, and are modifying to a greater or less extent, all the moral, social, and other characteristics of our population.

It seems to me, then, to be of the utmost importance that in our censuses, and in all our statistical investigations, we should be able to classify the population *not only by nativity*, *but also by parentage;* that we should be able to show not only the facts relating to persons of foreign birth, but also those relating to their children, as distinguished from the children of American parents.

And yet, notwithstanding the importance of these facts, no national or State census, in this country, previous to the census of Rhode Island, in 1865, has ever given this classification, or hardly alluded to it.

If we refer to these censuses, to study the facts relating to the American and foreign population, we find that, according to birthplace, the only classification given in them, the American class includes all the Americans and their children, and also all the children born in this country, of foreign parents, while the foreign class includes only persons of foreign birth.

The American class includes all the children in the community, and nearly all of the aged persons, while the foreign class is composed mostly of persons in the prime of life.

If we extend our inquiries to criminal statistics, we find that nearly all the juvenile crime in the community is committed by the American class, and that the truants, and the inmates of all our reform schools and other similar institutions, belong almost exclusively to this class.

If we look at educational statistics, we find that nearly all those who are growing up in ignorance, and cannot read and write, under 20 years of age, belong to the American population, by nativity.

If we turn to vital statistics, we find that the average age of those who die of the American population, according to nativity, is less than half the average age of those who die of the foreign population.

In relation to cholera infantum, and other diseases of childhood which are caused to a great extent by filth, improper food, and other defects in home life, we find that those who die, belong, almost exclusively, to the American population, and that almost none of the foreign population die from these causes.

If we wish to study the comparative increase of the American and foreign population, we find, for example, in the City of Boston, in 1865, that an American population, by nativity, of 126,304, had only 1,650 children, while a foreign population of 66,020 had 3,587 children in the same year. We also find that in the same city, in the same year, 3,127 died of the American population, by birth, and only 1,381 of the foreign population, showing an immense loss in the American, and a great gain in the foreign population.

It is not necessary to state that all the conclusions given above are utterly false and deceptive, and yet, they are all true, if we depend upon our censuses for our information. There has never been a national or State census in this country, until the recent census of Rhode Island, in which it is possible to find the facts which will give us any different conclusions.

They all ignore, entirely, the subject of parentage, and give us no facts by which the children of foreign parents can be distinguished from the American population.

PARENTAGE.

In the census of Rhode Island, in 1865, in addition to the full particulars relating to the nativity, or birth-place of the population, I have given the facts in relation to the parentage, by which we can show how many children of foreign parents, and of each class of foreign parents, there are living in the State. I have also shown how many persons there are in the State, of mixed parentage, that is, of whom one parent was of American and the other of foreign birth.

These particulars are given, for each town in the State and for each ward in the cities of Providence and Newport, in tables XV to XVIII inclusive, pages 23 to 27 inclusive, of the present volume. I have, also, added tables XX and XXII, which show the sex, according to parentage, and the age, according to parentage, of the population of each ward in the City of Providence.

Referring to these tables, we are able to see the difference between the nativity and parentage of the population, which, for the whole State, is as follows:

ACCORDING TO NATIVITY.

Americans	145,262, or	78.54 per cent. of all.
Foreigners	39,703, or	21.46 per cent. of all.
Total population	184,965,	100.00

ACCORDING TO PARENTAGE.

American	117,316, or	63.43 per cent. of all.
Foreign	67,649, or	36.57 per cent. of all.
Total population	184,965	100.00

In this statement, those of mixed parentage are given according to the birth-place of their fathers.

It seems that, *according to parentage*, the American population is 27,946 less, and the foreign population is the same number greater, than according to nativity. These 27,946 individuals are the children born in this country, of foreign parents.

In this classification, according to parentage, the American class includes those born in the United States with their children; while the foreign class includes those born in foreign countries with their children. It is obvious that this is the correct classification, and the only classification that is of any value in investigations relating to these divisions of the population.

Table XV, page 23, shows the number of each foreign class, according to parentage, in each town, and in the whole State.

The following table shows the number of each foreign class of the population, both according to nativity and according to parentage, in the whole State. The first column of figures shows the number according to birth-place; the second column, the number according to parentage; and the third column shows the difference between the other two, which is the number of children, born in this country, of each class. The population of mixed parentage are necessarily omitted in this table.

	Number by Nativity.	Number by Parentage.	Difference, children born in this country.
Irish	27,030	48,136	21,106
English	6,478	9,781	3,303
Scotch and Welsh	1,403	2,344	941
German	897	1,626	729
French	146	247	101
British American	3,384	3,259	....
Portuguese	75	140	65
Italian	37	61	24
Other foreign	253	256	3

It will be noticed that the number born in British America exceeds the number of British American parentage. The explanation of this is, that many of those born in British America, are of Irish, English, Scotch, or other parentage.

MIXED PARENTAGE.

It seems, from table XV, that there are 1,759 persons in the State, whose fathers were born in the United States, and whose mothers were born in some foreign country; there are, also, 1,799 persons with fathers born in some foreign country, and mothers born in the United States, making a total of 3,558 persons of "mixed" parentage, in the whole State.

The subject of the intermingling, by marriage, of persons born in different countries, is of considerable interest in this State, as well as throughout the country, and will become much more important in future. A census in which the nativity alone of the population is given, can give us no information upon this subject.

In the City of Providence, during eleven years, 1855 to 1865 inclusive, there were 1,371 children born of "mixed" parentage, or precisely 8 per cent. of the whole number of children born. During the same period, the annual number of "mixed" marriages was from 8.84 to 14.63 per cent. of the whole number.

Table XVII on page 26, shows us the number of persons, American and foreign, both by nativity and by parentage, in each town in the State; and also the percentage of American and of foreign parentage, in each town. It will be seen that the proportion of foreign population differs greatly in different towns; the greatest proportion being in the cities and manufacturing towns. The least percentage of foreign is in Exeter, only 1.47 in each 100 of the total population, while in North Providence, 56.17 in each 100 are of foreign parentage. In 3 towns, Cumberland, North Providence and Pawtucket, the population of foreign parentage exceeds that of American parentage; and in Burrillville, Cranston and Smithfield there is but a small difference.

In all the above towns, and in the aggregate for all the towns of Providence county, the percentage of the population of foreign parentage is greater than in the City of Providence.

The census of the City of Providence, in 1855, was taken like that, in 1865, so as to show the parentage as well as the nativity of the population. We are, therefore, able to compare the results, in this respect, of an interval of ten years, in the history of the city. They are as follows:

AMERICAN POPULATION.

Providence.	Total Population.	Number born in U. S.	Percentage.	Number of American Parentage.	Percentage.
1855	47,785	33,682	70.48	27,897	58.94
1865	54,595	41,193	75.45	30,702	56.24
Ten years	gain 6,810	gain, 7,511	gain, 4.97	gain, 2,805	loss, 2.70

FOREIGN POPULATION.

Providence.	Total Population.	Number born in foreign countries.	Percentage.	Number of Foreign Parentage.	Percentage.
1855	47,785	13,232	27.69	19,432	41.06
1865	54,595	13,402	24.55	23,893	43.76
Ten years	gain, 6,810	gain, 170	loss, 3.14	gain, 4,461	gain, 2.70

In the figures for 1855, in the above statement, those of unknown birth-place or parentage, are omitted. This fact makes an apparent discrepancy in the figures as given above. In the census of 1865, there were none of unknown nativity, or parentage, in the city or in the State.

The percentages given above are the proportions of the total population of the city. Looking at the actual gain of the two classes of the population, we have the following:

Birthplace.	1855.	1865.	Gain.	Gain per cent.
United States	33,682	41,193	7,511	22.30
Foreign Countries	13,232	13,402	170	1.28
Parentage.				
American	27,897	30,702	2,805	10.05
Foreign	19,432	23,893	4,461	22.95

This shows that, *according to nativity* or birth-place, the American population is increasing far more rapidly than the foreign; a fact which might be expected, as, by this classification, all the children born in this country, of foreign parents, are counted with the American population.

It also shows that, *according to parentage*, the foreign population is increasing much faster than the American; a fact which might be expected, as it is well known that the class of persons of foreign birth, who live in this country, has more children in proportion to its numbers, than the population of American birth.

Some persons, looking at this last fact, have concluded that the females of the native American population of New England, as a class, are degenerating, and that this population, as a class, is decreasing and must soon run out.

Without discussing the subject at length, at this time, we may observe that it is easy to explain why, without any degeneracy, the native American population now living in New England should have less children in proportion to its numbers, than the foreign population now living here.

In the first place, we should recollect the enormous emigration, during the last thirty years, of natives of New England to the Western States. By the census of 1860, there were 560,336 natives of the New England States living in other States, and the increase, from 1850 to 1860, of natives of New England, living in other States, was equal to an emigration of 10,645 *annually*. This only includes the actual increase in the number of natives of New England, living in other States, between 1850 and 1860, as shown by the censuses of those periods. To know the actual emigration from New England, during that time, we should add the number of natives of New England who were living in other States in 1850, and who died between 1850 and 1860. Remember too, that these emigrants are almost exclusively young persons, or persons in the prime of life,—precisely the class to which we must look for the natural increase of the population.

The result of this is, that the native American population which is left in New England is not, so to speak, a normal population; that is, it does not comprise the natural proportions of youth, middle age, and old age; but has a larger proportion than natural of aged persons, and a smaller proportion than natural of persons in the periods of life in which we may expect the production of children.

The foreign population living in New England, on the contrary, is composed almost entirely of young persons and of persons in the prime of life, with an exceedingly small proportion of aged persons. Such a population, as a class, will have, of course, more children in proportion to its numbers, than a population made up as the American population of New England is at present.

It will be seen, from table XXII, on page 38, that 92.47 per cent. of the American population, in 1865, in the City of Providence, according to parentage, was under 60 years of age, and 7.53 per cent. was of the age of 60 and over; while of the foreign population, 96.39 per cent. was under 60, and only 3.61 per cent, was 60 years and over. In the country towns, the true home and origin of the native American population of New England, the proportion of aged persons is very much greater, and that of young persons is very much smaller, than in the cities.

SEX, NATIVITY AND PARENTAGE.

In the registration of deaths, in the City of Providence, it has been found that there is a marked difference between the American and foreign population, in the proportions of the sexes of decedents from consumption. Of the decedents from consumption, of American parentage, a large excess is females, while of the decedents of foreign parentage, the proportion of the sexes is nearly equal, with sometimes an excess of males.

For this reason, and others which might be named, it is of considerable interest and importance to know the proportion of the sexes, according to nativity and parentage, among the living population.

This is given in tables XIX and XX, on page 28, for the City of Providence. The result is as follows:

ACCORDING TO NATIVITY.

Birth-Place.	Males.	Females.	Males.	Females.
Born in the United States	19,511	21,682,	or 47.37,	and 52.63 in each 100.
Born in Foreign Countries	5,708	7,694,	or 42.59,	and 57.41 in each 100.

ACCORDING TO PARENTAGE.

Parentage.	Males.	Females.	Males.	Females.
American	14,444	16,258,	or 47.05,	and 52.95 in each 100.
Foreign	10,775	13,118,	or 45.10,	and 54.90 in each 100.

Those of mixed parentage are given according to the birth-place of their fathers.

The above figures show that, both by birth-place and by parentage, the proportion of females is greater among the foreign than among the American population of Providence. We must look farther for the explanation of the greater proportion of female decedents, from consumption, among the American than among the foreign population.

AGE AND SEX.

The number of persons of each sex, in each division of ages, in each town and county in Rhode Island, and in each ward in the cities of Providence and Newport, is given in table XXI, pages 29 to 37 inclusive.

This table contains all the information usually given in modern censuses, in relation to the ages of the population, and will be found to contain much that is interesting and important, respecting the population of each town, and of the whole State.

Many other classifications and divisions, in connection with age, might have been given, all of which would be found useful to those interested in the investigation of the present condition and future prospects of the population of the State; but it seemed necessary to place a limit upon the number of tables given, and I have, therefore, omitted many which my own inclinations would have led me to insert.

The subject of the ages of the living is of very great importance in studying the existing characteristics and future prospects of the population of any community or State. The number and proportion of the sexes at different ages, the proportions of different classes of the population at different ages, the proportions of the dependent and productive classes, as shown by age, the longevity of the population, the probable and comparative mortality, and many other subjects, may be illustrated by tables of ages of the population, and all are important for a full understanding of the interests and characteristics of a community.

As has been said by an eminent statistical writer:

"The ages of a population are among the most important elements of information, and form some of the best means of comparing the people of one place with those of another; or the people of one place, at one period, with those of the same place at another period. A census in which the ages are not taken is comparatively useless. A people may be more or less healthy or unhealthy, efficient or inefficient, happy or unhappy, according as a greater or less number is found of one age or another. * * * These truths will be apparent to all who study the laws of health, life and longevity, and compare the operations of these laws in different places."

Notwithstanding the importance of the subject, I feel compelled, in its examination, to limit myself to a very few points. It would be extremely interesting to show the differences, in respect to age, and proportions at different ages, which exist between the different towns and divisions of the State; but this must be omitted. Those interested in the subject and in the population of the several towns, will be rewarded by an examination of the tables given, with reference to this point. I propose, only, to give a few facts and comparisons, relating to the ages of the population of the State as a whole.

The following table shows the number and proportions of each sex, and of the total population, in each division of ages, in the whole State, by the census of 1865. Those of "unknown" ages, numbering 41 in the whole State, are omitted:

TABLE.—*Proportions at different ages in Rhode Island*, 1865.

AGES.	MALES.		FEMALES.		TOTAL POPULATION.	
	Number.	Per Cent.	Number.	Per Cent.	Number.	Per Cent.
Under 1 year........	1,930	2.19	1,914	1.98	3 844	2.08
1 and under 2.......	1,607	1.82	1,668	1.72	3,275	1.77
2 " " 5.	5,915	6.70	5,835	6.04	11,750	6.35
Total under 5.......	9,452	10.71	9,417	9.74	18,869	10.20
5 and under 10.....	10,143	11.49	10,029	10.37	20,172	10.91
10 " " 15.....	9,358	10.60	9,258	9 58	18,616	10.07
15 " " 20.....	9,039	10.24	9,562	9.89	18,601	10.06
20 " " 30.....	15,004	17.00	18,474	19.11	33,478	18.10
30 " " 40.....	12,236	13.87	14,324	14.81	26,560	14.36
40 " " 50.....	10,234	11.60	10,472	10.83	20,706	11.20
50 " " 60.....	6,776	7.68	7,405	7.66	14,181	7.67
60 " " 70.....	3,888	4.41	4,762	4.93	8,650	4.68
70 " " 80.....	1,674	1.90	2,199	2.27	3,873	2.09
80 " " 90.....	407	0.46	696	0.72	1,103	0.60
90 and over.........	32	0.04	83	0.09	115	0.06
	88,243	100.00	96,681	100.00	184,924	100.00

At all ages, under 20, the proportions of males, to the whole number of males, are greater than the proportions of females to the whole number of females, though in the division, 1 and under 2, the number of females exceeds the number of males. In other words, of all the persons living in the State, there is a greater proportion of males than of females under 20 years of age. The proportions are as follows: Under 20 years of age, males, 43.04 per cent.; females, 39.58 per cent.

In the population, of 60 years of age and over, there is a large excess of females, both in numbers and in percentages. Thus, sixty years and over, males, 6,001, or 6.81 per cent.; females, 7,740, or 8.01 per cent.

Various classifications, according to age, have been suggested in order to show more plainly the different characteristics, or qualifications which exist in the population.

Among others, it has been proposed to divide the population with reference to the ability, as depending upon age, to labor and to assist

9

in increasing the productions of a community. This division makes three classes: those under 15 years of age; those of the age of 15 and under 60; and those of the age of 60 and over. Those under 15 compose the *dependent* class; those from 15 to 60, the *productive* class; and those of 60 and over, the *aged* class; or the first and last, combined, make the unproductive, and the other, the productive class.

Applying this classification to the population of Rhode Island, in 1865, we have the following:

	Under 15.		15 to 60.		60 and over.	
	Number.	Percentage.	Number.	Percentage.	Number.	Percentage.
Males	28,953	32.80	53,289	60.39	6,001	6.31
Females	28,704	29.69	60,237	62.30	7,740	8.01
Total population	57,657	31.18	113,526	61.39	13,741	7.43

It seems that 61.39 in each 100 of the population of the State, are in the productive class, and 38.61 in each 100 are in the unproductive classes. A larger proportion of the females than of the males, is in the productive class, probably on account of the large number of females employed in the manufacturing establishments in the State.

We shall understand the figures of the census of 1865 better, and see more clearly their value, by comparing them with those of other dates, and with those of other States and countries. The following table shows the proportions of the population at different ages in several places and at several dates, as named:

PERIODS OF LIFE.	R. I. 1865. Per cent.	R. I. 1860. Per cent.	Prov. 1865. Per cent.	Prov. 1855. Per cent.	U. S. 1860. Per cent.	Mass. 1860. Per cent.	England. 1851. Per cent.	France. 1851. Per cent.	Lower Canada. 1852. Per cent.
Under 5	10.20	11.81	9.73	12.93	15.43	12.28	13.06	9.29	18.89
5 to 10	10.91	10.39	10.46	10.58	13.29	10.43	11.68	9.22	14.29
10 " 15	10.07	9.94	9.60	9.11	11.85	9.28	10.72	8.80	11.86
15 " 20	10.06	10.23	9.87	10.02	10.71	9.81	9.88	8.81	11.62
20 " 30	18.10	19.34	19.70	23.52	18.24	19.82	17.52	16.34	16.28
30 " 40	14.36	14.47	16.03	15.61	12.81	14.91	13.08	14.75	10.28
40 " 50	11.20	10.37	11.57	9.09	8.33	10.19	9.82	12.47	7.45
50 " 60	7.67	6.72	7.22	5.02	5.05	6.61	6.90	10.17	4.95
60 " 70	4.68	4.12	3.86	2.65	2.83	4.05	4.51	6.46	2.73
70 " 80	2.09	1.98	1.53	1.08	1.11	1.91	2.22	3.01	1.26
80 " 90	.60	.55	.39	.35	.30	.55	.56	.63	.34
90 and over	.06	.08	.04	.04	.05	.05	.05	.05	.05
Total	100.	100.	100.	100.	100.	100.	100.	100.	100.

An examination and study of the preceding table will be found interesting, and will show great differences in the proportions of population at different periods of life in different places. Lower Canada far exceeds any other of the places given, in the proportion of the population in the early periods of life. The small percentage under 5 years of age, in 1865, in Providence; and the decreased percentage, at the same age, in Rhode Island in 1865, as compared with 1860, are what might be expected from the great decrease in the number of births, during the war of the last five years.

Those interested in the subject will find much that is suggestive and instructive in the table, which we have not space to show at this time.

Recurring to the classification of the population into the *productive* and *unproductive* classes, the following more extended comparisons of different dates and different places, will be found interesting, and valuable.

STATES OR PLACES.	Dates.	Under 15. Per cent.	15 to 60. Per cent.	60 and over Per cent.
Rhode Island	1865	31.18	61.39	7.43
Rhode Island	1860	32.14	61.13	6.73
Rhode Island	1850	32.80	60.98	6.22
Massachusetts	1860	32.02	61.36	6.62
Massachusetts	1850	31.70	62.14	6.16
Massachusetts	1840	33.99	59.65	6.36
Providence	1865	29.79	64.39	5.82
Providence	1860	30.98	63.95	5.07
Providence	1855	32.62	63.26	4.12
Providence	1850	32.18	63.61	4.21
Boston	1860	31.81	64.91	3.28
Boston	1850	31.02	65.76	3.22
Boston	1840	32.40	64.66	2.94
United States	1860	40.57	55.14	4.29
United States	1850	40.92	54.83	4.20
United States	1840	43.71	52.35	3.94
England	1851	35.46	57.20	7.34
England	1841	36.10	56.70	7.20
France	1851	27.31	62.54	10.15
Lower Canada	1852	45.04	50.58	4.38
Lowell	1860	26.36	69.97	3.67
Lowell	1840	25.00	73.68	1.32

It is not necessary to extend this list. Very great differences will be noticed in the percentages in different places, all having reference to some peculiarity in the population of the places named. Under 15 years of age, the highest percentage is 45.04, in Lower Canada; the lowest 25.00, in Lowell, in 1840. From 15 to 60, the highest is

73.68, in Lowell; the lowest, 50.58, in Lower Canada. Of the age of 60 and over, the highest percentage is 10.15, in France; the lowest, 1.32, in Lowell, in 1840. The reasons for most of these differences will be readily understood.

AGE AND PARENTAGE.

The foregoing illustrations show sufficiently the differences which exist, in respect to age, between the population of Rhode Island and some other States. Another interesting comparison on this subject would be to show the differences which exist at the same date, between different classes of the population of the State. We have already shown this in relation to the sexes in Rhode Island.

Table XXII., on page 38, shows the population of the City of Providence, according to age and parentage, in 1865. We see from that table that, in all the periods of life, under 10 years, in Providence, the population of foreign parentage exceeds that of American parentage, while at all periods above that, the population of American parentage is the most numerous.

Looking at the division into productive and unproductive classes, we find the population according to parentage, in Providence, in 1865, to be as follows:

	Under 15.		15 to 60.		60 and over.	
Parentage.	Number.	Per Cent.	Number.	Per Cent.	Number.	Per Cent
American	7,693	25.06	20,696	67.41	2,313	7,53
Foreign	8,573	35.88	14,458	60.51	862	3.61

This shows a large actual and proportional excess of persons of American parentage, in the productive and aged classes, in Providence; and a large excess of persons of foreign parentage, in the dependent class, under 15 years. Other interesting results will be found, in relation to this subject, by an examination of the figures in this, and the preceding tables.

AGED PERSONS IN RHODE ISLAND.

In connection with the subject of age, I have thought it might be interesting to publish the following list of all the persons of 90 years of age and over, in Rhode Island, reported in the census as living on the first of June, 1865:

Persons in Rhode Island of ninety years of age and over.

RESIDENCE.	NAME.	AGE.	BIRTH-PLACE.
Barrington	Nancy Smith	91	Providence.
Bristol	William Pearse	92	Bristol.
"	Joseph Ralph	91	North Providence.
"	Mary C. Reynolds	90	Massachusetts.
"	John Bullock	90	Connecticut.
"	Jerusha Kent	93	Massachusetts.
"	Gideon Vaughn	91	Exeter.
Warren	Fanny Burrows	95	Connecticut.
"	Lydia Johonnot	90	Barrington.
Coventry	Jonathan Whaley	91	Coventry.
"	Lydia Williams	95	East Greenwich.
"	Huldah Wood	93	Coventry.
East Greenwich	Rebecca Reynolds	90	South Kingstown.
" "	Lucy Tibbitts	94	East Greenwich.
" "	Lydia Williams	95	" "
West Greenwich	Barbara Spink	99	Coventry.
" "	Solomon Brown	99	West Greenwich.
Warwick	Sarah Manchester	92	North Kingstown.
"	Elizabeth Littlefield	90	Warwick.
"	Mary J. Pettis	91	"
"	Elizabeth Ladd	94	Providence.
"	Jesse Brown	90	South Kingstown.
"	Samuel Coultny	90	Ireland.
Little Compton	Mary A. Taylor	90	Wales.
Newport	Hope Spooner	93	Portsmouth.
"	James Hart	98	Newport.
"	Deborah Mitchell	90	"
"	Sarah Norton	99	"
New Shoreham	Bartlett Ball	90	New Shoreham.
Portsmouth	Bathsheba Coggeshall	90	Portsmouth.
Cranston	Rebecca B. Smith	90	Massachusetts.
"	Sarah Taylor	97	Hopkinton.
"	Lucy Gardner, (colored)	97	Coventry.
Cumberland	Sally Joslin	91	Cumberland.
"	Mary Grant	90	"
East Providence	William Hamlin	92	Providence.
" "	Martin Page	92	"

Persons in Rhode Island of ninety years of age and over. Continued.

RESIDENCE.	NAME.	AGE.	BIRTHPLACE.
Glocester	Ann Smith	95	Glocester.
"	Deborah Brown	90	"
"	Jesse Steere	92	"
"	William Thornton	91	Johnston.
Johnston	Penelope Waterman	93	Johnston.
North Providence	Edward McVey	94	Ireland.
" "	Matthew King	93	"
" "	Mary McDonough	93	"
" "	Amy Jenks	91	Massachusetts.
" "	Desire Hicks	90	Scituate.
Pawtucket	Patrick Derwin	95	Ireland.
"	John McKelvey	94	"
"	Mary McGuire	92	"
"	William West	92	Massachusetts.
"	Nancy Binford	90	"
"	Lucy Jerauld	90	Warwick.
"	Ann Hyde	90	England.
"	Felix Hughes	90	Ireland.
Scituate	Mary Smith	93	Glocester.
"	Patience Simmons	92	Cranston.
"	Abigail Tanner	91	Scituate.
Smithfield	Sylvia Whipple	102	Smithfield.
"	Hannah Gully	100	"
"	Mary McCabe	95	Ireland.
"	Hannah Smith	94	Smithfield.
"	Lucina Butler	94	"
"	Jonathan Buxton	93	"
"	Saloma Buxton	93	Burrillville.
"	Drusilla Sayles	93	Smithfield.
"	George Buffum	92	"
"	Annabel McIntie	92	Glocester.
"	Thankful Spaulding	92	Cumberland.
"	John G. Whipple	92	Massachusetts
"	Anna Sayles	91	Smithfield.
"	Catharine Grancy	90	"
"	Amy Jencks	90	"
"	Elizabeth Brown	90	"
Providence	John Williams, (colored)	99	Africa.
"	Thomas Carroll	91	Ireland.
"	Sarah Sheldon	93	Providence.

Persons in Rhode Island of ninety years of age and over. Concluded.

RESIDENCE.	NAME.	AGE.	BIRTHPLACE.
Providence	Bridget Gavin	97	Ireland.
"	Ellen Sullivan	90	"
"	Betsey Hubbard	90	Warwick.
"	Hannah Bowers	94	Massachusetts.
"	Abby Harding	92	Providence.
"	Lydia M. Billings	91	"
"	Sally Sweeting	90	"
"	Susan Manton	91	Cranston.
"	Mary Manchester	99	Providence.
"	Elizabeth Flanagan	93	Wales.
"	Rhoda Balcom	90	Providence.
"	Elizabeth Goff	90	Ireland.
"	Caleb Mosher	92	Massachusetts.
"	Abby T. Millard	93	"
"	Elizabeth Tallman	90	Connecticut.
"	Lydia Field	90	Providence.
"	Lucy Tillinghast	90	North Kingstown.
"	Mary McDonough	93	Ireland.
Charlestown	Preserved Davis	94	Massachusetts.
"	Jemima Nye	93	South Kingstown.
"	Elizabeth Allen	93	Connecticut.
"	Susannah Sheffield	91	"
Exeter	Hannah Bates	96	Richmond.
"	Amy Hazard	94	Exeter.
"	Gershom Palmer	92	Connecticut.
"	Othniel Shearman	91	Exeter.
Hopkinton	Rowse Collins	91	Richmond.
North Kingstown	Sybil Mitchell	95	North Kingstown.
" "	Polly Thomas	90	" "
" "	Esther M. Northup	91	East Greenwich.
" "	Mary Livingston	97	North Kingstown.
South Kingstown	Ebenezer Adams	93	Charlestown.
" "	Bethany, Robinson, (colored)	95	South Kingstown.
" "	Sarah N. Perry	92	" "
Richmond	Honor T. Reynolds	96	Richmond.
"	Rhoda Peterson	91	"
Westerly	Catharine Barber	92	Westerly.
"	Sarah Watson, (colored)	93	Charlestown.

EDUCATION.

The twenty-third table, on page 39, shows the number of children in each town in Rhode Island, between the ages of 5 and 15; and the number of all ages, reported by the census, as having attended school, more or less, during the year ending June 1, 1865. It also shows the number attending the three classes of schools, public, select, and catholic.

In the whole State, the number of children between 5 and 15 years of age, was 38,788; the number who had attended school during the year, was 33,774, showing that there was 5,014 children in the State who had not attended school during the year. This is 12.9 per cent. of the whole number of children between 5 and 15 years of age. But as the number reported as having attended school, included some who were under 5 years, or over 15, the number absent from school between these ages, must have been considerably greater than 5,014. It is probable that at least one in seven of all the children in the State, between 5 and 15 years of age, did not attend any school during the year.

It will be noticed that there are very great differences in the several towns, in the proportions of children who did not attend school, and that the greatest percentage of absentees is in those towns which have the largest foreign population, by parentage.

We have already seen that in three towns, Cumberland, North Providence, and Pawtucket, the population of foreign parentage exceeds that of American parentage; and in three other towns, Burrillville, Cranston and Smithfield, the foreign population, by parentage, nearly equals the American.

The proportion of children, in these towns, who did not attend any school during the year, is much larger than in other towns in the State, and is as follows:

Absent from school, Cumberland, 17.1 per cent.; North Providence 28.1 per cent.; Pawtucket, 18 per cent.; Burrillville, 26.8 per cent.; Cranston, 15.8 per cent.; Smithfield, 20.5 per cent.

It is a startling fact, and one which demands the earnest and immediate attention of our legislators, and of every citizen, that so large a proportion of the children is growing up in ignorance. It is of special importance to the citizens of those towns like North Providence, and Burrillville, where more than one-fourth of all the children, between 5 and 15 years of age, did not attend any school during a whole year.

It may be, and is probable, that the large percentage of children absent from school, in some towns, is not altogether owing to a disinclination of the population to attend school; but is owing to the want of sufficient, or of sufficiently convenient school accommodations.

In the City of Providence, where the proportion of foreign population is nearly as large as in Smithfield, the proportion of absentees from school was only 9.6 per cent., while in Smithfield it was 20.5 per cent.

In Providence, the school accommodations have been largely increased during the last twenty years, and they are now abundant, convenient, and free to children in every portion of the city. The effect has been in the highest degree satisfactory, and notwithstanding the indifference of some, and the persistent opposition of others to the free schools, the number of children in schools has largely increased, and the percentage of those who do not attend school, has largely diminished.

The city censuses enable us to show the results, in Providence, for the last thirty years, and they are most encouraging, as will be seen from the following statement:

CITY OF PROVIDENCE.

DATE.	Attending School 5 to 15 Years of Age.				Absent from Schools.	Percentage of Absentees.
	Public Schools.	Select Schools.	Catholic Schools.	Total all Schools.		
1835	1,456	2,135	....	3,591	1,604	30.8
1845	....	....	....	3,435	2,909	45.8
1855	5,730	680	606	7,016	2,984	32.4
1865	7,401	1,215	1,273	9,889	1,057	9.6

The percentage of absentees in 1865, should be slightly increased by deducting from the number reported as attending school, those who were over 15 years of age. After, however, making all possible corrections, the percentage of children who did not attend school during the year, by the census of 1865, was not much more than one-third as great as by the census of 1855.

In the census of 1835, the figures, as given above, were of children between 4 and 18 years of age.

In 1845, the number "attending school," only included those who were actually attending school at the time the census was taken,

10

Recurring to the table on page 39, it will be noticed that in nine towns, Barrington, Little Compton, Middletown, Newport, New Shoreham, East Providence, Foster, Charlestown, and Exeter, the number who had attended school during the year, is greater than the whole population between the ages of 5 and 15 years. In some other towns, the number of absentees from school is very small.

With the exception of Newport, these are all towns in which there are very few children of foreign parentage, and it will be found, in all cases, that there is a direct relation between the number of absentees from school, and the number of children of foreign parentage.

The exception in Newport is apparent, not real. In that city, the pupils of the United States Naval Academy, located there at that time, were included among the persons attending select schools, in the fourth ward. If we deduct these from the number reported as attending school, it leaves a considerable percentage of absentees from school in that city. In the fifth ward, where the largest percentage of foreign population resides, more than 16 per cent. of the children, between 5 and 15 years of age, did not attend school during the year. The particulars relating to this subject, for the cities of Providence and Newport, by wards, are given in table XXIV, on page 40.

It is certain that the subject is of the utmost importance in its connection with the future interests of the State, and the statistics obtained by the census furnish the data for a better understanding of it.

IGNORANCE.

The preceding pages have shown something of what is done, and what is left undone, with reference to the education of the rising generation. The facts they have given relate to the population under the age of 15 years. In our busy community, the chances are that unless an education, or at least the *rudiments* of an education, are obtained before the age of 15 years, they will be neglected for life. The few who commence the rudiments of an education, after that age, must be considered only as exceptions to the general rule.

It becomes, then, a matter of great interest and importance to the State, to know how many of its population, of the age of 15 years and over, have totally neglected or failed to obtain the first rudiments of an education:—how many can neither read nor write, and how many can read but cannot write.

The facts upon this subject, as obtained by the census of 1865, for each town in Rhode Island, will be found in table XXVI, on pages 42 and 43; and for each ward in Providence and Newport, on page 44.

It seems from the table that there are 10,181 persons in the State, of the age of 15 years or over, who can neither read nor write, and 4,582 more, who can read but cannot write.

If we refer to the table of ages of the population, we find the number of persons living in the State, of the age of 15 years and over, to be 127,308. It appears, therefore, that of all the persons in the State, of these ages, one in 12.5 can neither read nor write; and after deducting those who can neither read nor write, one in 25.5 of the remainder can only read, but cannot write.

If we add the two classes together, we find there are 14,763 persons in the State, who cannot write. This is one in 8.6 of the whole number of persons in the State, of the age of 15 years and over.

It is probable that some persons will be surprised to know that more than one in nine of all the inhabitants of the State, who have passed the age when the rudiments of an education are usually acquired, are unable to write their names; and that more than one in thirteen can neither read nor write.

When we recollect that the probabilities are, that the greater portion of these persons will remain in this condition of ignorance through life, the subject is certainly of the utmost importance in its relations to the future welfare of the State, and should not only awaken the deepest solicitude of our legislators and every citizen, but should also arouse them to immediate and earnest exertion.

Much more may be and should be done, than is done at the present time, to educate those above 15 years of age, and to save them from a life of ignorance; and, certainly, much greater and more efficient exertions may be made to prevent truancy and absenteeism from school, and thus to prevent those under 15 years of age from swelling the ranks of ignorance.

It is possible that some persons may, without reflection, be inclined to doubt the correctness of the figures of the census, upon this subject, particularly, if they compare them with those of the United States censuses of 1850 and 1860.

In 1850, the number of persons in Rhode Island, over 20 years of age, who could not read and write, was given as 3,607, of whom

1,248 were native, and 2,359 were foreign, by birth; 3,340 were whites, and 267 were colored.

In 1860, the number reported by the census, who could not read and write, over 20 years of age, was 6,112. Of these there were 1,202 natives and 4,910 foreigners, by birth; 5,852 whites, and 260 colored.

This shows a large increase in the number of ignorant persons, from 1850 to 1860, and from 1860 to 1865, part of which, in the latter period, is accounted for by including those between 15 and 20 years of age.

When we recollect the natural disinclination to ask and to answer questions upon this point, it must be certain to every mind, that the figures obtained by the census, do not exceed the truth. On the contrary, the number given by the census, who cannot read and write, is undoubtedly less than the actual number.

Recurring to the census of 1865, let us examine more particularly the statistics upon this subject, and endeavor to learn more exactly the sources and causes of this mass of ignorance.

The whole number of persons in the State, in 1865, who could neither read nor write, was 10,181. These were divided among the classes of the population, by parentage, as follows:

COULD NEITHER READ NOR WRITE.

	Number		In each 100 of the whole number
American Parentage.			
Whites	1,085,	or	10.65 in each 100 of the whole number.
Blacks	467,	or	4.59 in each 100 of the whole number.
Total American	1,552,	or	15.24 in each 100 of the whole number.
Foreign Parentage.			
Irish	7,313,	or	71.83 in each 100 of the whole number.
English, Scotch and Welsh	391,	or	3.84 in each 100 of the whole number.
German	44,	or	.43 in each 100 of the whole number.
Other foreign	881,	or	8.66 in each 100 of the whole number.
Total foreign	8,629,	or	84.76 in each 100 of the whole number.
Whole number	10,181,	or	100.00.

A glance at these figures shows at once, and unmistakably, the source of this mass of ignorance, and indicates the direction in which efforts should be made for its removal. Nearly 85 in each 100 of those over 15 years of age, who cannot read and write, are of foreign parentage, leaving 15 in each 100, of American parentage.

Of the whole population of the State, 63.4 in each 100 are of American, and 36.6 are of foreign parentage.

The larger portion of these persons of foreign parentage, who cannot read and write, is of foreign birth, and they are persons who, in their childhood, did not enjoy the opportunities for education that children do in this State. Of course, their ignorance is often more their misfortune than their fault.

Unfortunately the ignorance of parents, in connection with the open opposition of their spiritual advisers to the free schools, begets, on the part of a considerable portion of our foreign population, a great indifference, or even opposition, to the education of their children. In this way, there is great danger that this alarming amount of ignorance in the State, will be perpetuated, and increased.

The preceding figures and remarks refer to the actual number of persons in the State, of the age of 15 years and over, who cannot read and write, and show what proportion of the whole number belongs to each class of the population; but they do not show the relative proportions which belong to the several classes. In order to show this exactly, it would be necessary to know how many persons, of the age of 15 years and over, there are living in the State, in each of the several classes of the population.

This we are unable to show exactly, from our tables, and here again we have to regret that a table was not prepared showing the ages of the population, by parentage.

We may ascertain this, approximately, by assuming that the population of foreign birth is all over 15 years of age, and by deducting the whole number, under 15, from the population born in the United States. Of course, this is not exact; but it is probable that the errors will balance each other, and that the results will be not far from the truth.

The whole population of the State is 184,965. Born in the United States, 145,262; born in foreign countries, 39,703. The whole number, under 15 years of age, is 57,657. Deducting this number from the population of American birth, we have, of the age of 15 years and over, in the State, the following numbers:

Americans, 87,605 ; foreigners, 39,703 ; total, 127,308. Referring to the number of persons in Rhode Island, of the age of 15 years and over, who can neither read nor write, we have the following:

Population 15 years and over.		Number who can neither read nor write.	
Americans	87,605	1,552, or one in	56.4
Irish	27,030	7,313, or one in	3.7
English, Scotch and Welsh	7,881	391, or one in	20.1
Germans	897	44, or one in	20.4
Other foreign	3,895	881, or one in	4.4
Total foreign	39,703	8,629, or one in	4.6
All classes	127,308	10,181, or one in	12.5

It seems that the proportion of the American population, of the age of 15 years and over, who can neither read nor write, is one in 56.4, while the proportion of the foreign population is one in 4.6.

It should be remembered that of the 1,552 persons of the age of 15 years and over, of American parentage, who can neither read nor write, 467, or 30.1 per cent. are colored persons, while this class comprises only 3.5 per cent. of the population of American parentage.

According to the best estimate that we can make, in relation to the number of whites, and colored, of American parentage, in the State, over 15 years of age, we have the following results:

American Parentage.	Population 15 years and over.	Number who can neither read nor write.	
Whites	84,556	1,085, or one in	78.0
Colored	3,049	467, or one in	6.5
Total	87,605	1,552, or one in	56.4

I have no doubt that the relative proportions of persons who can neither read nor write, among the different classes of the population in the State, as given above, are very nearly correct, and they confirm what we have already stated in relation to the sources of the great amount of ignorance which exists in the community, and the direction in which efforts are most needed for its removal and prevention.

WANT OF EDUCATION IN PROVIDENCE.

A table is given on page 38, which shows the ages of the population, by parentage, in the City of Providence, in 1865. This enables us to give the exact figures upon this subject, for that city; and as a similar table of ages was given in the census of the city, in 1855, we can show the statistics for the two periods, though the different division of ages, adopted in 1855, in relation to those who can neither read nor write, prevents exact comparisons on the subject. The following are the statistics for the two periods:

CITY OF PROVIDENCE, 1865.

Parentage.	Population 15 years and over.	Number who can neither read nor write.	
American	23,009	163, or one in	141.1
Foreign	15,320	2,768, or one in	5.5
Total	38,329	2,931, or one in	13.1

CITY OF PROVIDENCE, 1855.

Parentage.	Population 10 years and under 20.	Number who can neither read nor write.	
American	5,822	8, or one in	655.2
Foreign	3,617	420, or one in	8.6
Total	8,939	428, or one in	20.9

CITY OF PROVIDENCE, 1855.

Parentage.	Population 20 years and over.	Number who can neither read nor write.	
American	16,294	105, or one in	155.1
Foreign	10,471	2,134, or one in	4.9
Total	26,765	2,239, or one in	11.9

As near as we can judge from these figures, there would seem to have been a slight improvement, in respect to the want of education, among the foreign population of Providence, during the ten years, from 1855 to 1865.

In connection with the subject of the want of education among the people, the returns of marriages furnish some interesting statistics. The marriage law of Rhode Island requires the parties about to be married, to sign their names to the return of the marriage. Those who cannot write, sign with their mark.

In the City of Providence, the statistics upon this subject, are collected and published in the annual reports of the City Registrar. The following are the aggregate results, in Providence, for the seven years, 1859 to 1865 inclusive:

1859—1865.	Whole number married.	Signed with a mark.	
Males of American birth	2,721	102,	or one in 26.7
Females of American birth	2,694	155,	or one in 17.3
Total of American birth	5,415	257,	or one in 21.1
Males of foreign birth	1,662	651,	or one in 2.5
Females of foreign birth	1,689	961,	or one in 1.8
Total of foreign birth	3,351	1,612,	or one in 2.1

About two-thirds of those persons of American birth, who signed with a mark, were colored, or children, born in this country, of foreign parents.

Referring to the census of 1865, it will be seen that the proportion of persons, of the age of 15 years and over, who can neither read nor write, is considerably greater in the whole State, including the city, than in the City of Providence alone.

Thus, the proportion of persons of American parentage who can neither read nor write, is one in 56.4, in the whole State; and one in 141.1 in the city.

The proportion of persons of foreign parentage, who can neither read nor write, is one in 4.6 in the whole State; and one in 5.5 in the city.

If we separate the statistics for the city, from those for the State, the results are as follows:

	Can neither read nor write, 15 years and over.	
Americans	in Providence, one in 141.1;	in rest of the State, one in 46.5
Foreign	in Providence, one in 5.5;	in rest of the State, one in 4.1

It is probable that the superior school accommodations in Providence, as compared with the more thinly populated towns, have some influence in decreasing the percentage of ignorance in the city. The winter evening schools, in Providence, have also met with a wonderful success, and have been of incalculable utility by furnishing large numbers of persons, over 15 years of age, with the rudiments of an education.

In the preceding remarks upon this subject, we have omitted those reported in the census of 1865, who could read, but could not write. If these are added to the number who could neither read nor write, we have the number who cannot write, and the percentage of ignorance is considerably increased.

Reviewing this subject, and considering it in connection with the subject of absence from school, a few conclusions may be summed up, as follows:

1. A greater proportion of the truancy and absenteeism from school, is among the children of foreign parentage, and is greater in the country towns, which have a large foreign population, than in the City of Providence.

2. The greater portion of those in the State, who cannot read and write, is among the foreign population, and, chiefly, among those born in foreign countries.

3. The colored population, which includes many who have come to the State from the South, furnishes, in proportion to its numbers, a very large percentage of persons who can neither read nor write.

4. It is evident that the subject should arrest attention, and excite immediate and efficient action in every portion of the State, and especially in those towns which have a large foreign population, and have not sufficient, nor easily accessible school accommodations for all their population.

DEAF AND DUMB, BLIND, INSANE, ETC.

Table XXV, on page 41, shows the number in 1865, as reported by the census, of deaf and dumb, blind, insane, idiotic, paupers, and convicts, in each town and county in the State.

It will be noticed that more than half the insane, in the State, and nearly all the convicts, are in the City of Providence, where the Butler Hospital for the insane, and the State prison, are located.

The facts respecting the condition and numbers of the several classes of the population, referred to in the table, are more fully shown in the annual, and in special reports to the General Assembly, than in the returns of the census. It is not, therefore, important to dwell upon the subject in this report.

11

It will be sufficient to give the following, which shows the numbers of the several classes, in the whole State, as returned by the censuses of 1850, 1860, and 1865 :

In Rhode Island.	1850.	1860.	1865.
Deaf and Dumb	65	56	89
Blind	67	85	120
Insane	217	288	287
Idiotic	114	101	140
Paupers	not stated	613	543
Convicts	not stated	181	114

It is probable that there are omissions in the returns of some of these classes of the population, and that the numbers should be larger than given.

NATURALIZED VOTERS.

The table, on page 45, shows the number, in each town in the State, of persons born in foreign countries, who have become voters, under the constitution and laws of Rhode Island.

The whole number in the State, as reported by the census of 1865, was 1,260. Three-fourths of the whole number were natives of Ireland. More than one-third of all were in the City of Providence. In four towns, Barrington, Jamestown, Charlestown, and Exeter, none were reported ; and in four other towns, West Greenwich, Middletown, Tiverton, and North Kingstown, there was only one each.

According to a table on page 28, the proportion of males and females, among the population of foreign birth, in the City of Providence, was 42.6 males, and 57.4 females in each 100. If the same proportion holds good throughout the State, there are in Rhode Island, 16,910 males, and 22,793 females, born in foreign countries.

Of the 16,910 males, 1,260 are voters, or one in 13.4 of the whole number. As the greater portion of these males of foreign birth, are more than 21 years of age, it is probably true that not more than one in twelve or thirteen of the males of foreign birth, over 21 years of age, are voters in Rhode Island.

These 1,260 naturalized voters are all owners of real estate, and as the whole foreign population of the State, by birth, male and female, is only 39,703, it seems that, at least, one in 31.5 of the whole number is an owner of real estate. If we take the whole population of American birth, men, women, and children, it is doubtful if the owners of real estate compose a greater proportion than this.

MILITARY AND NAVAL SERVICE.

In taking the census of 1865, provision was made for ascertaining how many of the inhabitants of each town in the State, who were living, June 1, 1865, were at that time, or had been since 1860, in the military or naval service of the United States; and also, the States in which they had enlisted.

The statistics obtained upon this subject, are given in tables XXX, and XXXI, on pages 47 and 48.

Of course, the number reported in the whole State, bears no relation to the whole number of troops furnished by the State, as the number furnished by the State, included many from other States.

But with reference to the inhabitants of each town and county, who enlisted in the army or navy, the tables give some facts which may be of interest.

The whole number of inhabitants of the State, who enlisted in the army and navy, as reported by the census, was 7,521.

The number and proportion to the whole population of each county, were as follows:

Bristol County	population, 8,469;	enlisted, 346,	or one in	24.5
Kent "	population, 15,319;	enlisted, 639,	or one in	24.0
Newport "	population, 20,687;	enlisted, 607,	or one in	34.1
Providence County, Towns	population, 67,427;	enlisted, 2,829,	or one in	23.8
Providence City	population, 54,595;	enlisted, 2,499,	or one in	21.8
Washington County	population, 18,468;	enlisted, 601,	or one in	30.7
Whole State	population, 184,965;	enlisted, 7,521,	or one in	24.6

A comparison of the proportions in the several towns of the State, would show much greater differences than these; but of course, with the same desire to enlist, the proportion which would do so, would depend upon the proportion of males living, within the ages suitable for military service.

The tables prepared from the census returns, do not show the number living between the military limits, 18 to 45; but we may ascertain, approximately, the proportions which enlisted, in different parts of the State, by taking the number of males between the ages of 20 and 50, as shown in table XXI.

The number of males, between the ages of 20 and 50, in each county of the State, in 1865; and the number and proportion, who enlisted in the army and navy during the war of the rebellion, were as follows :

Counties.	Male Population 20 to 50.	Enlisted Army and Navy.		
Bristol	1,608	346	one in 4.6, or 21.5	per cent.
Kent	2,900	639	one in 4.5, or 22.0	per cent.
Newport	4,152	607	one in 6.8, or 14.6	per cent.
Providence County, Towns	13,730	2,829	one in 4.8, or 20.6	per cent.
Providence City	11,599	2,499	one in 4.6, or 21.5	per cent.
Washington	3,485	601	one in 5.8, or 17.2	per cent.
Whole State	37,474	7,521	one in 4.9, or 20.1	per cent.

The full statistics in relation to the whole number of troops furnished by the State, are shown more completely by reports presented to the General Assembly, and from other sources, than by the returns of the census.

It should be remembered that the number of inhabitants of the State, reported by the census as having enlisted in the army and navy, includes only those who were living on the first day of June, 1865. Those who had enlisted, and had lost their lives during the war, are not included.

Table XXXI shows in what States the inhabitants of Rhode Island enlisted, who served in the army and navy. Of the whole number, (7,521,) who enlisted, 6,365 enlisted in Rhode Island regiments, and 1,156 in regiments of other States. There were 576 in Massachusetts regiments, 231 in New York regiments, and 133 in Connecticut regiments. The remainder were divided among the regiments of 21 different States, besides 2 in the District of Columbia, 26 in the United States "Regulars," and 2 in the rebel service.

OCCUPATIONS.

The occupations of persons of the age of 15 years and over, in Rhode Island, as reported by the census of 1865, are given in table XXXII, pages 49 to 51 inclusive.

The following shows the number of persons reported as engaged in several of the most prominent occupations, in Rhode Island, by the national census of 1860, and by the State census of 1865 :

Occupations.	1860.	1865.
Blacksmiths	653	861
Bakers	130	182
Book-keepers		378
Butchers	252	299

Occupations.	1860.	1865.
Carpenters	2,137	2,457
Cigar makers	205	227
Clergymen	231	230
Clerks	1,783	1,927
Dressmakers		692
Engineers	210	311
Farmers	10,385	10,754
Fishermen	322	497
Gardeners	223	271
Gunsmiths	28	330
Grocers	566	631
Jewelers	1,407	1,215
Laborers	7,360	5,440
Lawyers	96	124
Machinists	1,630	2,193
Merchants	754	1,155
Mariners	1,085	1,070
Masons	646	767
Moulders	410	441
Millers	87	120
Operatives (all kinds)	6,650	13,604
Painters and Glaziers	752	708
Physicians	221	251
Printers	152	196
Servants	4,916	3,503
Shoemakers	555	513
Silversmiths	144	175
Stone Cutters	237	258
Students	477	312
Tailors and Tailoresses	895	828
Tanners and Curriers	27	89
Teachers	753	856
Teamsters	651	692
Tinsmiths	161	130
Wheelwrights	150	154

The number of different occupations, given by the census of 1865, was 348, and the number of persons whose occupation was given, was 65,059.

In the United States census of 1860, the number of different occupations given, in Rhode Island, was 264, and the number of persons whose occupation was given, was 62,886.

Tables of occupations, in censuses, are extremely unsatisfactory, on account of the impossibility of obtaining uniformity in the manner of reporting the occupations. For reasons given, and suggested, on page 52, the returns of occupations, by the census of 1865, are not given with as much minuteness, as some might desire; and, for the same reasons, I do not consider it important to dwell upon the subject at this time.

III. COMMENTS UPON THE TABLES,—CONTINUED.

2. AGRICULTURAL STATISTICS.

The statistics of the agricultural interests, and productions of Rhode Island, as returned by the census of 1865, will be found in Tables XXXIII and XXXIV, on pages 54 to 64 inclusive.

These statistics were collected for the year ending June 1, 1865; and the value of farms, number of cattle and some other items are for that date. Some of the minor crops are given for the year 1865, while the figures given for the principal products, represent the crops of the year 1864.

A slight examination of the figures given in the table, will be sufficient to show that the agricultural interests of Rhode Island comprise no unimportant portion of the industrial pursuits of the State. An industry which has $24,389,242 invested in "farms including buildings"; $2,666,488, in "stock"; and $717,127 in "tools and implements"; and which employs 10,764 "farmers," is certainly not an unimportant item in a State of little more than 1,000 square miles of territory, though the figures may not approach in magnitude, those of the States of the West, which are many times larger in territory.

We have already intimated the opinion that, in New England, a community which depends exclusively upon general farming, cannot be expected to increase in population, to any great extent. In this respect, New England must yield to the more abundant lands, the richer soil, and the more favorable climate of the West.

We have also said, that the growth and prosperity of Rhode Island, so far at least as relates to population, has, for many years, depended chiefly upon its manufacturing interests.

While this is true, it may also be said, that in Rhode Island, the growth and prosperity of the agricultural interests themselves have depended, chiefly, upon the growth and prosperity of the manufacturing interests.

The results of the growth of manufactures have been that the cities have been increased, numerous villages have been built up, home markets for every variety of agricultural products have been multiplied, and though the character of the crops, and the modes of farming operations have been somewhat changed, it is probable that never before were agricultural pursuits so well remunerated, and of so much importance in Rhode Island, as at the present time.

Let us then examine the returns of agricultural products, in Rhode Island, as given by the census of 1865. We must leave to those interested, the study of the returns for each town and division of the State, and confine ourselves to the aggregates for the State as a whole.

In the first place it may be of interest to compare the statistics of the census of 1865, with those obtained by the previous national censuses.

The following shows the aggregates of the several items, in the whole State, as obtained by the national censuses of 1850 and 1860, and by the State census of 1865:

Items.	1865.	1860.	1850.
Farmers, number	10,754	10,385	8,398
Acres improved, number	291,486	335,128	356,487
Acres unimproved, number	201,090	186,096	197,451
Farms, 3 acres and over, number	6,280	5,364	Not stated.
Farms and buildings, value	$24,389,242	$19,550,553	$17,070,802
Stock, value	$2,666,488	$2,042,044	$1,532,637
Tools and implements, value	$717,127	$586,791	$497.201
Hay produced, tons	75,894	82,722	74,818
Clover seed, pounds	4,712	1,221	1,328
Other grass seed, bushels	2,404	4,237	3,708
Wheat, bushels	753	1,131	49
Rye, bushels	29,161	28,259	26,409
Indian corn, bushels	466,633	461,497	539,201
Oats, bushels	175,944	244,453	215,232
Irish potatoes, bushels	710,627	542,909	651,029
Sweet potatoes, bushels	284	946	
Barley, bushels	46,500	40,993	18,875
Buckwheat, bushels	2,369	3,573	1,245
Horses, number	11,133	7,121	6,168
Asses and Mules, number	71	10	1
Sheep, number	40,717	32,624	44,296
Wool, pounds	114,781	90,699	129,692
Swine, number	16,269	17,478	19,509
Milch Cows, number	17,518	19,700	28,698
Working Oxen, number	6,133	7,857	8,189
Other cattle, number	8,143	11,548	9,375
Cattle sold or killed, during year	$758,463	$711,728	$667,486
Butter, pounds	857,466	1,021,767	995.670
Cheese, pounds	136,130	181,511	316,508
Milk sold, gallons	2,223,272	1,297,753	Not stated.
Tobacco raised, pounds	33,548	705	
Wine, gallons	3,401	507	1,013
Orchard products, value	$143,585	$83,691	$63,994

Items.	1865.	1860.	1850.
Market-garden products, value	$341,831	$140,291	$98,298
Onions, bushels	152,603	161,764	Not stated.
Carrots, bushels	90,020	122,639	" "
Beets, bushels	25,600	Not stated	" "
Turnips, all kinds, bushels	202,480	" "	" "
Green peas, bushels	14,077	" "	" "
String beans, bushels	7,631	" "	" "
Garden seeds, value	$12,917	" "	" "
Strawberries, quarts	66,492	" "	" "
Eggs and poultry, value	$311,794	$173,416	" "
Poultry on hand, value	$129,187	$69,642	" "
Honey produced, pounds	14,830	5,261	6,347
Hops, pounds	679	50	277
Flax, pounds	245		85
Peat dug, cords	9,522	2,235	Not stated.
Manures bought, value	$111,219	Not stated.	" "

It will be seen that the census of 1865 gives a considerable number of items, some of them quite important, which were not given in the national censuses. Several of the items named above, in the census of 1860, were obtained through the efforts of the "Rhode Island Society for the Encouragement of Domestic Industry," and are not given in the report of the census by the United States Government. The importance of these and of other items not obtained by the national census, is shown in the report made to the General Assembly, by a Committee of the Rhode Island Society.

Those who examine the preceding list of agricultural statistics will find some apparent discrepancies, which, however, are susceptible of explanation. For example, the number of horses reported in 1860, was 4,012 less than in 1865. The number given for 1860, included only horses on farms, while in 1865, the number was intended to include all the horses in the State. An additional census taken in 1860, under the direction of the "Rhode Island Society for the Encouragement of Domestic Industry," reported 4,938 horses in the State, "not on farms." If we add these to the number reported by the national census, it makes 12,059 horses in 1860, or a greater number than in 1865.

But if we look at the returns, by towns, for 1865, it is evident that in some towns the horses were not all reported. Newport, which probably has seven or eight hundred horses, reported only 60, which included only the number on farms.

Other similar, apparent errors, might be named and explained; but it is not necessary. We may remark, generally, that it is well known that the figures obtained by a census, in relation to these subjects, are never exactly correct. Some persons, knowing this fact, are inclined to reject the results, and disparage the value of all census returns.

This would be a serious mistake. Though the items of a census may not be precisely accurate, they are generally less than the truth, and the results are not exaggerated. Besides, the errors are similar in different censuses, and, to some extent, correct each other, so that an examination of the aggregates for a State, and particularly a comparison of the returns for different years, will show that the errors are unimportant, and that the general results may safely be considered as reliable.

If we examine the preceding table comparing the results of three censuses, we find abundant evidence that the comparative results correspond with our general knowledge of the facts, and are therefore probably true.

For example, the increase, from 1860 to 1865, in the value of farms, stock, tools, &c., corresponds with our general knowledge of the rise in nominal value of these items; the increase in the value of the products of orchards, of market-gardens, of poultry, eggs, &c., is what we would expect from the great increase in the prices of these articles, and the consequent increase in production; the increase in the number of sheep, and in the amount of wool, and the decrease in the number of cattle and in the amount of butter and cheese, between 1860 and 1865, correspond with our general information upon the subject; and, finally, the enormous increase in the quantity of tobacco raised, is just what would be expected from the circumstances in which we have been placed.

These, and many other particulars which might be named, corroborate our general knowledge of the subject, from other sources, and confirm our opinion, that the general results of the census are reliable, and worthy of confidence, even though some errors may be found in the particulars.

Recurring to the agricultural statistics, obtained by the census of 1865, let us examine the values represented in the items given. We have obtained an estimate, intended to be low, in relation to the items the value of which is not stated in the table, and the general results may be given for the whole State as follows:

STATE OF RHODE ISLAND, 1865.

Farms, buildings, &c., value	$24,389,242
Sheep and cattle, value	2,666,488
Horses, mules, and swine, value	1,547,125
Poultry on hand, value	129,187
Tools and implements, value	717,127
Total invested	$29,449,169

PRODUCTIONS FOR THE YEAR.

Crops, not specified below, value	$5,657,489
Cattle sold and killed, value	758,463
Orchard products, value	143,585
Market-garden products, value	341,831
Garden seeds, value	12,917
Eggs, poultry, and miscellaneous, value	675,794
Total, productions	$7,590,079

The large sums given in the table on page 54, for the value of farms in Providence and Newport, do not fairly represent their value for agricultural purposes, and some deduction should be made on this account, for a correct understanding of the subject.

The tables of agricultural statistics show the average yield per acre, in Rhode Island, of some of the crops named. They are as follows:

Hay	101,243 acres,	75,894 tons;	average, 0.75 of a ton.
Wheat	53 acres,	753 bushels;	average, 14.2 bushels.
Rye	2,634 acres,	29,161 bushels;	average, 11.1 bushels.
Corn	16,518 acres,	466,633 bushels;	average, 28.2 bushels.
Oats	6,308 acres,	175,944 bushels;	average, 27.9 bushels.
Potatoes	7,602 acres,	710,627 bushels;	average, 93.4 bushels.

In the statistics for Rhode Island, obtained by the "Society for the Encouragement of Domestic Industry," in 1860, the averages obtained for a few products were as follows: Corn, 27 bushels per acre; rye, 15 bushels; oats, 26 bushels; hay, 1.05 tons; carrots, 500 bushels; onions, 354 bushels; barley, 22 bushels.

More attention should be given to this subject in censuses, and we should be able to show the average amount per acre, of all our crops, with the cost of production, and other particulars. Though it is contrary to the common opinion, I have no doubt that the average yield per acre, of some of the items which constitute the principal crops of the Western States, is greater in New England than in those States; though the greater cost of production in New England, may render the crops less profitable.

We have before us the report of the census taken by the State of Iowa, in 1865, and from it, make the following comparisons which confirm this opinion. The crops are for the same year, and the average products per acre in the two States, are as follows:

	Rhode Island.	Iowa.
Hay, per acre	0.75 of a ton	0.84 of a ton.
Wheat, Spring,	14.2 bushels.	8.6 bushels.
Wheat, Winter,		9.5 bushels.
Rye	11.1 bushels	13.5 bushels.
Corn	28.2 bushels	28.0 bushels.
Oats	27.9 bushels	27.5 bushels.
Potatoes	93.4 bushels	67.9 bushels.

The average of wool was the same in both States, 2.8 pounds to each sheep.

It is probable that the average yield of some of these crops is less in Rhode Island than in the other New England States.

In the report of the census of Iowa, the average yield per acre is given by counties, and varies greatly in different portions of the State. The extremes reported in the several counties, are as follows:

Spring wheat	from 2.90 lowest, to 23.24 highest,	bushels, per acre.
Winter wheat	from 4.91 lowest, to 34.77 highest,	bushels, per acre.
Oats	from 1.73 lowest, to 41.70 highest,	bushels, per acre.
Corn	from 3.51 lowest, to 52.22 highest,	bushels, per acre.
Rye	from 3.37 lowest, to 21.45 highest,	bushels, per acre.
Potatoes	from 16.10 lowest, to 153.92 highest,	bushels, per acre.

The tables of agricultural statistics of the census of Rhode Island in 1865, contain many items which it would be interesting to examine, and the examination of which would be of utility to the interests of agriculture in the State.

But the full investigation of the subject would require too much space for this report; and, besides, it would better be done by those whose familiarity with the subject renders them better qualified to do it justice. We commend the study of the tables to those persons.

III. COMMENTS UPON THE TABLES.—CONTINUED.

3. FISHERIES, AND SHORE STATISTICS.

The products of the fisheries, and the shore statistics of Rhode Island, as reported by the census of 1865, will be found in Table XXXV, pages 65 to 70 inclusive.

These statistics are a novelty in census returns in this country. Though of great importance in some States, no account of them has been obtained by the national censuses. Their importance in Rhode Island induced the "Rhode Island Society for the Encouragement of Domestic Industry" to make an attempt, in 1860, to obtain some of the statistics relating to them.

The results obtained at that time were presented to the General Assembly, in a report from the Society which was published in 1861.

The following extracts from this report show the importance of these statistics in Rhode Island, and the success of the Society in its attempt to obtain them:

"While the continental shore line of Rhode Island is only 45 miles, it has 320 miles of shore washed by the ebbing and flowing tides. Five out of the thirty-two towns that compose the State, are situated on islands. The bays embraced within the State abound with fish, many kinds of which are fitted for food, while others are only used for the manufacture of fish oil, and for manures. The shores and shoals of these bays and of the extensive salt ponds near the southern coast, abound with shell-fish. Besides this, every ebbing tide leaves, on almost every portion of these shores, a rich and valuable deposit of sea-weed and drift."

"The *annual value of the product of these salt waters*, has never been ascertained. The committee deemed it worth an attempt to procure it. These products are of great value and importance. They are secured at an outlay of time and labor, very small compared with their value. Many families derive a large part of their support from them. The amount of fish exported for food is very large, while other varieties are exported in larger quantities for manure, or to be manufactured into special manures, which are returned to the State, under long and learned names, as special fertilizers."

"To ascertain the value and amount of the various products of these salt waters, the committee instituted inquiries." * * * * "They regret to report that the returns made are not so full, nor as they believe, so accurate as they desired. Some of the assistant marshals construed the queries to extend only to the quantities taken and sold. Others have almost entirely omitted all returns on the subject." * * * * "The committee, however, are satisfied that they have commenced the inquiry. They did not expect full and accurate returns, but they have obtained enough to show the great importance of the inquiry, and thereby to secure future attention to it."

The plan and purpose of the committee, in 1860, were adopted with some modifications and additions, in the census of 1865. The results obtained in the latter year, seem to be much more full than in 1860, though evidently incomplete in some particulars. These statistics must, from the nature of the case, depend to some extent, upon estimates. For example, the clams on the shores are free to all the inhabitants of the State who choose to dig them. Persons come to the shores from all quarters, and often from distances of several miles, and dig as many clams as they choose, to eat or to carry home. Nothing is exactly known of the quantities thus removed. The only estimates which could be made, were from the opinions of the owners of shore farms. Much care and caution were used in obtaining the estimates, and it was the general opinion of the marshals that the quantities stated were less than the truth.

Difficulties, somewhat similar in extent; but of a different character, were met with in relation to some other statistics upon this subject.

We can only say, that the attempt to obtain correct information was faithfully made, and that the results do not exceed the truth; but are, probably, considerably less.

The following shows the statistics of fisheries, and other items, in Rhode Island, as obtained by the census of 1865, and compared with those obtained by the Rhode Island Society, in 1860:

	1865.	1860.
Salt Marsh, acres	3,531	1,279
Salt Hay, tons	2,116	1,540
Value of same	$18,545	$12,320
Sea drift, cords	34,146	34,927
Value of same	$38,083	$37,604
Fish seined for manure and oil, barrels	154,468	118,611
Value of same	$126,035	$27,817
Fish caught for food, pounds	2,462,360	Not stated.
Value of same	$121,094	$24,187
Clams dug, bushels	31,697	Not stated.

	1865.	1860.
Quahogs, bushels	9,241	Not stated.
Scallops, bushels	9,653	Not stated.
Oysters, bushels	72,895	Not stated.
Lobsters, pounds	42,900	Not stated.
Total value of all shell fish	$118,655	$11,692
Total value of fisheries, &c., as above	$422,412	$113,620

The statistics obtained in 1865, though imperfect, are sufficient to show that the fisheries and shore products in Rhode Island are of considerable importance to the State, and deserve the attention and care of our legislators.

At the present time the fish which abound in the waters of the State, are taken without restriction, by every means that the invention of man, stimulated by avarice, can devise. This is done without reference to season or to the natural habits of the fish, so that there is supposed to be great danger that some varieties of fish, which have heretofore been abundant, will soon be exterminated, or banished from the waters of the State.

Whether this danger exists or not, to the extent that is feared, with reference to the fish in the salt waters of the State, it is certain that the same result has been accomplished in relation to several kinds of fresh-water fish. Some of the most valuable varieties of fish which formerly abounded in the fresh-water rivers and ponds in Rhode Island, are now unknown in them.

Within a few years past, much attention has been given to the subject of the propagation of fish, in some of the States of New England, as well as in other countries, and it seems to be established that their propagation is easy; and that salmon and shad may be easily restored to our rivers, if a free passage be provided for them, to and from the ocean.

It is also shown that many other kinds of valuable fish may be multiplied without limit, if attention is given to their natural habits, and if they are protected until they have time to grow.

There is no State which should have a greater interest in this subject than Rhode Island. In addition to our bays and arms of the ocean, we have numerous small rivers; every portion of the State is dotted with fresh-water ponds of all sizes, and our Southern coast is lined with extensive salt-water ponds.

These features of the State furnish natural and favorable resorts for every species of shell and other fish that can exist on this coast.

They are all capable of indefinite multiplication, and the expense of propagation and of gathering the products is much less, in proportion to the results, than in other branches of industry.

It is probable that with intelligent, scientific culture, and with a comparatively slight expense, the products of the shell and other fisheries in Rhode Island, might, in a few years, be made to rival in importance those of agriculture. The subject is certainly worthy the attention of our legislators.

III. COMMENTS UPON THE TABLES.—Continued.

4. MANUFACTURES.

The statistics of the manufactures of Rhode Island, for the year ending June 1, 1865, as obtained by the census, will be found on pages 72 to 96 inclusive; and a table, on page 97, shows the number and other particulars of the manufactures reported in each town of the State.

For reasons given on page 72, I am not able to present the statistics of manufactures with as much minuteness, or in as interesting form as might be desired. Instead of giving the particulars of each manufacture, in each town or county, I am obliged to confine the items to the aggregates for the State, and, in some cases, to combine several kinds of manufactures together.

The results will be found, however, to be highly interesting, and the total value of the products largely exceeds that of any previous census.

It is probable that the manufactures of the State were more fully and more correctly reported, by the census of 1865, than by that of 1860. The promises that were made in 1865, that nothing should be published which would show the private business of any individual, probably resulted in obtaining more correct information, than was obtained by the census of 1860.

While, then, we regret that we cannot show many particulars which would be highly interesting, we feel confident that the resources and productive wealth of the State, in connection with manufactures, are more fully, and more correctly shown by the census of 1865, than ever before.

The full discussion of the topics suggested by the statistics of manufactures given, would properly require a volume instead of the few pages we can give it. We must leave the study of the facts, and their application to the numerous interests involved, to those whose familiarity with the subject renders them better qualified to do it justice. It will be my object, solely, to present the statistics of manufactures, as obtained by the census of 1865, as fully and clearly as possible, so that others may be able to make the use of them which their importance deserves.

The total value of the products of manufactures, for the year ending June 1, 1865, was $103,106,395, which was equal to $557 for every man, woman, and child in the State.

The capital invested in manufactures, was $32,646,603, equal to $176 for each inhabitant.

The following shows the general results, by the censuses of 1860, and 1865, and the increase between the two dates. It should be remembered that the figures, at each date, are for a single year:

	U. S. Census, 1860.	State Census, 1865.	Increase.
Number of Manufacturers	1,191	1,459	268
Capital stock invested	$24,278,295	$32,646,603	$8,368,308
Value of raw materials, used	$19,858,515	$63,861,552	$44,003,037
Value of products for the year	$40,711,298	$103,106,395	$62,395,097
Hands employed	32,490	36,993	4,503

The enormous increase in the value of raw materials used, and in the total value of the annual products, since 1860, is partly owing to the increase in the quantity of some items; but more to the great advance in prices, since that date.

Before making further comparisons in relation to the statistics of the two censuses, let us present in a more condensed, tabular form, some of the statistics of manufactures, obtained by the census of 1865.

The following table shows the kinds of manufactures reported, the number of establishments, the capital stock invested, the value of raw materials used, the total value of the products, and the number of hands employed, (male and female,) in the whole State, for the year ending June 1, 1865:

Manufactures in Rhode Island for the year ending June 1, 1865.

KIND OF MANUFACTURES.	No. of Establishments Reported.	Capital Stock.	Value of Raw Materials.	Total Value of Products.	Hands Employed.
Agricultural Implements	6	$8,500	$7,160	$13,200	15
Ale and Lager Beer	3	22,200	35,300	68,700	12
Artificial Teeth	23	21,500	21,800	81,000	41
Baskets	8	....	12	928	8
Blank Books	2	12 500	22,000	35,000	31
Bobbins and Spools	10	62,800	40,950	106,530	117
Boots and Shoes	120	119,785	210,422	450,404	483
Brass Castings	6	26,000	46,300	115,900	22
Blocks, Pumps, &c	2	2,500	3,450	21,500	15
Bread, Crackers, &c	15	77,300	358,088	498,500	152
Bricks	3	233,000	6,000	120,500	205
Brushes	3	10 800	6,700	16,700	14
Cabinet Ware and Upholstery	14	88,000	83,670	238,970	180
Carriages and Wagons	56	103,400	83,100	208.319	211
Carpentry	59	126.900	473,650	939,550	534
Coffins	14	20,200	43,338	68,233	26
Cooperage	6	34,600	30,000	63,315	37
Charcoal	47	....	....	48,680	115
Cigars	29	52,350	90,597	208,870	179
Clothing.					
Clothing, Mens'	51	178,315	470,158	810,357	666
Dresses and Cloaks	48	10,250	141,900	196,200	181
Hoop Skirts and Corsets	5	18,300	27,500	41,800	81
Total, Clothing	104	206,865	639,558	1,048,357	928
Coffee and Spices	3	22,500	65,000	95,000	18
Coffin Trimmings	2	3,000	15,010	23,775	20
Confectionery and Ice Cream	6	7,300	28,080	41,000	24
Coppersmithing and Plumbing	7	46,300	87,300	123,600	59
Cotton Manufactures.					
Cotton Cloth	74	9,884,000	15,347,839	24,723,988	11,826
Cotton Yarn, Twine, Thread, &c	45	1,645,800	4,035,820	5,598,219	1,504
Cotton Wicking	3	41,000	72,000	114,300	38
Calico Printing	6	3,230,000	19,272,973	23,551,216	1,876
Dyeing and Bleaching	6	432,400	255,400	482,387	277
Shoe and Corset Lacings, &c	6	871,700	443,650	787,600	476
Wadding and Batting	2	112,000	146,400	220,800	52
Total Cotton Manufactures	142	15,716,900	39,574,082	55,478,510	16,049
Drugs and Chemicals	4	139,500	180,900	357,000	136
Fancy Goods, Book Clasps, &c	2	7,000	19,400	36,000	31
Fish Oil and Guano	19	128,350	105,460	222,150	198
Gas,—Illuminating	5	1,067,700	143,864	349,336	131
Gas Pipe, Fixtures and Burners	6	118,000	145,500	221,000	87
Gold and Silver Refining, &c	4	12,000	25,500	516,000	14
Granite Work	3	1,900	1,650	5,000	8
Grist Mills	30	341,700	....	....	94

Manufactures in Rhode Island for the year ending June 1, 1865, Continued.

KIND OF MANUFACTURES.	No. of Establishments Reported.	Capital Stock.	Value of Raw Materials.	Total Value of Products.	Hands Employed.
Hair Cloth	3	$185,000	$429,118	$1,091,666	197
Harnesses, Trunks and Valises	36	58,950	94,010	222,336	214
Hats and Caps	4	5,350	14,700	25,742	16
Iron Manufactures.					
Blacksmithing	100	53,715	96,900	212,220	213
Edge Tools	5	66,400	77,650	222,200	99
Files	3	215,000	78,200	226,500	156
Fire Arms	3	430,000	680,000	1,940,000	1,040
Horse Shoes, Nails, Cable, &c	8	801,450	761,750	952,700	488
Iron Castings	12	606,000	536,360	830,600	664
Jewelers' Tools	5	1,000	1,200	5,000	5
Machinery, Steam Engines, &c	22	842,000	604,300	1,962,800	1,612
" Cotton, Wool and Flax	18	543,300	439,755	1,183,000	1,124
Spiral Springs, Hardware, &c	4	254,000	383,500	654,672	271
Wood Screws	2	1,370,000	834,782	1,460,870	591
Total Iron Manufactures	182	5,182,865	4,494,397	9,650,562	6,263
Jewelry and Jewelers' Findings	45	261,000	576,922	1,200,025	724
Leather	9	85,000	244,405	409,000	85
Loom Pickers and Belting	4	129,813	265,400	354.130	74
Lime and Casks	3	42,000	56,011	74,133	44
Lumber	47	58,725	14,614	92,442	87
Marble	14	82,650	72,583	168,206	153
Millinery	26	23,250	25,200	57,400	59
Mattresses	2	3,600	6,000	11,400	10
Newspaper, Book and Job Printing	10	213,000	186,000	421,000	173
Oils	5	186,500	132,000	182,000	47
Paper Boxes, Cards and Envelopes	3	11,500	38,525	71,063	97
Paper Cop Tubes	2	300	2,450	8,622	13
Patent Medicines	7	75,800	150,800	304,600	31
Photographs	20	38,900	51,300	119,000	73
Planing and Box Making	13	176,500	160,300	290,000	93
Patterns	3	900	1,000	7,500	7
Planes	2	200	400	2,000	2
Picture Frames	4	10,300	6,850	16,500	15
Pyroligneous Acid	2	8,100	4,800	20,140	8
Pearl Works and Shell Combs	2	8,500	7,500	23,000	25
Ropes and Lines	4	11,200	20,500	30,300	17
Rubber Goods	2	175,000	750,000	944,832	281
Sail Making	3	1,100	4,100	10,150	8
Sashes, Blinds and Doors	12	69,700	48,140	115,500	78
Ships, Yachts and Boats	24	93,400	102,270	230,760	142
Short and Kindling Wood	10	2,800	22,700	29,350	23
Silver Ware	3	348,000	390,000	725,000	304
Soap and Candles	13	188,700	216,550	527,770	82
Stucco Work	2	1,500	1,162	12,100	5
Straw Goods	2	4,000	4,200	8,500	48
Sugar Refining	2	175,000	1,417,000	1,550,000	115

Manufactures in Rhode Island for the year ending June 1, 1865, Concluded.

KIND OF MANUFACTURES.	No. of Establishments Reported.	Capital Stock.	Value of Raw Materials.	Total Value of Products.	Hands Employed.
Tin and Sheet Iron Ware..........	46	$102,650	$82,752	$179,854	135
Top Roll Covering...............	3	1,600	4,500	9,000	5
Toys and Tobacco Pipes...........	4	32,400	12,800	38,000	60
Washing & Wringing Machines, &c.	2	253,000	18,300	30,000	23
Wooden Ware and Harness Hames.	2	5,800	2,690	6,849	8
Wood Turning	4	5,700	....	11,500	19
Willow Ware....................	2	3,100	2,500	4,700	8
Weavers Harnesses and Reeds.....	5	49,000	36,750	79,960	68
Wine, Grape.....	2	1,800	1,450	4,000	2
Woolen Manufactures.					
Satinets, Flannels, &c............	32	1,373,000	3,632,170	6,048,210	1,873
Shoddy........	4	4,300	21,060	33,000	14
Wool Carding....	3	2,800	....	2,200	4
Woolen Goods................ ...	32	3,415,000	6,068,177	13,127,086	3,734
Woolen Yarn..	7	297,000	912,280	1,728,700	794
Worsted Braid and Lacings........	5	141,000	154,880	232,955	176
Total Woolen Manufactures.......	83	5,233,100	10,788,567	21,172,151	6,595
Other Manufactures..............	19	276,000	305,995	758,125	265

The preceding list includes all the manufactures reported in the State, in 1865. It would be interesting to compare all the items with those of the national census of 1860; but the different arrangements and combinations, made in the two censuses, render it difficult to do so, and it is not, perhaps, necessary for the objects of this report. It will be sufficient to make a comparison of three of the most important of the manufacturing interests of the State.

An examination of the table shows that of the $32,646,603 invested in manufactures, in 1865, in Rhode Island, the sum of $26,132,865 was invested in manufactures of cotton, wool, and iron. Let us compare the statistics of the two censuses, in relation to these manufactures.

COTTON MANUFACTURES.

In the statistics of cotton manufactures, by the census of 1865, as given on page xcvii, we have included the following: cotton cloth; cotton yarn, twine, thread, &c.; cotton wicking; calico printing; bleaching and dyeing; shoe and corset lacings; and wadding and batting.

In the census of 1860, the combinations are different, and we only find the following items named, of cotton manufactures: calico printing; cotton goods; cotton batting; cotton yarns, &c.; bleaching and dyeing.

The statistics of the two periods are as follows:

COTTON MANUFACTURES, RHODE ISLAND.

	1860.	1865.
Number of establishments	170	142
Capital invested	$11,367,500	$15,716,900
Cost of raw materials	$6,590,025	$39,574,082
Annual value of products	$15,168,681	$55,478,510
Hands employed	15,900	16,049
Cotton used, pounds	41,614,797	28,959,626
Spindles employed	814,554	839,695
Looms employed	17,315	16,548
Cotton cloth made, yards	147,652,300	104,865,978
Yarn and twine, pounds		2,725,950
Cotton thread, spools, dozen		1,565,000
Yarn and thread, pounds	5,072,114	

The particulars for the several branches, included in the cotton manufactures in 1865, are given on page xcvii.

The great increase in the cost of raw materials, and in the total value of products, between 1860 and 1865, is evidently owing to the enormous increase of prices between the two periods. The quantity of cotton used, and the amount of cloth made, were much less in 1865 than in 1860.

The comparison of the statistics of cotton manufactures, at the two periods named, suggests many topics which are of importance to those interested in these manufactures.

The want of time and space, and, more than this, the want of sufficient acquaintance with the subject, render it advisable to leave the discussion to those more capable of doing it justice.

WOOLEN MANUFACTURES.

In the statement given in relation to the manufactures of Rhode Island, as reported by the census of 1865, the following branches are included under the head of woolen manufactures, viz.: satinets, flannels, &c.; shoddy; wool carding; woolen goods; woolen yarn; worsted braid and lacings.

Selecting, so far as possible, the same branches from the returns of the census of 1860, we have the following comparative statistics:

WOOLEN MANUFACTURES, RHODE ISLAND.

	1860.	1865.
Number of establishments	59	83
Capital invested	$3,176,000	$5,233,100
Cost of raw materials	$4,077,914	$10,788,567
Annual value of products	$6,929,205	$21,172,151
Hands employed	4,239	6,595
Wool used, pounds	6,832,600	13,343,228
Cotton used, pounds	3,056,200	1,461,813
Cloth made, yards	19,343,600	14,625,477
Woolen yarn, pounds	112,800	1,047,600
Shawls, number	100,000	43,359
Blankets, number		159,143
Woolen Hoods, dozen		15,000
Hosiery, dozen pairs		10,000
Worsted braid and lacings, yards		9,747,000
Shoddy, pounds		134,000

IRON MANUFACTURES.

In the statement on page xcviii, we have included the following in the iron manufactures of Rhode Island, as returned by the census of 1865, viz.: blacksmithing; edge tools; files; fire arms; horse shoes; nails, cables, &c.; iron castings; jewelers' tools; machinery; steam engines, &c.; spiral springs, hardware, &c., and wood screws.

We have collected the same items, so far as possible, from the returns of the census of 1860, and find the following comparative results, for the two periods:

IRON MANUFACTURES, RHODE ISLAND.

	1860.	1865.
Number of establishments	134	182
Capital invested	$3,620,200	$5,182,865
Cost of raw materials	$1,769,377	$4,494,397
Annual value of products	$4,689,115	$9,650,562
Hands employed	3,942	6,263

These comparisons show that, in cotton manufactures, there was an enormous increase between 1860 and 1865, in the annual value of raw materials used, and in the annual value of the products, though there was a large decrease in the quantity of both; but in the woolen and iron manufactures, there was a great increase both in the quantity and in the value of the raw materials used, and of the products.

The following table will show the statistics of all the manufactures reported, in the several counties of Rhode Island, by the censuses of 1860 and 1865:

COUNTIES.		Number of Establishments.	Capital invested.	Cost of Raw Materials.	Annual value of Products.	Hands Employed.
Bristol........	1860.......	62	$824,650	$1,621,960	$2,692,092	975
	1865.......	69	1,058,980	2,379,091	3,132,683	1,300
Kent.....	1860.......	73	2,766,760	1,667,183	3,601,141	3,779
	1865.......	111	3,303,675	6,900,418	10,250,052	4,731
Newport.......	1860.......	85	799,100	548,193	1,213,625	1,224
	1865.......	129	890,500	777,430	1,675,519	987
Providence....	1860.......	894	17,961,985	13,655,956	29,211,478	23,769
	1865.......	1,038	25,023,098	48,156,274	78,538,135	27,143
Washington ...	1860.......	77	1,925,300	2,365,223	3,992,960	2,743
	1865.......	112	2,370,350	5,648,339	9,510,006	2,832
Whole State...	1860... ...	1,191	24,278,295	19,858,515	40,711,296	32,490
	1865... ...	1,459	32,646,603	63,861,552	103,106,395	36,993

The United States census of 1860 does not show the statistics of manufactures, for the City of Providence, separately from the rest of the county. The particulars for each town and city, by the census of 1865, are given on page 97, of the tabular portion of this volume.

PRODUCTS OF MANUFACTURES.

The following list comprises the greater portion of the products of all kinds of manufactures in Rhode Island, as reported by the census of 1865, for the year ending on the first of June of that year:

It would be interesting to compare the figures given for each item, with those of the census of 1860; but I am able to find only a small portion of the items in the report of the census of that year, and cannot, therefore, make a full comparison.

PRODUCTS OF MANUFACTURES, IN RHODE ISLAND, DURING THE YEAR ENDING JUNE 1, 1865.

Article	Quantity
Ale and lager beer, barrels	4,250
Ambrotypes and tintypes	57,500
Articles for jewelry, gross	50
Artificial teeth, sets	2,310
Assortments of hardware, dozen	60
Awnings	150
Axes	200
Bags	30,200
Balmoral skirts	30,000
Barrels and casks	85,350
Baskets	2,660
Block alphabets, sets	300
Blankets	159,144
Bobbins and spools, gross	433,161
Book clasps	126,600
Boards, feet	4,912,742
Boots and shoes, pairs	272,423
Bricks	12,100,000
Boxes	197,500
Brushes	14,000
Bonnets	13,650
Boats and ships	261
Butt hinges, dozen	277,598
Buttons, gross	7,000
Calf-skins	5,100
Candles, pounds	106,000
Candy, pounds	118,000
Cards cut	1,570,790
Cartes de visite	222,500
Cartridges	15,000,000
Chain cable, tons	1,000
Charcoal, bushels	580,800
Cloaks and Mantillas	4,000
Cigars	8,844,970
Coal tar, barrels	3,222
Coke, bushels	321,900
Coal mined, tons	11,338
Coffins	2,705
Coffin trimmings, gross	23,200
Coats	14,314
Corn knives	8,400
Cotton cloth made, yards	104,865,978
Cotton thread, spools, dozen	1,565,000
Cotton thread spooled, spools	720,000
Cotton rope, pounds	260
Cotton lines, dozen	13,500
Cotton tape, yards	2,380,400
Cotton braid, balls, dozen	200,000
Cotton wicking, pounds	188,880
Cotton wicking, gross	150,000
Cotton cloth printed, yards	95,814,863
Cotton cloth bleached and dyed, yards	30,867,518
Cotton yarn and twine, pounds	2,725,950
Cotton warps, yards	3,875,000
Cotton shoe and corset lacings, gross	800,000
Corsets	600
Cut nails, casks	80,000
Dresses	8,780
Dyewoods ground, tons	500
Envelopes	500,000
Files	540,000
Fire engines	3
Flax Picking, pounds	184
Grain ground, bushels	624,400
Gravestones and monuments	5,316
Guano, tons	2,825
Hair cloth, yards	1,271,500
Hand rakes	3,000
Horse rakes	200
Handles for cutlery, gross	150
Hemp rope, tons	11
Harnesses	1,187
Hats and caps	6,000
Hoop skirts	39,750
Hoop skirt braid, pounds	83,200
Harness hames, pairs	2,500
Horse shoes	3,026,000
Horse shoe nails, pounds	407,100
Illuminating gas, cubic feet	91,222,000
Iron castings, tons	710
Iron Sinks	4,000
Lacing Leather, dozen	250
Leather Belting, feet	263,182
Leather, sides	29,650
Loom pickers, dozen	21,949
Lumber planed, feet	1,050,000
Lime, casks	29,487
Linen lines, dozen	662
Marble furniture tops and mantles	1,075
Marine engines	14
Mattresses	1,500
Musket bands, sets	15,000
Newspapers printed	5,410,000
Nail kegs	49,553

Oil, gallons	226,976	Staves	2,269,000
Pails and buckets	1.300	Soap, pounds	5,515,440
Pants	37,094	Soft soap, barrels	2,358
Paper boxes	467,711	Shirts	6,000
Plows and cultivators	565	Stoves	5,270
Paper cop tubes, pounds	22,500	Sugar refined, pounds	4,984,000
Planes	200	Syrup and molasses, barrels	13,718
Photographs	16,800	Short and kindling wood, cords	2,850
Picture frames	4,600	Straw hats	14,000
Printing presses	346	Toys, sets	1,200
Pyroligneous acid, gallons	95,000	Toys, gross	4,000
Rifles and muskets	81,000	Tobacco pipes, gross	12
Refined iron, tons	5,000	Trunks	2,600
Rear sights for muskets	60,000	Valises and traveling bags	32,400
Sabres	13,500	Vests	35,533
Salt ground, bushels	10,000	Wire rod, tons	1,000
Screw machines	105	Wood screws, gross	3,652,748
Scythes	118,000	Woolen cloth, yards	14,625,477
Sewing Machines	10,000	Woolen hoods, dozen	15,000
Shoddy, pounds	134,000	Woolen hosiery, pairs, dozen	10,000
Spermaceti, pounds	20,000	Wool carded, pounds	7,100
Steam boilers	157	Weavers' harnesses, sets	16,780
Steam Engines	144	Weavers' reeds	7,200
Snaths	1,000	Wine, gallons	2,400
Sashes, blinds and doors	8,130	Washing and wringing machines	1,644
Shawls	43,359	Water elevators	500
Sheepskins	64,400	Worsted braid & lacings, yards	9,747,000
Shingles	2,636,000	Woolen yarn, pounds	1,047,600

The preceding list is, by no means complete, for all the articles manufactured in the State. In some establishments, a great variety of articles is made, and while it is comparatively easy to obtain the total value of the products, it is difficult, and sometimes impossible, to obtain the exact number or quantity of all the different articles manufactured.

The same remarks are true, and to a still greater extent, in relation to the articles used in the various manufactures. Almost every important substance known, in the animal, vegetable, and mineral kingdoms, is used in the manufactures of the State, and of some of them, the quantities required are very great.

The manufacture of a single product, in some cases, requires the use of some scores of different kinds of substances,—drugs, chemicals, dyes, &c. In taking the census, it was found impracticable to obtain these items in full, and though the amount was given in the returns in many cases, it is probable that the quantities of only a few of the most important substances, are fully stated, for all the manufactures.

From the returns, we select only a few of the substances used in the manufactures of the State, during the year ending June 1, 1865, as follows:

Cotton, pounds	30,434,989	Tin, pounds	164,000
Wool, pounds	13,343,228	Tobacco, pounds	189,595
Coal, tons	42,566	Tallow, pounds	752,500
Iron, tons	41,498	Potash, pounds	81,600
Steel, pounds	634,617	Resin, pounds	117,500
Brass, pounds	257,000	Hair, pounds	34,334
Copper, pounds	66,097	Pearl shell, pounds	12,000
Lead, pounds	1,212,002	Leather, pounds	163,540

Perhaps a better idea of the quantities of some of these substances used in manufactures, may be obtained from the daily consumption. Estimating the working days of the year at three hundred, the quantities used, *daily*, in the manufactures of the State, were as follows, for the year ending June 1, 1865:

DAILY CONSUMPTION IN MANUFACTURES.

Cotton, pounds	101,350	Iron, tons	138
Wool, pounds	44,477	Steel, pounds	2,115
Coal, tons	142	Lead, pounds	4,040

Let us apply the same illustration to the products of the manufactures. We have already given the annual quantities of most of the products of manufactures. The following shows the quantities produced *daily*, of a few of the articles manufactured in Rhode Island, during the year ending June 1, 1865:

DAILY PRODUCTS IN RHODE ISLAND.

Cotton cloth, yards	349,553	Horse shoe nails, pounds	1,357
Cotton yarn and twine, pounds	9,086	Cut nails, pounds	26,667
Cotton thread, spools	62,600	Hoop skirts, number	132
Calicoes printed, yards	319,383	Shoe and corset lacings, dozens	32,000
Files, number	1,800	Butt hinges, dozens	925
Hair cloth, yards	4,238	Woolen cloths, yards	48,751
Rifles and muskets, number	270	Balls of braid, number	8,000
Horse shoes, number	10,087	Worsted braid, yards	32,490
Tape, yards	7,933	Shawls, number	145
Wood screws, gross	12,176	Stockings, pairs	400
Blankets, number	530	Woolen yarns, pounds	3,492

If we call the working days, ten hours each, the production of cotton cloth in the State, was equal to 583 yards *per minute;* of calico, 532 yards per minute; of woolen cloths, 81 yards per minute; and of wood screws, 2,922 per minute, during all the working hours of the year.

The total production for the year, amounted to 67,893 *miles* of cotton and woolen cloths; and 54,440 miles of calicoes. The aggregate of cotton and woolen cloths and calicoes, produced during the year, was sufficient for a web of cloth nearly five times around the globe; or 941 times around the State of Rhode Island; or equal to 1,164 yards for every man, woman, and child in the State. It was equal to 69.5 square miles of cloth, or nearly sufficient to cover the whole surface of a town 10 miles long and 7 miles wide.

These illustrations will give to some persons a clearer idea of the magnitude of the manufacturing interests of the State, than the simple statement of the quantities of the articles made.

It should be remembered that, during the year ending June 1, 1865, the amount of products of some of the most important branches of manufacture, was much less than it was five years previous. This was especially true in relation to manufactures of cotton. The high prices and difficulty of obtaining cotton during the war, caused the suspension of some of the mills, and reduced largely the quantity of the products. Some other branches of manufacture were also much depressed, at the time the census was taken, in the summer of 1865.

SPINDLES AND LOOMS.

The number of spindles, looms, &c., reported in use in the manufactures of Rhode Island, June 1, 1865, was as follows:

In *cotton manufactures* ....839,695 spindles, and 16,548 looms.
In *woolen manufactures* ....8,866 spindles, 2,756 looms, and 381 sets of machinery.
In the manufacture of *hair cloth*.......................................585 looms.
In the manufacture of *braid, lacings*, &c...............................1,180 braiders.

POWER USED IN MANUFACTURES.

The number of steam engines used in the manufactures of Rhode Island, as reported by the census of 1865, was 263, with 726 boilers, and with a total horse power of 16,092. In addition to this, 3 caloric engines with 11 horse power, were reported in Providence.

It is well known that the statement of the horse power of steam engines is very indefinite, and that the power of any engine may be increased or diminished, within wide limits. It is probable that the amount of horse power, as given for the steam engines in the following table might be greatly increased, and would be whenever occasion required.

Only nine windmills were reported: one in Bristol, one in Jamestown, 2 in Little Compton, and 5 in Portsmouth. It is well known that there are more than this in the State.

In 258 manufacturing establishments in the State, water power was used; in 24, horse power was used; in 828, manual labor was the power used; and 104 used hired steam power. Of the number using hired steam power, 103 were in Providence, and 1 in Cumberland.

The table on the next page shows the number of steam engines, the horse power of the engines, the number of steam boilers, the number of establishments using water power, the number using horse power, and the number carried on by manual labor, in each town in Rhode Island, as reported by the census, June 1, 1865.

TABLE, *Showing the power used in the manufactures, in each town in Rhode Island, as reported by the census of* 1865.

TOWNS AND DIVISIONS OF THE STATE.	Number of Steam Engines.	Total Horse Power.	Number of Steam Boilers.	Establishments using Water Power.	Establishments using Horse Power.	Establishments using Manual Labor.
Barrington	5	100	5	1	......	8
Bristol	7	390	19	......	1	27
Warren	3	490	23	......	......	26
BRISTOL COUNTY	15	980	47	1	1	61
Coventry	2	15	2	14	......	8
East Greenwich	3	265	8	2	1	17
West Greenwich	1	60	4	12	......	5
Warwick	6	516	19	11	......	14
KENT COUNTY	12	856	33	39	1	44
Jamestown	......	......	......	......	......	......
Little Compton	2	8	2	......	1	6
Middletown	......	......	......	......	......	2
Newport	14	521	32	......	1	64
New Shoreham	......	......	......	......	......	......
Portsmouth	6	250	16	......	......	11
Tiverton	1	5	1	4	......	10
NEWPORT COUNTY	23	784	51	4	2	93
Burrillville	1	8	1	21	......	12
Cranston	6	611	43	2	......	6
Cumberland	11	1,150	41	19	2	35
East Providence	2	40	3	1	......	9
Foster	......	......	......	2	......	12
Glocester	......	......	......	15	1	19
Johnston	2	220	9	8	......	3
North Providence	39	3,028	109	29	1	11
Pawtucket	11	636	28	7	......	14
Scituate	......	......	......	24	......	16
Smithfield	17	1,259	48	23	......	21
PROVIDENCE COUNTY, TOWNS	89	6,952	282	151	4	158
PROVIDENCE CITY	105	5,831	270	1	11	447
Charlestown	......	......	......	2	......	1
Exeter	......	......	......	20	......	7
Hopkinton	2	21	2	19	4	8
North Kingstown	7	187	15	2	1	9
South Kingstown	7	291	12	4	......	......
Richmond	1	60	4	12	......	......
Westerly	2	130	10	3	......	......
WASHINGTON COUNTY	19	689	43	62	5	25
WHOLE STATE	263	16,092	726	258	24	828

This completes our statement of the statistics relating to the manufactures of the State of Rhode Island, for the year ending June 1, 1865. We regret that the statement could not be made more complete; that we could not present more particulars of the numerous manufactures of the State; and that we could not show a multitude of facts relating to the improvements in machinery, and the history of the various manufactures, which would tend to render the statistics more interesting. A full exhibition of the manufactures of the State, in all their relations, would show that there is hardly a subject, financial, moral, scientific, sanitary, or political, with which they are not intimately connected; that there is hardly any matter relating to the prosperity and welfare of the State, that is not intimately connected with, and affected by the manufactures within its limits.

It is probable that this would be admitted as a general truth, in relation to every civilized State and community; but we cannot avoid the conviction that the statistics of manufactures, as given by the census of 1865, demonstrate that it is especially true in Rhode Island, and of especial importance to the welfare of the State.

The strictly manufacturing interests of Rhode Island, are probably greater, in proportion to its population, than those of any other State in the Union; and the influence of these interests upon the character of the population, and upon its moral and sanitary condition, is probably greater, and more distinctly felt here, than in any other State.

It is important then, that the statistics of the manufacturing interests, and their influence upon the community, should be thoroughly studied, and understood by our legislators, and by every citizen who has any regard for the best welfare of the community and of the State.

The interests of the manufacturer, and of the State are, in most cases, identical in long periods of time, though there may be temporary circumstances which may seem to render them antagonistic. There may be, for example, a temporary necessity for our manufacturers to bring into the State large numbers of persons who are very ignorant, and entirely different in their all social characteristics, from our native population. But intelligent, skillful labor, which can only be obtained in an educated population, would be far more valuable to the manufacturers, and their interests are identical with those of the State, that this population should be made intelligent, skillful, and educated, as speedily as possible.

There may be a temporary necessity, (though very rarely,) for our manufacturers to neglect proper sanitary precautions in the construction of tenements, and in the location and arrangement of their villages. But, in time, disease is sure to find it out, and to show the manufacturers that their interests are identical with those of the State, that the laws of sanitary science should be obeyed, and that the health of the population should be protected.

Similar illustrations might be given in relation to other interests of the State, which are identical with those of the manufacturers; but it is not necessary. It is not my purpose to discuss these questions only so far as to show the importance of statistics, upon which all intelligent discussion of them, and all correct decisions in relation to them, must depend.

It is important, for a complete understanding of these subjects, that full statistics of manufactures should be collected; that they should be collected frequently; and that they should be obtained correctly. This has never been done under any census in this country. Those who have had experience in taking a census, know well that no portion of it is so unsatisfactory; none in which there is so great a liability to errors, as in that relating to manufactures.

The infinite variety of products; the temptation to misrepresent the facts, either to conceal profits, or to conceal losses; the want of accurate knowledge from the lack of accurate accounts; the liability to errors where the facts depend upon memory, though the intentions may be honest; these, and many other reasons, cannot but impair our confidence in the *details* of our statistics of manufactures, though, as we have already shown elsewhere, the general results, and the comparison of the census of one date with that of another, may be of very great value.

There are three most urgent needs, in relation to the collection of statistics in this country:

1. A more perfect arrangement, and classification of the facts to be obtained; particularly those relating to manufactures.
2. An entirely different, and better system of obtaining the facts.
3. The education of the people to the habit of giving the information, and to an appreciation of its value.

These objects may be attained, to a great extent, by the national government, by making the census department a permanent organization, so that the experience of one census may be made available for the next. So far as relates to manufactures, however, these objects would be much better attained by State statistical bureaus, which could collect the statistics much more frequently, and could better adapt their plans and machinery to the special institutions, wants, and peculiarities of each State.

CONCLUSION, RECAPITULATORY.

The total population of Rhode Island, by the census of 1865, was 184,965. The total value of the products of the State, for the year ending June 1, 1865, was as follows:

Products of agriculture	$7,590,079
Products of fisheries	422,412
Products of manufactures	103,106,395
Total value of products	$111,118,886

This shows an annual production of 601 dollars for each man, woman, and child in the State.

In Massachusetts, the State census for the same year, shows a population of 1,267,239, and the value of all the products for the year, was $517,240,613, equal to 408 dollars for each inhabitant. In the Massachusetts report there are large sums for whale, cod, and mackerel fisheries, coastwise freights, and other items, which are not found in the productions as reported in Rhode Island.

CENSUS OF RHODE ISLAND,

JUNE 1, 1865.

TABLES.

PART I.

POPULATION.

TABLE I.—*Showing the population, number of dwelling houses, number of families to each dwelling, and number of persons to each dwelling and each family in each town of the State.*

Towns and Divisions of the State.	Total Population.	Dwelling Houses.				Empty Dwelling Houses.	Whole No. Families.	Families to each dwell'g.	Persons to each dwell'g.	Persons to each Family.
		Wood.	Brick.	Stone.	Whole No.					
Barrington......	1,028	163	7	1	171	13	186	1.08	6.01	5.52
Bristol..........	4,649	826	11	9	846	24	1,054	1.24	5.49	4.41
Warren.........	2,792	451	12	1	464	15	612	1.32	6.02	4.56
Bristol County	8,469	1,440	30	11	1,481	52	1,852	1.25	5.71	4.57
Coventry........	3,995	803	.....	1	804	21	921	1.14	4.96	4 33
East Greenwich..	2,400	389	1	....	390	8	514	1.31	6.15	4.67
West Greenwich.	1,228	277	......	....	277	14	273	.98	4.43	4.49
Warwick........	7,696	1,413	3	1	1,417	95	1,666	1.17	5.43	4.62
Kent County...	15,319	2,882	4	2	2,888	138	3,374	1.16	5.30	4.54
Jamestown......	349	75	1	...	76	7	72	.94	4.60	4.84
Little Compton..	1,197	261	......	3	264	6	294	1.11	4.53	4.07
Middletown......	1,019	184	.....	..	184	9	193	1.04	5.53	5.28
Newport........	12,688	1,861	26	22	1,909	120	2,549	1.33	6.64	4.97
New Shoreham..	1,308	234	......	....	234	5	259	1.10	5.59	5.05
Portsmouth......	2,153	345	2	....	347	9	440	1.26	6.20	4.89
Tiverton........	1,973	354	1	2	357	4	424	1.18	5.52	4.65
Newport Co...	20,687	3,314	30	27	3,371	160	4,231	1.25	6.13	4.88
Burrillville......	4,861	804	......	3	807	30	1,088	1.34	6.02	4.47
Cranston.... ...	9,177	1,383	4	6	1,393	21	2,066	1.48	6.59	4.44
Cumberland.....	8,216	1,119	94	6	1,219	61	1,726	1.41	6.74	4.76
East Providence.	2,172	348	6	6	360	7	458	1.27	6.03	4.74
Foster..........	1,873	388	......	2	390	24	426	1.09	4.80	4.39
Glocester........	2,286	496	1	1	498	29	517	1.03	4.59	4.42
Johnston........	3,436	526	.....	24	550	31	708	1.28	6.25	4.85
North Providence	14,553	1,786	37	12	1,835	16	2,940	1.60	7.93	4.95
Pawtucket......	5,000	1,065	7	6	1,078	7	1,077	1.00	4.64	4.64
Scituate.........	3,538	755	......	17	772	89	821	1.06	4.58	4-31
Smithfield.......	12,315	1,588	2	104	1,694	33	2,531	1.49	7.27	4.86
Towns Prov. Co	67,427	10,258	151	187	10,596	348	14,358	1.35	6.36	4.69
Prov. City.....	54,595	6,527	211	35	6,773	27	11,393	1.68	8.06	4.79
Charlestown.....	1,134	230	......	....	230	12	244	1.06	4.93	4.64
Exeter....... ...	1,498	376	......	....	376	46	341	.90	3.98	4.39
Hopkinton......	2,512	482	...	3	485	26	580	1.19	5.18	4.33
North Kingstown	3,166	594	1	....	595	19	696	1.17	5.32	4.55
South Kingstown	4,513	850	2	10	862	43	950	1.10	5.23	4.75
Richmond.......	1,830	417	......	....	417	41	410	.98	4.38	4.46
Westerly	3,815	589	3	....	592	14	779	1.31	6.44	4.89
Washington Co	18,468	3,538	6	13	3,557	201	4,000	1.12	5.19	4.61
Whole State ..	184,965	27,959	432	275	28,666	926	39,208	1.40	6.45	4.72

TABLE II.—SEX AND COLOR. *Showing the sex and color of the population in each town and division of the State.*

TOWNS AND DIVISIONS OF THE STATE.	WHITES.			COLORED.			Whole No. of Males.	Whole No. of Females	Total Population.
	Males.	Females	Total.	Males	Feml's	Total.			
Barrington........	567	438	1,005	15	8	23	582	446	1,028
Bristol............	2,072	2,432	4,504	60	85	145	2,132	2,517	4,649
Warren............	1,233	1,517	2,750	17	25	42	1,250	1,542	2,792
BRISTOL COUNTY...	3,872	4,387	8,259	92	118	210	3,964	4,505	8,469
Coventry..........	1,855	2,108	3,963	15	17	32	1,870	2,125	3,995
East Greenwich.....	1,095	1,223	2,318	44	38	82	1,139	1,261	2,400
West Greenwich....	639	587	1,226	2	.....	2	641	587	1,228
Warwick...........	3,538	4,017	7,555	73	68	141	3,611	4,085	7,696
KENT COUNTY......	7,127	7,935	15,062	134	123	257	7,261	8,058	15,319
Jamestown.........	168	163	331	11	7	18	179	170	349
Little Compton.....	573	620	1,193	1	3	4	574	623	1,197
Middletown........	508	501	1,009	5	5	10	513	506	1,019
Newport...........	5,725	6,258	11,983	277	428	705	6,002	6,686	12,688
New Shoreham.....	647	631	1,278	15	15	30	662	646	1,308
Portsmouth.........	1,115	1,032	2,147	4	2	6	1,119	1,034	2,153
Tiverton...........	953	988	1,941	14	18	32	967	1,006	1,973
NEWPORT COUNTY..	9,689	10,193	19,882	327	478	805	10,016	10,671	20,687
Burrillville.........	2,363	2,478	4,841	8	12	20	2,371	2,490	4,861
Cranston...........	4,574	4,362	8,936	122	119	241	4,696	4,481	9,177
Cumberland........	3,873	4,322	8,195	9	12	21	3,882	4,334	8,216
East Providence....	1,038	1,111	2,149	12	11	23	1,050	1,122	2,172
Foster.............	921	951	1,872	1	....	1	922	951	1,873
Glocester...	1,162	1,115	2,277	6	3	9	1,168	1,118	2,286
Johnston...........	1,744	1,667	3,411	11	14	25	1,755	1,681	3,436
North Providence...	6,990	7,503	14,493	33	27	60	7,023	7,530	14,553
Pawtucket.........	2,348	2,638	4,986	8	6	14	2,356	2,644	5,000
Scituate............	1,729	1,797	3,526	6	6	12	1,735	1,803	3,538
Smithfield..	5,811	6,458	12,269	24	22	46	5,835	6,480	12,315
TOWNS PROV. CO..	32,553	34,402	66,955	240	232	472	32,793	34,634	67,427
PROVIDENCE CITY..	24,505	28,379	52,884	714	997	1,711	25,219	29,376	54,595
Charlestown........	495	489	984	65	85	150	560	574	1,134
Exeter............	745	722	1,467	14	17	31	759	739	1,498
Hopkinton..........	1,219	1,272	2,491	11	10	21	1,230	1,282	2,512
North Kingstown...	1,486	1,609	3,095	40	31	71	1,526	1,640	3,166
South Kingstown...	2,081	2,153	4,234	121	158	279	2,202	2,311	4,513
Richmond..........	841	953	1,794	16	20	36	857	973	1,830
Westerly,..........	1,857	1,914	3,771	19	25	44	1,876	1,939	3,815
WASHINGTON CO...	8,724	9,112	17,836	286	346	632	9,010	9,458	18,468
WHOLE STATE.....	86,470	94,408	180,878	1,793	2,294	4,087	88,263	96,702	184,965

TABLE III.—*Showing the particulars of tables I. and II., in the Cities of Providence and Newport, by Wards.*

CITY OF PROVIDENCE. TABLE I. *By Wards.*

Wards.	Total Population.	Dwelling Houses.				Empty Dwelli'g Houses.	Whole No. Families	Families to each Dwelli'g	Persons to each Dwelli'g	Persons to each Family.
		Wood.	Brick.	Stone.	Whole No.					
First.......	10,668	1,257	16	4	1,277	8	2,159	1.69	8.35	4.94
Second	4,618	508	82	6	596	3	783	1.31	7.75	5.90
Third......	8,034	912	31	3	946	4	1,673	1.76	8.49	4.80
Fourth.....	4,667	569	40	7	616	3	989	1.60	7.57	4.72
Fifth.......	7,695	872	17	11	900	2	1,619	1.80	8.55	4.75
Sixth......	10,513	1,342	15	2	1,359	4	2,352	1.73	7.73	4.47
Seventh....	8,400	1,067	10	2	1,079	3	1,818	1.68	7.78	4.62
Whole City.	54,595	6,527	211	35	6,773	27	11,393	1.68	8.06	4.79

CITY OF NEWPORT. TABLE I. *By Wards.*

Wards.	Total Population.	Dwelling Houses.				Empty Dwelli'g Houses.	Whole No. of Famili's	Famili's to each Dwelli'g	Persons to each Dwelli'g	Persons to each Family.
		Wood.	Brick.	Stone.	Whole No.					
First.......	1,944	320	......	2	322	14	399	1.24	6.04	4.87
Second	2,558	420	3	2	425	15	559	1.31	6.02	4.57
Third......	2,059	334	4	1	339	12	442	1.30	6.07	4.66
Fourth.....	2,730	308	5	2	315	10	448	1.42	8.66	6.09
Fifth.......	3,397	479	14	15	508	69	701	1.38	6.68	4.84
Whole City.	12,688	1,861	26	22	1,909	120	2,549	1.33	6.64	4.97

CITY OF PROVIDENCE. TABLE II. *By Wards.*

Wards.	Whites.			Colored.			Whole No. of Males.	Whole No. of Females	Total Population.
	Males.	Females	Total.	Males.	Females	Total.			
First.......... ...	4,820	5,412	10,232	189	247	436	5,009	5,659	10,668
Second	1,840	2,322	4,162	180	276	456	2,020	2,598	4,618
Third.............	3,709	4,205	7,651	52	68	120	3,761	4,273	8,034
Fourth............	2,016	2,494	4,510	69	88	157	2,085	2,582	4,667
Fifth..............	3,649	4,002	7,651	14	30	44	3,663	4,032	7,695
Sixth.............	4,635	5,457	10,092	176	245	421	4,811	5,702	10,513
Seventh...........	3,836	4,487	8,323	34	43	77	3,870	4,530	8,400
Whole City.......	24,505	28,379	52,884	714	997	1,711	25,219	29,376	54,595

CITY OF NEWPORT. TABLE II. *By Wards.*

Wards.	Whites.			Colored.			Whole No. of Males.	Whole No. of Females	Total Population.
	Males.	Females	Total.	Males.	Females	Total.			
First..	907	968	1,875	25	44	69	932	1,012	1,944
Second	1,027	1,311	2,338	101	119	220	1,128	1,430	2,558
Third.............	779	1,161	1,940	38	81	119	817	1,242	2,059
Fourth............	1,446	1,071	2,517	81	132	213	1,527	1,203	2,730
Fifth	1,566	1,747	3,313	32	52	84	1,598	1,799	3,397
Whole City.......	5,725	6,258	11,983	277	428	705	6,002	6,686	12,688

TABLE IV.—NATIVITY. *Showing in general terms the birth places of the population.*

Towns and Divisions of the State.	Birth Place.					
	In the Town.	Out of the Town and in the State	Out of the State and in the U.S.	Total born in the United States.	Born in Foreign Countries.	Total Population.
Barrington	404	193	191	788	240	1,028
Bristol	2,620	555	694	3,869	780	4,649
Warren	1,424	392	455	2,271	521	2,792
BRISTOL COUNTY	4,448	1,140	1,340	6,928	1,541	8,469
Coventry	1,725	1,443	353	3,521	474	3,995
East Greenwich	933	914	265	2,112	288	2,400
West Greenwich	736	362	107	1,205	23	1,228
Warwick	2,822	2,454	813	6,089	1,607	7,696
KENT COUNTY	6,216	5,173	1,538	12,927	2,392	15,319
Jamestown	193	131	14	338	11	349
Little Compton	726	156	258	1,140	57	1,197
Middletown	535	322	83	940	79	1,019
Newport	6,255	1,081	2,634	9,970	2,718	12,688
New Shoreham	1,199	60	42	1,301	7	1,308
Portsmouth	1,097	469	267	1,833	320	2,153
Tiverton	1,577	113	228	1,918	55	1,973
NEWPORT COUNTY	11,582	2,332	3,526	17,440	3,247	20,687
Burrillville	1,682	915	770	3,367	1,494	4,861
Cranston	2,231	3,005	1,582	6,818	2,359	9,177
Cumberland	2,723	1,103	1,623	5,449	2,767	8,216
East Providence	120	703	1,105	1,928	244	2,172
Foster	1,276	373	208	1,857	16	1,873
Glocester	1,297	569	324	2,190	96	2,286
Johnston	1,151	1,193	355	2,699	737	3,436
North Providence	3,781	3,149	2,817	9,747	4,806	14,553
Pawtucket	1,441	918	1,146	3,505	1,495	5,000
Scituate	1,757	1,235	349	3,341	197	3,538
Smithfield	4,013	2,324	2,424	8,761	3,554	12,315
TOWNS PROVIDENCE COUNTY	21,472	15,487	12,708	40,662	17,765	67,427
PROVIDENCE CITY	21,124	8,124	11,945	41,193	13,402	54,595
Charlestown	612	396	96	1,104	30	1,134
Exeter	862	522	107	1,491	7	1,498
Hopkinton	1,170	864	379	2,413	99	2,512
North Kingstown	1,983	762	193	2,938	228	3,166
South Kingstown	3,101	838	293	4,232	281	4,513
Richmond	769	764	181	1,714	116	1,830
Westerly	1,716	750	754	3,220	595	3,815
WASHINGTON COUNTY	10,213	4,896	2,003	17,112	1,356	18,468
WHOLE STATE	75,055	37,152	33,055	145,262	39,703	184,965

TABLE V.—NATIVITY. *Showing how many of the inhabitants of each town were born in each town and county in Rhode Island.*

PRESENT RESIDENCE.	PLACE OF BIRTH IN RHODE ISLAND.								
	Barrington.	Bristol.	Warren.	BRISTOL Co.	Coventry.	East Greenwi'h	West Greenw'h	Warwick.	KENT COUNTY.
Barrington	404	7	24	435	....	1	1	6	8
Bristol	4	2,620	103	2,727	9	25	3	21	58
Warren	52	88	1,424	1,564	2	10	1	7	20
BRISTOL COUNTY	460	2,715	1,551	4,726	11	36	5	34	86
Coventry	1	9	....	10	1,725	78	242	297	2,342
East Greenwich	2	9	....	11	62	933	37	195	1,227
West Greenwich	...	....	....	....	119	32	736	50	937
Warwick	...	14	6	20	365	259	118	2,822	3,564
KENT COUNTY	3	32	6	41	2,271	1,302	1,133	3,364	8,070
Jamestown	...	....	....	....	....	....	1	....	1
Little Compton	1	....	....	1	1	....	....	1	2
Middletown	...	2	....	2	....	4	2	1	7
Newport	3	66	21	90	10	29	3	18	60
New Shoreham	...	1	1	2	....	3	1	3	7
Portsmouth	...	33	4	37	3	2	6	6	17
Tiverton	...	6	1	7	....	2	....	2	4
NEWPORT COUNTY	4	108	27	139	14	40	13	31	98
Burrillville	1	1	6	8	8	....	....	11	19
Cranston	1	31	24	56	113	49	33	277	472
Cumberland	2	9	5	16	32	13	4	41	90
East Providence	24	21	17	62	24	2	7	27	60
Foster	...	1	....	1	32	7	9	14	61
Glocester	2	....	....	2	9	1	8	7	25
Johnston	1	6	4	11	27	9	3	54	93
North Providence	6	37	26	69	113	42	24	149	328
Pawtucket	2	11	11	24	19	8	1	52	80
Scituate	1	3	1	5	156	17	22	61	256
Smithfield	5	9	11	25	67	37	13	90	207
TOWNS PROVIDENCE COUNTY	45	129	105	279	600	185	123	783	1,691
PROVIDENCE CITY	105	297	268	670	317	247	82	828	1,474
Charlestown	...	1	1	2	11	....	6	19	36
Exeter	...	4	....	4	27	36	86	19	168
Hopkinton	...	....	....	....	58	11	32	37	138
North Kingstown	1	8	1	10	31	56	30	86	203
South Kingstown	...	8	....	8	6	8	5	26	45
Richmond	1	....	2	3	23	12	42	21	98
Westerly	...	1	....	1	10	11	12	48	81
WASHINGTON COUNTY	2	22	4	28	166	134	213	256	769
WHOLE STATE	619	3,303	1,961	5,883	3,379	1,944	1,569	5,296	12,188

TABLE V. NATIVITY.—CONTINUED. *Showing how many of the inhabitants of each town were born in each town and county in Rhode Island.*

PRESENT RESIDENCE.	PLACE OF BIRTH IN RHODE ISLAND.										
	Jamestown.	Little Compton	Middletown.	Newport	New Shoreham	Portsmouth.	Tiverton.	NEWPORT Co.	Burrillville.	Cranston.	Cumberland.
Barrington	2	1	...	6	....	2	3	14	....	5	7
Bristol	...	5	7	57	13	55	14	151	1	2	12
Warren	...	...	1	35	4	18	10	68	....	6	2
BRISTOL COUNTY	2	6	8	98	17	75	27	233	1	13	21
Coventry	...	1	...	10	5	....	3	19	10	81	13
East Greenwich	...	5	2	26	32	3	2	70	....	20	13
West Greenwich	...	...	1	8	....	....	....	9	....	11	....
Warwick	3	2	1	40	15	14	11	86	27	209	20
KENT COUNTY	3	8	4	84	52	17	16	184	37	321	46
Jamestown	193	...	11	23	4	15	2	248	....	....	...
Little Compton	...	726	20	5	....	13	97	861	....	4	1
Middletown	6	10	535	131	27	84	8	801	....	....	....
Newport	47	22	136	6,255	55	112	39	6,666	....	11	7
New Shoreham	2	1	...	9	1,199	2	8	1,221	....	....	....
Portsmouth	11	15	94	86	15	1,097	80	1,398	....	6	7
Tiverton	...	36	9	14	....	32	1,577	1,668	....	....	1
NEWPORT COUNTY	259	810	805	6,523	1,300	1,355	1,811	12,863	....	21	16
Burrillville	...	...	1	8	....	6	2	17	1,682	7	73
Cranston	9	3	2	91	12	21	7	145	17	2,231	37
Cumberland	1	12	1	13	....	2	1	30	60	23	2,723
East Providence	4	1	...	17	3	20	7	52	....	19	9
Foster	...	...	...	4	....	....	....	4	3	23	2
Glocester	...	2	...	....	....	2	....	4	99	10	20
Johnston	...	...	1	10	1	3	2	17	5	103	17
North Providence	3	10	6	62	3	17	19	120	45	85	217
Pawtucket	2	6	7	19	....	2	12	48	5	22	85
Scituate	1	1	...	13	1	4	....	20	42	86	21
Smithfield	2	8	6	37	1	6	11	71	151	74	453
TOWNS PROV. CO.	22	43	24	274	21	83	61	528	2,109	2,683	3,657
PROVIDENCE CITY	29	74	24	659	37	91	97	1,011	122	549	404
Charlestown	1	...	...	4	14	....	....	19	....	3	....
Exeter	...	1	...	12	3	2	....	18	....	7	3
Hopkinton	...	...	2	14	1	4	....	21	2	16	4
North Kingstown	15	...	3	25	19	3	1	66	....	14	6
South Kingstown	7	2	9	81	24	20	3	146	3	8	1
Richmond	2	1	1	2	2	1	....	9	1	11	....
Westerly	...	1	...	25	22	1	....	49	4	7	2
WASHINGTON COUNTY	25	5	15	163	85	31	4	328	10	66	16
WHOLE STATE	340	946	880	7,801	1,512	1,652	2,016	15,147	2,279	3,653	4,160

TABLE V. NATIVITY.—CONTINUED. *Showing how many of the inhabitants of each town were born in each town and county in Rhode Island.*

PRESENT RESIDENCE.	PLACE OF BIRTH IN RHODE ISLAND.									
	E. Providence.	Foster.	Glocester.	Johnston.	N. Providence.	Pawtucket.	Scituate.	Smithfield.	PROVIDENCE CO. TOWNS.	PROV. CITY.
Barrington	...	....	1	1	1	7	2	2	26	111
Bristol	2	1	2	4	14	7	4	21	70	129
Warren	...	2	....	7	3	5	4	7	36	107
BRISTOL COUNTY	2	3	3	12	18	19	10	30	132	347
Coventry	...	86	19	39	10	4	233	30	525	59
East Greenwich	...	4	4	6	7	....	22	29	105	78
West Greenwich	...	4	....	1	....	....	19	....	35	6
Warwick	...	60	10	59	22	6	178	51	642	288
KENT COUNTY	...	154	33	105	39	10	452	110	1,307	431
Jamestown	...	....	....	....	1	....	2	....	3	4
Little Compton	1	....	....	....	....	....	....	1	7	8
Middletown	...	....	....	....	....	1	1	4	6	18
Newport	...	....	4	1	18	1	7	8	57	197
New Shoreham	...	1	....	....	....	....	1	....	2	14
Portsmouth	...	1	1	....	1	4	2	1	23	27
Tiverton	...	....	1	....	....	4	1	....	7	.....
NEWPORT COUNTY	1	2	6	1	20	10	14	14	105	268
Burrillville	...	19	379	18	22	....	85	189	2,474	56
Cranston	2	62	33	184	45	7	148	91	2,857	1,520
Cumberland	...	14	40	18	87	....	36	467	3,468	160
East Providence	120	3	1	13	35	....	11	49	260	347
Foster	...	1,276	44	19	11	....	151	12	1,541	21
Glocester	...	102	1,297	51	18	....	76	121	1,794	37
Johnston	...	63	71	1,151	69	....	97	90	1,666	229
North Providence	1	39	60	182	3,781	11	137	532	5,090	1,103
Pawtucket	33	4	13	17	155	1,441	23	208	2,006	166
Scituate	...	334	109	96	22	1	1,757	79	2,547	89
Smithfield	6	61	159	147	249	59	168	4,013	5,540	321
TOWNS PROV. CO.	162	,1977	2,206	1,896	4,494	1,519	2,689	5,851	29,243	4,049
PROVIDENCE CITY	6	226	277	435	722	....	601	717	4,059	21,124
Charlestown	...	....	1	....	5	....	....	2	11	9
Exeter	...	4	1	4	....	....	15	4	38	15
Hopkinton	...	1	1	2	4	....	4	2	36	24
North Kingstown	...	4	4	2	3	6	9	12	60	45
South Kingstown	...	....	6	....	5	4	6	8	41	51
Richmond	...	1	1	1	10	....	4	1	30	16
Westerly	...	4	1	3	1	1	4	8	35	37
WASHINGTON COUNTY	...	14	15	12	28	11	42	37	251	197
WHOLE STATE	171	2,376	2,540	2,461	5,321	1,569	3,808	6,759	35,097	26,416

TABLE V.—*Continued.* NATIVITY.—*Showing how many of the inhabitants of each town were born in each town and county in Rhode Island.*

PRESENT RESIDENCE.	PLACE OF BIRTH IN RHODE ISLAND.									
	Charlestown.	Exeter.	Hopkinton.	N. Kingstown.	S. Kingstown.	Richmond.	Westerly.	WASHINGTON COUNTY.	R. I., no town given.	Whole State.
Barrington	.....	2	.....	1	.....	.....	.....	2	...	597
Bristol	7	3	4	16	9	.....	.....	39	1	3,175
Warren	6	.....	1	8	4	2	.....	21	...	1,816
BRISTOL COUNTY	13	5	5	25	13	2	.....	63	1	5,588
Coventry	7	69	16	53	46	11	11	213	...	3,168
East Greenwich	12	57	4	177	76	17	13	356	...	1,847
West Greenwich	5	55	10	12	13	11	3	109	2	1,098
Warwick	31	133	34	237	152	52	10	649	27	5,276
KENT COUNTY	55	314	64	479	287	91	37	1,327	29	11,389
Jamestown	2	2	.....	15	46	2	1	68	...	324
Little Compton	.....	1	.....	1	1	.....	.....	3	...	882
Middletown	.....	2	2	2	15	1	1	23	...	857
Newport	10	11	11	38	165	3	19	257	9	7,336
New Shoreham	3	.....	.....	4	5	1	.....	13	...	1,259
Portsmouth	1	7	.....	7	23	.....	2	40	24	1,566
Tiverton	2	.....	1	.....	1	.....	.....	4	...	1,690
NEWPORT COUNTY	18	23	14	67	256	7	23	408	33	13,914
Burrillville	1	4	2	1	11	2	2	23	...	2,597
Cranston	10	33	11	62	38	17	11	182	4	5,236
Cumberland	1	13	3	20	23	1	1	62	...	3,826
East Providence	.....	8	2	9	15	7	1	42	...	823
Foster	.....	5	.....	3	5	6	2	21	...	1,649
Glocester	.....	3	1	.....	.....	.....	.....	4	...	1,866
Johnston	2	11	.....	4	2	4	.....	23	305	2,344
North Providence	7	32	5	46	33	34	11	168	52	6,930
Pawtucket	.....	7	3	10	10	4	1	35	...	2,359
Scituate	2	25	4	21	10	8	3	73	2	2,992
Smithfield	7	43	11	57	39	6	4	167	0	6,337
TOWNS PROV. CO.	30	184	42	233	186	89	36	800	369	36,959
PROVIDENCE CITY	35	84	35	341	179	73	37	784	126	29,248
Charlestown	612	26	42	15	71	112	53	931	...	1,008
Exeter	12	862	31	97	56	78	5	1,141	...	1,384
Hopkinton	74	138	1,170	21	82	194	134	1,813	2	2,034
North Kingstown	7	160	7	1,983	178	18	8	2,361	...	2,745
South Kingstown	121	117	24	145	3,101	103	37	3,648	...	3,939
Richmond	106	128	161	23	158	769	25	1,370	7	1,533
Westerly	144	29	156	19	126	72	1,716	2,262	1	2,466
WASHINGTON CO.	1,076	1,460	1,591	2,303	3,772	1,346	1,978	13,526	10	15,109
WHOLE STATE	1,227	2,070	1,751	3,448	4,693	1,608	2,111	16,908	568	112,207

TABLE VI. NATIVITY.—*Showing how many of the inhabitants of each town and county of the State were born in each of the United States.*

TOWNS AND DIVISIONS OF THE STATE.	PLACE OF BIRTH.—UNITED STATES.													
	Alabama.	Arkansas.	California.	Connecticut.	Delaware.	Florida.	Georgia.	Illinois.	Indiana.	Iowa.	Kansas.	Kentucky.	Louisiana.	Maine.
Barrington	..	..	1	13	..	..	....	2	1	..	..	..	..	3
Bristol	1	..	4	31	1	..	6	2	..	..	..	1	1	22
Warren	..	..	3	13	..	.	....	1	..	..	..	..	..	12
BRISTOL COUNTY	1	..	8	57	1	..	6	5	1	..	..	1	1	37
Coventry	..	..	..	166	1	..	....	1	..	..	..	1	..	5
East Greenwich	..	..	1	84	4	..	2	1	..	..	..	..	..	9
West Greenwich	..	..	..	73	..	..	....	....	..	..	..	..	..	......
Warwick	..	..	1	267	..	1	8	3	4	2	..	..	4	27
KENT COUNTY	..	..	2	590	5	1	10	5	4	2	..	1	4	41
Jamestown	..	..	..	2	..	..	....	....	..	..	..	..	..	1
Little Compton	..	..	..	9	..	..	1	....	..	..	..	..	..	3
Middletown	..	..	1	10	..	..	5	....	..	..	..	..	..	4
Newport	3	1	5	121	23	3	21	25	28	14	3	24	15	84
New Shoreham	..	..	..	8	..	..	....	....	..	..	..	..	..	7
Portsmouth	..	..	..	21	..	3	....	....	..	2	..	..	1	10
Tiverton	..	..	..	8	..	..	....	....	..	..	..	..	2	4
NEWPORT COUNTY	3	1	6	179	23	6	27	25	28	16	3	24	18	113
Burrillville	..	..	..	160	..	..	1	1	..	3		..	..	19
Cranston	..	..	2	181	2	2	2	6	..	3	1	1	.	54
Cumberland	1	..	..	167	..	..	....	4	1	..	..	1	..	66
East Providence	..	..	1	59	..	..	3	9	..	1	..	..	..	33
Foster	..	1	..	136	..	..	1	....	..		..	..	..	......
Glocester	..	4	2	182	..	..	....	....	..	..	..	..	..	1
Johnston	..	..	..	86	..	..	....	3	..	..	..	..	..	10
North Providence	..	..	1	304	..	..	5	12	1	..	..	1	2	135
Pawtucket	2	..	..	66	..	..	3	5	5	2	4	1	..	37
Scituate	..	..	..	120	..	..	....	....	..	..	..	1	..	18
Smithfield	..	..	..	295	1	..	1	7	2	3	..	1	2	122
TOWNS PROVIDENCE COUNTY	3	5	6	1,756	3	2	16	47	9	12	5	6	4	495
PROVIDENCE CITY	8	..	12	1,683	60	9	45	25	7	10	3	11	6	592
Charlestown	..	..	..	75	..	..	....	....	..	..	..	..	1	......
Exeter	..	..	..	71	..	..	....	....	..	..	..	..	1	......
Hopkinton	..	..	..	255	..	..	....	1	..	1	..	..	..	3
North Kingstown	..	..	..	53	..	..	1	....	..	..	..	1	1	10
South Kingstown	..	..	1	114	..	..	3	1	..	2	..	..	..	6
Richmond	..	..	..	109	..	..	....	....	..	..	..	..	..	1
Westerly	..	..	..	497	6	..	....	5	..	2	..	..	..	12
WASHINGTON COUNTY	..	..	1	1,174	6	..	4	7	..	5	..	1	3	32
WHOLE STATE	15	6	35	5,439	98	18	108	114	49	45	11	44	36	1,310

TABLE VI.—*Continued.* NATIVITY.—*Showing how many of the inhabitants of each town and county of the State were born in each of the United States.*

TOWNS AND DIVISIONS OF THE STATE.	PLACE OF BIRTH.—UNITED STATES.										
	Maryland.	Massachusetts.	Michigan.	Minnesota.	Mississippi.	Missouri.	New Hampshire.	New Jersey.	New York.	North Carolina	Ohio.
Barrington	3	135	..	..	..	..	3	....	22	1	2
Bristol	13	429	4	1	.	..	13	3	107	..	4
Warren	2	368	..	..	..	..	8	2	25	..	7
BRISTOL COUNTY	18	932	4	1	..	..	24	5	154	1	13
Coventry	....	109	..	..	..	1	2	1	36	1	2
East Greenwich	....	81	..	..	1	..	11	3	42	..	2
West Greenwich	....	9	..	..	..	..	1	....	9	..	...
Warwick	5	308	..	..	..	..	10	8	86	3	2
KENT COUNTY	5	507	..	..	1	1	24	12	173	4	6
Jamestown	....	4	..	..	..	..	....	1	4	..	....
Little Compton	....	226	..	..	..	..	1	3	9	2	....
Middletown	4	26	..	..	..	..	1	....	20	..	3
Newport	218	821	21	6	9	12	41	67	613	17	48
New Shoreham	...	18	..	..	..	..	2	1	5	..	....
Portsmouth	1	158	1	..	..	..	13	9	31	3	1
Tiverton	....	189	..	..	..	..	4	2	10	..	....
NEWPORT COUNTY	223	1,442	22	6	9	12	62	83	692	22	52
Burrillville	2	478	..	..	..	..	24	1	38	1	1
Cranston	71	632	..	..	..	..	54	31	201	6	5
Cumberland	....	1,100	1	1	..	..	80	7	101	1	7
East Providence	10	897	1	..	..	..	21	9	33	..	....
Foster	....	42	1	..	..	..	1	...	14	..	2
Glocester	...	98	..	..	..	..	5	1	19	..	1
Johnston	1	178	..	..	1	..	14	4	41	..	....
North Providence	7	1,852	2	..	..	..	115	33	217	9	8
Pawtucket	6	841	1	..	..	1	43	11	70	..	9
Scituate	4	146	..	..	..	1	11	1	15	..	....
Smithfield	4	1,512	6	1	..	1	82	12	165	..	18
TOWNS PROVIDENCE COUNTY	105	7,776	12	2	1	3	450	110	914	17	51
PROVIDENCE CITY	259	6,344	15	3	5	13	503	138	1,219	36	59
Charlestown	...	8	1	..	..	..	1	....	7	..	....
Exeter	...	20	1	..	..	..	2	....	9	..	....
Hopkinton	...	34	1	..	..	..	....	....	69	1	2
North Kingstown	1	71	..	2	..	..	5	4	28	..	2
South Kingstown	3	61	..	..	1	2	9	5	59	..	3
Richmond	1	38	..	..	1	1	....	5	19	..	1
Westerly	1	87	..	..	..	..	2	9	112	..	....
WASHINGTON COUNTY	6	319	3	2	2	3	19	23	303	1	8
WHOLE STATE	616	17,320	56	14	18	32	1,082	371	3,455	81	189

TABLE VI.—*Continued.* NATIVITY.—*Showing how many of the inhabitants of each town and county of the State were born in each of the United States.*

TOWNS AND DIVISIONS OF THE STATE.	PLACE OF BIRTH.—UNITED STATES.										Total born in United States.
	Pennsylvania.	Rhode Islsnd.	South Carolina	Tennessee.	Texas.	Vermont.	Virginia.	Wisconsin.	District of Columbia.	United States. No State given.	
Barrington	1	597	..	..	..	2	2	..	....	....	788
Bristol	18	3,175	7	..	..	14	10	1	1	...	3,869
Warren	4	1,816	..	..	..	8	1	..	...	1	2,271
BRISTOL COUNTY	23	5,588	7	..	..	24	13	1	1	1	6,928
Coventry	5	3,168	..	..	..	11	2	1	....	8	3,521
East Greenwich	8	1,847	1	1	..	5	....	2	1	6	2,112
West Greenwich	1	1,098	..	..	..	3	1	..	....	10	1,205
Warwick	33	5,276	1	..	..	17	10	5	....	8	6,089
KENT COUNTY	47	11,389	2	1	..	36	13	8	1	32	12,927
Jamestown	....	324	..	..	..	....	1	..	...	1	338
Little Compton	....	882	..	..	..	4	....	..	....	....	1,140
Middletown	2	857	..	..	..	....	4	..	..	3	940
Newport	199	7,336	11	5	1	20	71	10	45	29	9,970
New Shoreham	1	1,259	..	..	..	....	....	..	....	....	1,301
Portsmouth	2	1,566	..	..	..	1	2	8	....	....	1,833
Tiverton	....	1,690	..	..	..	7	1	..	....	1	1,918
NEWPORT COUNTY	204	13,914	11	5	1	32	79	18	45	34	17,440
Burrillville	6	2,597	..	..	..	31	1	2	...	1	3,367
Cranston	36	5,236	2	..	1	48	14	17	3	207	6,818
Cumberland	10	3,826	..	..	..	70	5	..	....	....	5,449
East Providence	7	823	3	..	..	16	2	..	....	....	1,928
Foster	4	1,649	..	..	..	4	2	..	....	....	1,857
Glocester	1	1,866	1	..	..	3	2	..	....	4	2,190
Johnston	1	2,344	2	..	..	9	2	1	2	....	2,699
North Providence	26	6,930	4	..	..	60	9	5	1	8	9,747
Pawtucket	22	2,359	..	1	..	9	4	3	....	....	3,505
Scituate	14	2,992	..	..	..	7	2	..	...	9	3,341
Smithfield	19	6,337	..	..	..	95	5	7	....	63	8,761
TOWNS PROVIDENCE CO.	146	36,959	12	1	1	352	48	35	6	292	49,662
PROVIDENCE CITY	292	29,248	37	6	1	280	102	9	37	116	41,193
Charlestown	....	1,008	..	..	..	2	1	..	....	....	1,104
Exeter	2	1,384	..	..	..	1	....	..	....	....	1,491
Hopkinton	4	2,034	..	..	..	6	2	..	....	....	2,413
North Kingstown	1	2,745	..	..	..	6	4	..	....	3	2,938
South Kingstown	13	3,939	1	..	..	4	....	1	....	4	4,232
Richmond	....	1,533	..	..	..	2	2	..	....	1	1,714
Westerly	5	2,466	..	..	..	3	8	4	1	....	3,220
WASHINGTON COUNTY	25	15,109	1	..	..	24	17	5	1	8	17,112
WHOLE STATE	737	112,207	70	13	3	748	272	76	91	483	145,262

TABLE VII. NATIVITY.—*Showing how many of the inhabitants of each town in the State were born in each foreign country.*

TOWNS AND DIVISIONS OF THE STATE.	PLACE OF BIRTH.—FOREIGN COUNTRIES.											
	Asia.	Africa.	Australasia.	Belgium.	British America.	China.	Denmark.	East Indies.	England.	France.	Germany.	Greece.
Barrington	..	..	..	..	156	..	..	..	10	1	....	....
Bristol	..	3	..	2	32	..	..	..	142	1	46	....
Warren	2	1	..	..	43	..	1	..	75	4	3	....
BRISTOL COUNTY	2	4	..	2	231	..	1	..	227	6	49	....
Coventry	..	..	..	..	140	..	..	..	105	1	11	....
East Greenwich	..	1	..	..	18	..	..	..	62	...	....	....
West Greenwich	..	..	..	..	1	..	..	..	1	....	....	....
Warwick	..	..	..	..	314	1	..	..	313	1	2	....
KENT COUNTY	..	1	..	..	473	1	..	..	481	2	13	....
Jamestown	..	..	..	..	......	..	..	..	3	....	....	....
Little Compton	..	..	..	..	3	..	..	..	7	....	....	....
Middletown	..	..	..	..	6	..	..	..	9	....	1	....
Newport	..	4	1	..	69	..	1	1	461	56	112	....
New Shoreham	..	..	..	..	2	..	..	..	4	....	1	....
Portsmouth	..	..	..	..	3	..	..	..	28	3	10	....
Tiverton	..	..	..	..	7	..	..	..	9	....	7	....
NEWPORT COUNTY	..	4	1	..	90	..	1	1	521	59	131	....
Burrillville	..	..	..	..	325	..	1	..	261	1	12	....
Cranston	..	..	..	..	110	..	..	..	410	4	51	....
Cumberland	..	..	..	..	539	..	..	..	346	1	8	....
East Providence	..	..	..	..	22	..	3	..	27	1	2	...
Foster	..	..	..	..	3	..	..	..	3	....	....	....
Glocester	..	..	..	..	15	..	..	..	22	....	....	..
Johnston	..	..	..	..	9	..	..	1	191	....	14	...
North Providence	..	..	..	..	100	..	2	..	942	8	91	....
Pawtucket	..	..	..	..	34	..	..	..	369	....	16	....
Scituate	..	..	..	..	1	..	..	..	43	....	....	....
Smithfield	..	..	..	..	695	..	..	..	698	6	22	....
TOWNS PROVIDENCE COUNTY	..	..	..	..	1,853	..	6	1	3,312	21	216	....
PROVIDENCE CITY	2	4	4	..	589	..	5	4	1,606	53	416	5
Charlestown	..	..	..	..	......	..	..	..	6	....	11	....
Exeter	..	..	..	..	1	..	..	..	1	....	....	....
Hopkinton	..	1	..	..	19	..	..	..	41	....	2	....
North Kingstown	..	..	..	..	92	..	..	..	16	....	6	....
South Kingstown	..	..	..	..	3	..	1	..	36	5	15	....
Richmond	..	..	..	..	20	..	..	..	23	....	11	....
Westerly	..	..	..	..	13	..	..	..	208	....	27	....
WASHINGTON COUNTY	.	1	..	..	148	..	1	..	331	5	72	....
WHOLE STATE	4	14	5	2	3,384	1	14	6	6,478	146	897	5

TABLE VII.—*Continued.* NATIVITY.—*Showing how many of the inhabitants of each town in the State were born in each foreign country.*

TOWNS AND DIVISIONS OF THE STATE.	PLACE OF BIRTH.—FOREIGN COUNTRIES.									
	Holland.	Hungary.	Italy.	Ireland.	Mexico.	Norway.	Portugal and Western Islands.	Poland.	Russia.	Spain.
Barrington				69						
Bristol				490			8			
Warren	1			368			1			
BRISTOL COUNTY	1			927			9			
Coventry				165						
East Greenwich				183						
West Greenwich				19						
Warwick			1	867						
KENT COUNTY			1	1,234						
Jamestown				8						
Little Compton				32			8			
Middletown				58						
Newport			3	1,921	1		6		1	2
New Shoreham										
Portsmouth				274						
Tiverton			1	22			7			
NEWPORT COUNTY			4	2,315	1		21		1	2
Burrillville				873						
Cranston	1		2	1,693		7	13	1		
Cumberland				1,821						
East Providence				175			2			
Foster				10						
Glocester				57						
Johnston				450						
North Providence	5		4	3,490		2	1			
Pawtucket				1,033		2				
Scituate				147						
Smithfield			2	1,961		3			3	
TOWNS PROVIDENCE COUNTY	6		8	11,710		14	16	1	3	
PROVIDENCE CITY	10	1	24	10,130		15	28	4	4	1
Charlestown				8						
Exeter				3						
Hopkinton				27						
North Kingstown				111						1
South Kingstown				206			1			
Richmond				55						
Westerly				304						
WASHINGTON COUNTY				714			1			1
WHOLE STATE	17	1	37	27,030	1	29	75	5	8	4

TABLE VII.—*Continued.* NATIVITY.—*Showing how many of the inhabitants of each town in the State were born in each foreign country.*

TOWNS AND DIVISIONS OF THE STATE.	PLACE OF BIRTH.—FOREIGN COUNTRIES.								
	Sandwich Islands.	South America.	Scotland and Wales.	Sweden.	Switzerland.	St. Helena.	West Indies.	On the Ocean.	Total Foreign Born.
Barrington	....	....	2	....	....	1	1	....	240
Bristol	1	....	33	1	....	1	20	....	780
Warren	....	3	18	....	....	....	1	....	521
BRISTOL COUNTY	1	3	53	1	....	2	22	....	1,541
Coventry	....	....	52	....	....	....	....	....	474
East Greenwich	....	....	24	....	....	....	....	....	288
West Greenwich	....	....	2	....	....	....	....	....	23
Warwick	....	....	106	....	1	....	1	....	1,607
KENT COUNTY	....	....	184	....	1	....	1	....	2,392
Jamestown	....	....	....	....	....	....	....	....	11
Little Compton	....	....	6	....	1	....	....	....	57
Middletown	....	....	2	....	3	....	....	....	79
Newport	2	....	73	2	....	....	2	....	2,718
New Shoreham	....	....	....	....	....	....	....	....	7
Portsmouth	....	....	2	....	....	....	....	....	320
Tiverton	....	....	1	....	....	....	1	....	55
NEWPORT COUNTY	2	....	84	2	4	....	3	....	3,247
Burrillville	....	....	21	....	....	....	....	....	1,494
Cranston	....	....	53	14	....	....	....	....	2,359
Cumberland	....	....	52	....	....	....	....	....	2,767
East Providence	....	....	12	....	....	....	....	....	244
Foster	....	....	....	....	....	....	....	....	16
Glocester	....	....	2	....	....	....	....	....	96
Johnston	....	....	72	....	....	....	....	....	737
North Providence	....	....	160	....	....	....	1	....	4,806
Pawtucket	....	....	40	....	1	....	....	....	1,495
Scituate	....	....	6	....	....	....	....	....	197
Smithfield	....	....	157	....	7	....	....	....	3,554
TOWNS PROVIDENCE COUNTY	....	....	575	14	8	....	1	....	17,765
PROVIDENCE CITY	6	12	425	11	18	4	20	1	13,402
Charlestown	....	....	5	....	....	....	....	....	30
Exeter	....	....	2	....	....	....	....	....	7
Hopkinton	....	....	9	....	....	....	....	....	99
North Kingstown	....	....	2	....	....	....	....	....	228
South Kingstown	....	....	14	....	....	....	....	....	281
Richmond	....	....	7	....	....	....	....	....	116
Westerly	....	....	43	....	....	....	....	....	595
WASHINGTON COUNTY	....	....	82	....	....	....	....	....	1,356
WHOLE STATE	9	15	1403	28	31	6	47	1	39,703

TABLE VIII. NATIVITY.—*Showing the particulars of Table IV, in the cities of Providence and Newport, by Wards.*

CITY OF PROVIDENCE. TABLE IV. *By Wards.*

WARDS.	BIRTH PLACE.					Total Population.
	In the City.	Out of the City and in the State.	Out of the State and in the U. S.	Total born in the United States.	Born in Foreign Countries.	
First	3,911	1,282	2,275	7,468	3,200	10,668
Second	1,783	556	1,216	3,555	1,063	4,618
Third	3,561	746	1,685	5,992	2,042	8,034
Fourth	1,814	759	1,152	3,725	942	4,667
Fifth	2,921	992	1,704	5,617	2,078	7,695
Sixth	3,938	2,368	2,435	8,741	1,772	10,513
Seventh	3,196	1,421	1,478	6,095	2,305	8,400
Whole city	21,124	8,124	11,945	41,193	13,402	54,595

CITY OF NEWPORT. TABLE IV. *By Wards.*

WARDS.	BIRTH PLACE.					Total Population.
	In the City.	Out of the City and in the State.	Out of the State and in the U. S.	Total born in the United States.	Born in Foreign Countries.	
First	1,269	143	288	1,700	244	1,944
Second	1,346	315	447	2,108	450	2,558
Third	1,086	187	442	1,715	344	2,059
Fourth	1,092	219	969	2,280	450	2,730
Fifth	1,462	217	488	2,167	1,230	3,397
Whole city	6,255	1,081	2,634	9,970	2,718	12,688

TABLE IX. NATIVITY.—*Being table V for the City of Providence, by Wards; showing how many of the inhabitants of each Ward, in the City of Providence, were born in each town and county in Rhode Island.*

BIRTH PLACE IN RHODE ISLAND.	WARDS: CITY OF PROVIDENCE.							Whole City.
	I.	II.	III.	IV.	V.	VI.	VII.	
Barrington	10	6	34	19	9	17	10	105
Bristol	13	31	75	31	61	59	27	297
Warren	24	34	50	33	39	46	42	268
BRISTOL COUNTY	47	71	159	83	109	122	79	670
Coventry	43	11	19	24	44	108	68	317
East Greenwich	28	20	23	20	36	74	46	247
West Greenwich	18	8	5	2	9	34	6	82
Warwick	74	43	48	98	106	308	151	828
KENT COUNTY	163	82	95	144	195	524	271	1,474
Jamestown	4	....	4	3	1	17	....	29
Little Compton	7	6	14	19	10	14	4	74
Middletown	3	3	3	4	3	8	....	24
Newport	89	70	131	74	78	134	83	659
New Shoreham	2	3	9	11	2	5	5	37
Portsmouth	10	10	12	12	5	24	18	91
Tiverton	13	10	15	6	14	24	15	97
NEWPORT COUNTY	128	102	188	129	113	226	125	1,011
Burrillville	42	8	9	4	22	28	9	122
Cranston	44	17	35	42	89	234	88	549
Cumberland	121	40	43	41	43	67	49	404
East Providence	....	....	2	....	2	2	....	6
Foster	21	5	3	7	11	112	67	226
Glocester	42	22	9	31	17	99	57	277
Johnston	50	8	11	27	50	171	118	435
North Providence	227	55	44	55	87	117	137	722
Pawtucket	....	....	....	....	....	....	....	....
Scituate	52	16	26	46	56	242	163	601
Smithfield	201	46	44	66	74	160	126	717
TOWNS PROV. CO.	800	217	226	319	451	1,232	814	4,059
PROVIDENCE CITY	3,011	1,783	3,561	1,814	2,921	3,938	3,196	21,124
Charlestown	3	3	4	3	4	12	6	35
Exeter	10	3	5	5	12	32	17	84
Hopkinton	4	2	2	4	5	11	7	35
North Kingstown	57	27	23	30	45	116	43	341
South Kingstown	34	17	15	15	18	50	30	179
Richmond	13	1	8	4	12	27	8	73
Westerly	8	5	10	2	2	4	6	37
WASHINGTON COUNTY	129	58	67	63	98	252	117	784
R. I. town not given	15	26	11	21	26	12	15	126
WHOLE STATE	5,193	2,339	4,307	2,573	3,913	6,306	4,617	29,248

TABLE X. NATIVITY.—*Being table V for the City of Newport, by Wards; showing how many of the inhabitants of each Ward, in the City of Newport, were born in each town and county in Rhode Island.*

BIRTH PLACE IN RHODE ISLAND.	WARDS: CITY OF NEWPORT. I.	II.	III.	IV.	V.	Whole City.
Barrington	....	2	....	1	....	3
Bristol	12	21	11	9	13	66
Warren	2	9	2	4	4	21
BRISTOL COUNTY	14	32	13	14	17	90
Coventry	....	1	....	6	3	10
East Greenwich	2	4	9	12	2	29
West Greenwich	....	....	2	1	....	3
Warwick	3	....	5	4	6	18
KENT COUNTY	5	5	16	23	11	60
Jamestown	10	5	6	12	14	47
Little Compton	2	9	4	6	1	22
Middletown	11	79	16	11	19	136
Newport	1,269	1,346	1,086	1,092	1,462	6,255
New Shoreham	10	17	10	11	7	55
Portsmouth	10	41	26	10	25	112
Tiverton	8	4	11	4	12	39
NEWPORT COUNTY	1,320	1,501	1,159	1,146	1,540	6,666
Burrillville	....	....	....	....	....	....
Cranston	5	2	....	3	1	11
Cumberland	2	1	....	2	2	7
East Providence	....	....	....	....	....	....
Foster	....	....	....	....	....	....
Glocester	....	2	....	....	2	4
Johnston	....	....	....	1	....	1
North Providence	2	1	2	6	7	18
Pawtucket	1	....	....	....	....	1
Scituate	1	2	2	2	....	7
Smithfield	....	2	2	3	1	8
TOWNS PROVIDENCE COUNTY	11	10	6	17	13	57
PROVIDENCE CITY	26	44	42	53	32	197
Charlestown	1	1	5	1	2	10
Exeter	1	4	1	2	3	11
Hopkinton	3	1	1	4	2	11
North Kingstown	4	9	7	4	14	38
South Kingstown	24	51	17	34	39	165
Richmond	1	....	1	....	1	3
Westerly	2	3	5	4	5	19
WASHINGTON COUNTY	36	69	37	49	66	257
R. I. town not given	....	....	....	9	....	9
WHOLE STATE	1,412	1,661	1,273	1,311	1,679	7,336

TABLE XI. NATIVITY.—*Being table VI, for the City of Providence, by Wards; showing how many of the inhabitants of each Ward in the City of Providence, were born in each of the United States.*

BIRTH PLACE IN THE UNITED STATES.	WARDS: CITY OF PROVIDENCE.							Whole City.
	I.	II.	III.	IV.	V.	VI.	VII.	
Alabama	1	....	3	2	2	....	....	8
California	....	1	3	2	1	3	2	12
Connecticut	234	172	161	169	229	483	235	1,683
Delaware	26	13	3	3	1	6	8	60
Florida	....	1	2	3	....	3	....	9
Georgia	7	13	7	10	3	3	2	45
Illinois	4	4	3	....	9	1	4	25
Indiana	3	2	....	....	...	1	1	7
Iowa	2	....	2	....	2	3	1	10
Kansas	3	....	...	....	....	....	....	3
Kentucky	4	1	1	1	2	2	....	11
Louisiana	1	....	1	3	....	1	....	6
Maine	114	66	79	50	76	127	80	592
Maryland	39	62	26	18	9	91	14	259
Massachusetts	1,165	500	1,030	655	1,013	1,180	801	6,344
Michigan	5	1	....	....	....	7	2	15
Minnesota	1	....	....	....	....	2	....	3
Mississippi	1	1	....	1	1	1	....	5
Missouri	2	....	3	1	4	2	1	13
New Hampshire	99	55	52	57	81	97	62	503
New Jersey	37	31	13	8	12	19	18	138
New York	294	124	167	98	164	221	151	1,219
North Carolina	8	5	....	4	1	10	8	36
Ohio	10	4	6	11	5	15	8	59
Pennsylvania	76	59	39	17	23	47	31	292
Rhode Island	5,193	2,339	4,307	2,573	3,913	6,306	4,617	29,248
South Carolina	5	1	7	4	7	10	3	37
Tennessee	....	2	....	1	....	1	2	6
Texas	1	....	....	....	....	....	....	1
Vermont	50	28	41	26	47	56	32	280
Virginia	13	34	18	5	3	22	7	102
Wisconsin	....	....	2	...	3	4	....	9
District of Columbia	4	7	11	2	1	11	1	37
U. S. State not given	66	29	5	1	5	6	4	116
Totals born in U. S.	7,468	3,555	5,992	3,725	5,617	8,741	6,095	41,193

None born in Arkansas, Oregon, or in the Territories.

TABLE XII. NATIVITY.—*Being table VI, for the City of Newport, by Wards; showing how many of the inhabitants of each Ward in the City of Newport, were born in each of the United States.*

BIRTH PLACE IN THE UNITED STATES.	WARDS: CITY OF NEWPORT.					Whole City.
	I.	II.	III.	IV.	V.	
Alabama	....	....	1	2	....	3
Arkansas	....	....	....	1	....	1
California	....	....	....	5	....	5
Connecticut	22	24	17	43	15	121
Delaware	3	6	4	7	3	23
Florida	....	....	1	1	1	3
Georgia	1	11	5	1	3	21
Illinois	....	....	1	24	....	25
Indiana	....	8	1	17	2	28
Iowa	....	....	1	12	1	14
Kansas	....	....	....	1	2	3
Kentucky	3	1	2	14	4	24
Louisiana	3	4	1	2	5	15
Maine	13	9	15	30	17	84
Maryland	11	39	49	82	37	218
Massachusetts	140	178	150	181	172	821
Michigan	1	5	3	9	3	21
Minnesota	....	....	....	3	3	6
Mississippi	....	....	5	3	1	9
Missouri	....	....	....	12	....	12
New Hampshire	9	5	1	18	8	41
New Jersey	....	12	12	24	19	67
New York	47	89	110	233	134	613
North Carolina	6	1	3	5	2	17
Ohio	1	2	3	37	5	48
Pennsylvania	11	27	27	95	39	199
Rhode Island	1,412	1,661	1,273	1,311	1,679	7,336
South Carolina	1	4	5	....	1	11
Tennessee	3	....	...	2	....	5
Texas	....	....	....	1	....	1
Vermont	1	3	4	7	5	20
Virginia	12	9	8	38	4	71
Wisconsin	....	....	....	10	....	10
District of Columbia	....	7	13	24	1	45
U. S. State not given	....	1	....	25	1	27
Territories	....	2	....	....	....	2
Totals born in U. S.	1,700	2,108	1,715	2,280	2,167	9,970

None born in Oregon.

TABLE XIII. NATIVITY.—*Showing the particulars of table VII, in the City of Providence, by Wards; showing how many of the inhabitants of each Ward in the City of Providence were born in each foreign country.*

CITY OF PROVIDENCE. TABLE VII. *By Wards.*

BIRTH PLACE IN FOREIGN COUNTRIES.	WARDS: CITY OF PROVIDENCE.							Whole City.
	I.	II.	III.	IV.	V.	VI.	VII.	
Asia	....	2	....	....	....	....	....	2
Africa	1	1	....	...	1	....	1	4
Australasia	1	....	....	2	....	....	1	4
British America	146	87	116	48	67	51	74	589
Denmark	1	....	1	....	1	1	1	5
East Indies	1	1	....	2	....	....	....	4
England	412	114	176	116	277	209	302	1,606
France	9	7	9	12	7	3	6	53
Germany	50	31	38	44	54	103	96	416
Greece	....	4	....	1	....	....	....	5
Holland	5	....	2	....	3	....	....	10
Hungary	....	....	....	....	....	....	1	1
Italy	1	....	2	6	....	1	14	24
Ireland	2,455	755	1,615	677	1,570	1,341	1,717	10,130
Norway	2	....	4	3	3	3	....	15
Portugal & West'n Islands	....	....	22	....	1	1	4	28
Poland	3	1	....	....	....	....	....	4
Russia	....	4	....	....	....	....	....	4
Spain	....	....	....	....	....	1	....	1
Sandwich Islands	....	....	4	2	....	....	....	6
South America	1	....	5	3	1	2	....	12
Scotland and Wales	108	45	37	19	80	52	84	425
Sweden	....	2	3	1	3	1	1	11
Switzerland	1	3	1	2	9	....	2	18
St. Helena	....	1	....	....	1	2	....	4
West Indies	3	5	7	4	....	....	1	20
On the Ocean	....	....	....	....	....	1	....	1
Totals foreign born	3,200	1,063	2,042	942	2,078	1,772	2,305	13,402

TABLE XIV. NATIVITY.—*Showing the particulars of table VII, in the City of Newport, by Wards; showing how many of the inhabitants in each Ward of the City of Newport were born in each foreign country.*

CITY OF NEWPORT. TABLE VII. *By Wards.*

BIRTH PLACE IN FOREIGN COUNTRIES.	WARDS: CITY OF NEWPORT.					Whole City.
	I.	II.	III.	IV.	V.	
Africa	....	3	....	....	1	4
Australasia	....	....	....	....	1	1
British America	9	16	9	12	23	69
Denmark	....	1	....	....	....	1
East Indies	....	....	....	....	1	1
England	50	39	50	62	260	461
France	1	7	16	17	15	56
Germany	18	4	21	41	28	112
Italy	....	....	....	2	1	3
Ireland	152	379	240	308	842	1,921
Mexico	....	....	1	....	....	1
Portugal & Western Islands	2	...	....	....	4	6
Russia	....	....	....	....	1	1
Spain	....	....	....	....	2	2
Sandwich Islands	1	....	....	1	....	2
Scotland and Wales	9	1	7	7	49	73
Sweden	2	....	....	....	....	2
West Indies	....	...	....	....	2	2
Totals foreign born	244	450	344	450	1,230	2,718

TABLE XV. PARENTAGE.—*Showing the Parentage of the population, in each town and county in the State.*

TOWNS AND DIVISIONS OF THE STATE.	Total American.	Irish.	English.	Scotch & Welsh.	German.	French.	British American.
Barrington	711	116	26	4	....	1	157
Bristol	3,399	751	190	58	95	3	35
Warren	1,983	572	132	26	4	4	25
BRISTOL COUNTY	6,093	1,439	348	88	99	8	217
Coventry	3,278	271	168	54	17	2	161
East Greenwich	1,927	282	126	29	....	....	12
West Greenwich	1,172	47	1	2	....	....	....
Warwick	4,951	1,617	442	179	2	2	372
KENT COUNTY	11,328	2,217	737	264	19	4	545
Jamestown	330	8	4	....	....	....	....
Little Compton	1,104	44	12	9	1	....	....
Middletown	903	77	13	4	1	....	4
Newport	7,976	3,215	720	145	171	60	2
New Shoreham	1,286	7	5	....	1	....	1
Portsmouth	1,629	436	41	2	10	1	....
Tiverton	1,840	30	21	2	14	....	....
NEWPORT COUNTY	15,068	3,817	816	162	198	61	7
Burrillville	2,487	1,490	395	39	18	3	392
Cranston	4,540	3,397	676	90	101	11	60
Cumberland	3,799	3,132	442	57	13	....	721
East Providence	1,632	356	40	29	6	5	21
Foster	1,832	24	9	2	....	....	2
Glocester	2,112	108	26	2	....	....	18
Johnston	2,170	809	287	88	39	....	....
North Providence	6,217	6,123	1,365	255	151	17	90
Pawtucket	2,188	1,979	521	59	23	2	2
Scituate	3,217	237	52	9	....	....	....
Smithfield	6,618	3,389	1,002	234	40	8	805
TOWNS PROV. COUNTY	36,812	21,044	4,815	864	391	46	2,111
PROVIDENCE CITY	30,163	18,430	2,581	855	801	117	207
Charlestown	1,079	15	10	11	14	....	....
Exeter	1,473	5	8	4	1	....	....
Hopkinton	2,330	52	60	9	2	1	21
North Kingstown	2,813	164	22	2	14	...	122
South Kingstown	3,914	396	53	24	22	10	2
Richmond	1,604	96	52	9	14	....	23
Westerly	2,880	461	279	52	51	....	4
WASHINGTON COUNTY	16,093	1,189	484	111	118	11	172
WHOLE STATE	115,557	48,136	9,781	2,344	1,626	247	3,259

TABLE XV.—*Continued.* PARENTAGE.—*Showing the Parentage of the population, in each town and county in the State.*

TOWNS AND DIVISIONS OF THE STATE.	Portuguese.	Italian.	Other Foreign.	Total Foreign.	American Father and For'gn Mother.	Foreign Father and American Mother.	Total population.
Barrington	....	....	....	304	6	7	1,028
Bristol	12	....	12	1,156	38	56	4,649
Warren	1	....	5	769	15	25	2,792
BRISTOL COUNTY	13	....	17	2,229	59	88	8,469
Coventry	....	....	....	673	10	34	3,995
East Greenwich	....	....	1	450	11	12	2,400
West Greenwich	....	....	....	50	6	....	1,228
Warwick	...	....	3	2,617	84	44	7,696
KENT COUNTY	....	....	4	3,790	111	90	15,319
Jamestown	....	....	....	12	7	....	349
Little Compton	8	....	3	77	1	15	1,197
Middletown	....	....	....	99	16	1	1,019
Newport	18	3	14	4,348	178	186	12,688
New Shoreham	....	....	....	14	1	7	1,308
Portsmouth	...	....	....	490	26	8	2,153
Tiverton	7	1	....	75	52	6	1,973
NEWPORT COUNTY	33	4	17	5,115	281	223	20,687
Burrillville	....	3	1	2,341	20	13	4,861
Cranston	26	2	49	4,412	118	107	9,177
Cumberland	....	....	....	4,365	39	13	8,216
East Providence	2	....	10	469	46	25	2,172
Foster	....	....	....	37	....	4	1,873
Glocester	....	....	....	154	19	1	2,286
Johnston	....	....	....	1,223	36	7	3,436
North Providence	1	7	5	8,014	161	161	14,553
Pawtucket	....	....	2	2,588	71	153	5,000
Scituate	....	....	...	298	13	10	3,538
Smithfield	...	2	7	5,487	90	120	12,315
TOWNS PROV. COUNTY	29	14	74	29,388	613	614	67,427
PROVIDENCE CITY	64	43	141	23,239	539	654	54,595
Charlestown	....	....	....	50	4	1	1,134
Exeter	....	....	....	18	3	4	1,498
Hopkinton	....	....	1	146	14	22	2,512
North Kingstown	....	....	1	325	22	6	3,166
South Kingstown	1	....	1	509	51	39	4,513
Richmond	....	....	...	194	22	10	1,830
Westerly	....	....	....	847	40	48	3,815
WASHINGTON COUNTY	1	....	3	2,089	156	130	18,468
WHOLE STATE	140	61	256	65,850	1,759	1,799	184,965

TABLE XVI. PARENTAGE.—*Being table XV for Providence and and Newport, by Wards; showing the Parentage of the population in each Ward.*

CITY OF PROVIDENCE. TABLE XV. *By Wards.*

PARENTAGE.	WARDS. CITY OF PROVIDENCE.							Whole City.
	I.	II.	III.	IV.	V.	VI.	VII.	
TOTAL AMERICAN	4,659	3,160	3,973	3,134	3,979	7,254	4,004	30,163
Irish	4,568	1,020	3,282	1,085	2,780	2,430	3,265	18,430
English	669	169	285	178	387	356	537	2,581
Scotch and Welsh	207	105	104	38	168	96	137	855
German	113	52	77	82	92	173	212	801
French	26	11	15	24	22	7	12	117
British American	75	27	38	9	27	18	13	207
Portuguese	2	....	57	1	1	1	2	64
Italian	4	...	1	10	....	3	25	43
Other Foreign	28	14	21	13	39	14	12	141
TOTAL FOREIGN	5,692	1,398	3,880	1,440	3,516	3,098	4,215	23,239
American Father and Foreign Mother	147	26	94	32	105	54	81	539
Foreign Father and American Mother	170	34	87	61	95	107	100	654
TOTAL POPULATION	10,668	4,618	8,034	4,667	7,695	10,513	8,400	54,595

CITY OF NEWPORT. TABLE XV. *By Wards.*

PARENTAGE.	WARDS. CITY OF NEWPORT.					Whole City.
	I.	II.	III.	IV.	V.	
TOTAL AMERICAN	1,420	1,848	1,555	1,993	1,160	7,976
Irish	273	574	331	484	1,553	3,215
English	81	57	72	101	409	720
Scotch and Welsh	22	4	8	21	90	145
German	25	4	35	64	43	171
French	2	8	19	18	13	60
British American	1	....	....	....	1	2
Portuguese	10	....	...	....	8	18
Italian	....	1	....	1	1	3
Other Foreign	2	8	....	....	4	14
TOTAL FOREIGN	416	656	465	689	2,122	4,348
American Father and Foreign Mother	42	34	14	27	61	178
Foreign Father and American Mother	66	20	25	21	54	186
TOTAL POPULATION	1,944	2,558	2,059	2,730	3,397	12,688

TABLE XVII. NATIVITY AND PARENTAGE COMPARED; *showing the number and proportions of the population by Nativity and by Parentage in each town in the State. Mixed parentage given according to the birthplace of the fathers.*

TOWNS AND DIVISIONS OF THE STATE.	Total Population.	Number born in the United States.	Number of American Parentage.	Difference: Children of Foreigners born in the United States.	Number born in Foreign Countries.	Number of Foreign Parentage.	In each 100 of the Population there were of American Parentage.	Foreign Parentage.
Barrington	1,028	788	717	71	240	311	69.75	30.25
Bristol	4,649	3,869	3,437	432	780	1,212	73.93	26.07
Warren	2,792	2,271	1,998	273	521	794	71.56	28.44
BRISTOL COUNTY	8,469	6,928	6,152	776	1,541	2,317	72.64	27.36
Coventry	3,995	3,521	3,288	233	474	707	82.30	17.70
East Greenwich	2,400	2,112	1,938	174	288	462	80.75	19.25
West Greenwich	1,228	1,205	1,178	27	23	50	95.93	4.07
Warwick	7,696	6,089	5,035	1,054	1,607	2,661	65.42	34.58
KENT COUNTY	15,319	12,927	11,439	1,488	2,392	3,880	74.67	25.33
Jamestown	349	338	337	1	11	12	96.56	3.44
Little Compton	1,197	1,140	1,105	35	57	92	92.31	7.69
Middletown	1,019	940	919	21	79	100	90.19	9.81
Newport	12,688	9,970	8,154	1,816	2,718	4,534	64.27	35.73
New Shoreham	1,308	1,301	1,287	14	7	21	98.39	1.61
Portsmouth	2,153	1,833	1,655	178	320	498	76.87	23.13
Tiverton	1,973	1,918	1,892	26	55	81	95.89	4.11
NEWPORT COUNTY	20,687	17,440	15,349	2,091	3,247	5,338	74.20	25.80
Burrillville	4,861	3,367	2,507	860	1,494	2,354	51.57	48.43
Cranston	9,177	6,818	4,658	2,160	2,359	4,519	50.76	49.24
Cumberland	8,216	5,449	3,838	1,611	2,767	4,378	46.71	53.28
East Providence	2,172	1,928	1,678	250	244	494	77.26	22.74
Foster	1,873	1,857	1,832	25	16	41	97.81	2.19
Glocester	2,286	2,190	2,131	59	96	155	93.22	6.78
Johnston	3,436	2,699	2,206	493	737	1,230	64.20	35.80
North Providence	14,553	9,747	6,378	3,369	4,806	8,175	43.83	56.17
Pawtucket	5,000	3,505	2,259	1,246	1,495	2,741	45.18	54.82
Scituate	3,538	3,341	3,230	111	197	308	91.29	8.71
Smithfield	12,315	8,761	6,708	2,053	3,554	5,607	54.47	45.53
TOWNS PROV. COUNTY	67,427	49,662	37,425	12,237	17,765	30,002	55.50	44.50
PROVIDENCE CITY	54,595	41,193	30,702	10,491	13,402	23,893	56.24	43.76
Charlestown	1,134	1,104	1,083	21	30	51	95.50	4.50
Exeter	1,498	1,491	1,476	15	7	22	98.53	1.47
Hopkinton	2,512	2,413	2,344	69	99	168	93.31	6.69
North Kingstown	3,166	2,938	2,835	103	228	331	89.55	10.45
South Kingstown	4,513	4,232	3,965	267	281	548	87.86	12.14
Richmond	1,830	1,714	1,626	88	116	204	88.85	11.15
Westerly	3,815	3,220	2,920	300	595	895	76.54	23.46
WASHINGTON COUNTY	18,468	17,112	16,249	863	1,356	2,219	87.98	12.02
WHOLE STATE	184,965	145,262	117,316	27,946	39,703	67,649	63.43	36.57

TABLE XVIII. NATIVITY AND PARENTAGE COMPARED.—*Being table XVII for the cities of Providence and Newport, by Wards. Those of mixed parentage according to birthplace of their fathers.*

CITY OF PROVIDENCE. TABLE XVII. *By Wards.*

WARDS.	Total Population.	Number born in the United States.	Number of American Parentage.	Difference: Children of Foreigners, born in the United States.	Number born in Foreign countries.	Number of Foreign Parentage.	In each 100 of the Population there were of American Parentage.	Foreign Parentage.
I............	10,668	7,468	4,806	2,662	3,200	5,862	45.05	54.95
II............	4,618	3,555	3,186	369	1,063	1,432	68.99	31 01
III....	8,034	5,992	4,067	1,925	2,042	3,967	50.62	49.38
IV..........	4,667	3,725	3,166	559	942	1,501	67.84	32.16
V..........	7,695	5,617	4,084	1,533	2,078	3,611	53.07	46.93
VI..........	10,513	8,741	7,308	1,433	1,772	3,205	69.51	30.49
VII.........	8,400	6,095	4,085	2,010	2,305	4,315	48.63	51.37
Whole City...	54,595	41,193	30,702	10,491	13,402	23,893	56.24	43.76

CITY OF NEWPORT. TABLE XVII. *By Wards.*

WARDS.	Total Population.	Number born in the United States.	Number of American Parentage.	Difference: Children of Foreigners, born in the United States.	Number born in Foreign Countries.	Number of Foreign Parentage.	In each 100 of the Population there were of American Parentage.	Foreign Parentage
I............	1,944	1,700	1,462	238	244	482	75.21	24.79
II............	2,558	2,108	1,882	226	450	676	73.57	26.43
III...........	2,059	1,715	1,569	146	344	490	76.20	23.80
IV..........	2,730	2,280	2,020	260	450	710	73.99	26.01
V....	3,397	2,167	1,221	946	1,230	2,176	35.94	64.06
Whole City...	12,688	9,970	8,154	1,816	2,718	4,534	64.27	35.73

TABLE XIX. SEX OF FOREIGN BORN.—*Showing the Sex of the population of Foreign birth in each Ward of the City of Providence.*

WARDS CITY OF PROVIDENCE.	BIRTH PLACE.										
	Ireland.		England, Scotland and Wales.		Germany.		Other Foreign Countries.		Total Foreign Born.		
	Males.	Females	M.	F.	M.	F.	M.	F.	M.	F.	Total.
I.	1,093	1,362	256	264	30	20	74	101	1,453	1,747	3,200
II.	179	576	81	78	18	13	41	77	319	744	1,063
III.	704	911	100	113	26	12	80	96	910	1,132	2,042
IV.	213	464	69	66	31	13	39	47	352	590	942
V.	677	893	197	160	29	25	44	53	947	1,131	2,078
VI.	512	829	127	134	56	47	31	36	726	1,046	1,772
VII.	692	1,025	202	184	56	40	51	55	1,001	1,304	2,305
Whole City...	4,070	6,060	1,032	999	246	170	360	465	5,708	7,694	13,402

TABLE XX. SEX AND PARENTAGE.—*Showing the Parentage and Sex of the whole population in each Ward of the City of Providence.*

WARDS CITY OF PROVIDENCE.	PARENTAGE.										
	American.		Foreign.		Amer. Fath and For. Moth.		Foreign Fa. and Am. Mother		Total Population.		
	Males.	Females	M.	F.	M.	F.	M.	F.	M	F.	Totals.
I.	2,189	2,470	2,665	3,027	67	80	88	82	5,009	5,659	10,668
II.	1,534	1,626	460	938	11	15	15	19	2,020	2,598	4,618
III.	1,869	2,104	1,804	2,076	40	54	48	39	3,761	4,273	8,034
IV.	1,455	1,679	585	855	16	16	29	32	2,085	2,582	4,667
V	1,905	2,074	1,663	1,853	51	54	44	51	3,663	4,032	7,695
VI	3,389	3,865	1,332	1,766	28	26	62	45	4,811	5,702	10,513
VII	1,855	2,149	1,929	2,286	35	46	51	49	3,870	4,530	8,400
Whole City...	14,196	15,967	10,438	12,801	248	291	337	317	25,219	29,376	54,595

TABLE XXI. AGE AND SEX.—*Showing the number of each Sex, in each division of ages, in each town and county in Rhode Island, and in Providence and Newport, by Wards.*

TOWNS AND DIVISIONS OF THE STATE.		Under 1 year.	1 and under 2	2 and under 5	5 and under 10	10 and under 15	15 and under 20	20 and under 30	30 and under 40	40 and under 50	50 and under 60	60 and under 70	70 and under 80	80 and under 90	90 and over.	Age not given	Totals.
Barrington........	Males.....	11	4	25	45	49	114	121	69	59	44	29	10	2	....	....	582
	Females..	6	12	24	40	38	38	80	60	55	42	26	18	6	1	....	446
	Totals....	17	16	49	85	87	152	201	129	114	86	55	28	8	1	....	1,028
Bristol............	Males....	48	35	143	242	218	198	348	279	239	206	112	44	16	4	....	2,132
	Females..	41	35	131	249	228	239	479	374	267	234	151	67	20	2	....	2,517
	Totals...	89	70	274	491	446	437	827	653	506	440	263	111	36	6	....	4,649
Warren..	Males....	22	14	70	122	153	143	168	153	172	115	79	28	11	....	....	1,250
	Females..	28	21	90	139	155	167	258	218	182	130	90	46	16	2	....	1,542
	Totals ...	50	35	160	261	308	310	426	371	354	245	169	74	27	2	....	2,792
BRISTOL COUNTY..	Males....	81	53	238	409	420	455	637	501	470	365	220	82	29	4	....	3,964
	Females..	75	68	245	428	421	444	817	652	504	406	267	131	42	5	....	4,505
	Totals....	156	121	483	837	841	899	1,454	1,153	974	771	487	213	71	9	....	8,469
Coventry	Males....	34	31	114	222	205	183	302	216	225	159	109	60	9	1	....	1,870
	Females..	30	33	110	208	203	215	367	291	235	204	129	79	19	2	....	2,125
	Totals....	64	64	224	430	403	398	669	507	460	363	238	139	28	3	....	3,995
East Greenwich...	Males....	19	20	56	101	141	110	203	127	136	109	73	37	7	....	....	1,139
	Females..	17	15	54	101	107	119	250	152	158	131	85	53	16	3	....	1,261
	Totals....	36	35	110	202	248	229	453	279	294	240	158	90	23	3	....	2,400

TABLE XXI.—*Continued.* AGE AND SEX.

TOWNS AND DIVISIONS OF THE STATE.		Under 1 year.	1 and under 2	2 and under 5	5 and under 10	10 and under 15	15 and under 20	20 and under 30	30 and under 40	40 and under 50	50 and under 60	60 and under 70	70 and under 80	80 and under 90	90 and over.	Age not given	Totals.
West Greenwich..	Males....	12	14	56	62	73	69	87	61	59	63	52	21	11	1	....	641
	Females..	15	10	45	60	65	57	82	64	56	55	52	12	13	1	....	587
	Totals....	27	24	101	122	138	126	169	125	115	118	104	33	24	2	....	1,228
Warwick..	Males....	70	71	234	422	408	339	539	505	440	301	179	71	30	2	....	3,611
	Females .	60	68	232	444	443	420	734	583	436	324	193	100	44	4	....	4,085
	Totals....	130	139	466	866	851	759	1,273	1,088	876	625	372	171	74	6	....	7,696
KENT COUNTY.....	Males....	135	136	460	807	827	701	1,131	909	860	632	413	189	57	4	....	7,261
	Females .	122	126	441	813	818	811	1,433	1,090	885	714	459	244	92	10	....	8,058
	Totals....	257	262	901	1,620	1,645	1,512	2,564	1,999	1,745	1,346	872	433	149	14	....	15,319
Jamestown.........	Males....	4	4	10	14	24	24	25	14	21	19	14	5	1	....	....	179
	Females .	3	1	5	18	23	24	22	18	19	18	10	9	......	....	....	170
	Totals....	7	5	15	32	47	48	47	32	40	37	24	14	1	....	....	349
Little Compton	Males....	6	13	22	50	70	49	77	77	69	55	55	26	5	....	....	574
	Females .	12	5	30	53	62	56	104	78	72	59	58	23	10	1	....	623
	Totals....	18	18	52	103	132	105	181	155	141	114	113	49	15	1	....	1,197
Middletown..	Males....	6	15	28	60	52	67	92	55	72	30	26	6	4	....	....	513
	Females..	4	9	31	61	50	65	87	66	59	33	18	18	5	....	....	506
	Totals....	10	24	59	121	102	132	179	121	131	63	44	24	9	....	....	1,019

TABLE XXI.—*Continued.* Age and Sex.

Towns and Divisions of the State.		Under 1 year.	1 and under 2	2 and under 5	5 and under 10	10 and under 15	15 and under 20	20 and under 30	30 and under 40	40 and under 50	50 and under 60	60 and under 70	70 and under 80	80 and under 90	90 and over.	Age not given	Totals.
City of Newport. Wards. I.	Males	17	24	70	120	97	79	155	124	98	73	50	17	8	....	....	932
	Females	29	16	59	116	95	90	169	140	94	92	66	31	14	1	....	1,012
	Totals	46	40	129	236	192	169	324	264	192	165	116	48	22	1	....	1,944
II.	Males	31	19	86	119	101	97	214	172	136	76	55	18	3	1	....	1,128
	Females	42	20	89	135	106	139	289	222	157	123	54	40	14	....	....	1,430
	Totals	73	39	175	254	207	236	503	394	293	199	109	58	17	1	....	2,558
III.	Males	14	11	44	63	78	70	157	123	119	71	49	16	2	....	....	817
	Females	15	19	48	86	78	117	255	190	167	109	101	35	21	1	...	1,242
	Totals	29	30	92	149	156	187	412	313	286	180	150	51	23	1	....	2,059
IV.	Males	41	12	65	108	113	475	243	181	134	75	46	29	1	....	4	1,527
	Females	32	19	47	80	94	107	270	201	147	97	67	29	11	1	1	1,203
	Totals	73	31	112	188	207	582	513	382	281	172	113	58	12	1	5	2,730
V.	Males	51	36	139	236	140	116	260	247	186	118	50	17	2	....	....	1,598
	Females	59	44	135	196	152	151	334	282	210	126	71	32	7	....	....	1,799
	Totals	110	80	274	432	292	267	594	529	396	244	121	49	9	....	....	3,397
Whole City.	Males	154	102	404	646	529	837	1,029	847	673	413	250	97	16	1	4	6,002
	Females	177	118	378	613	525	604	1,317	1,035	775	547	359	167	67	3	1	6,686
	Totals	331	220	782	1,259	1,054	1,441	2,346	1,882	1,448	960	609	264	83	4	5	12,688

TABLE XXI.—*Continued.* Age and Sex.

Towns and Divisions of the State.		Under 1 year.	1 and under 2	2 and under 5	5 and under 10	10 and under 15	15 and under 20	20 and under 30	30 and under 40	40 and under 50	50 and under 60	60 and under 70	70 and under 80	80 and under 90	90 and over.	Age not given	Totals.
New Shoreham....	Males....	10	11	46	81	108	63	94	71	81	43	28	18	7	1	....	662
	Females..	10	12	40	83	78	82	104	87	50	45	29	17	9	....	....	646
	Totals....	20	23	86	164	186	145	198	158	131	88	57	35	16	1	....	1,308
Portsmouth	Males....	21	27	56	113	117	109	222	143	123	90	51	39	8	..	....	1,119
	Females..	22	21	94	104	84	94	195	125	107	80	50	37	20	1	....	1,034
	Totals....	43	48	150	217	201	203	417	268	230	170	101	76	28	1	...	2,153
Tiverton	Males....	14	28	57	105	106	103	158	100	109	78	65	37	7	....	....	967
	Females..	22	22	58	118	113	104	158	120	102	83	61	35	10	....	....	1,006
	Totals....	36	50	115	223	219	207	316	220	211	161	126	72	17	....	....	1,973
Newport County.	Males....	215	200	623	1,069	1,006	1,252	1,697	1,307	1,148	728	489	228	48	2	4	10,016
	Females..	250	188	636	1,050	935	1,029	1,987	1,529	1,184	865	585	306	121	5	1	10,671
	Totals....	465	388	1,259	2,119	1,941	2,281	3,684	2,836	2,332	1,593	1,074	534	169	7	5	20,687
Burrillville........	Males....	50	47	172	288	264	240	414	313	268	161	97	42	15	....	....	2,371
	Females..	52	59	199	292	258	274	467	334	234	153	109	38	21	....	....	2,490
	Totals....	102	106	371	580	522	514	881	647	502	314	206	80	36	....	....	4,861
Cranston..........	Males....	121	109	369	635	545	401	766	676	500	327	164	75	8	....	....	4,696
	Females..	115	92	356	626	427	380	780	674	454	297	177	76	24	3	...	4,481
	Totals....	236	201	725	1,261	972	781	1,546	1,350	954	624	341	151	32	3	....	9,177

TABLE XXI.—*Continued.* AGE AND SEX.

TOWNS AND DIVISIONS OF THE STATE.		Under 1 year.	1 and under 2	2 and under 5	5 and under 10	10 and under 15	15 and under 20	20 and under 30	30 and under 40	40 and under 50	50 and under 60	60 and under 70	70 and under 80	80 and under 90	90 and over.	Age not given	Totals.
Cumberland	Males ...	109	67	255	448	431	400	665	478	462	316	158	80	13	....	....	3,882
	Females..	92	70	258	432	410	492	848	612	487	317	208	94	12	2	....	4,334
	Totals....	201	137	513	880	841	892	1,513	1,090	949	633	366	174	25	2	....	8,216
East Providence...	Males....	30	15	84	120	110	109	152	147	116	90	48	21	6	2	....	1,050
	Females..	24	33	90	128	106	95	190	153	113	72	79	31	8	....	....	1,122
	Totals....	54	48	174	248	216	204	342	300	229	162	127	52	14	2	....	2,172
Foster............	Males....	23	20	49	93	95	86	129	101	114	95	65	38	14	....	....	922
	Females..	14	15	59	100	104	95	134	112	108	91	69	34	16	....	....	951
	Totals....	37	35	108	193	199	181	263	213	222	186	134	72	30	....	....	1,873
Glocester..........	Males....	17	15	78	132	91	129	162	133	136	110	89	65	9	2	....	1,168
	Females..	15	26	71	109	116	81	165	161	131	94	75	57	15	2	....	1,118
	Totals....	32	41	149	241	207	210	327	294	267	204	164	122	24	4	....	2,286
Johnston..........	Males....	42	34	122	209	173	164	313	232	194	149	82	32	9	....	....	1,755
	Females..	34	26	121	186	141	134	326	237	201	132	100	36	6	1	....	1,681
	Totals....	76	60	243	395	314	298	639	469	395	281	182	68	15	1	....	3,436
North Providence..	Males....	168	101	512	893	808	665	1,203	1,121	790	440	226	76	17	2	1	7,023
	Females..	162	119	493	863	778	783	1,469	1,171	775	473	284	125	25	3	7	7,530
	Totals....	330	220	1,005	1,756	1,586	1,448	2,672	2,292	1,565	913	510	201	42	5	8	14,553

TABLE XXI.—*Continued.* AGE AND SEX.

TOWNS AND DIVISIONS OF THE STATE.		Under 1 year.	1 and under 2	2 and under 5	5 and under 10	10 and under 15	15 and under 20	20 and under 30	30 and under 40	40 and under 50	50 and under 60	60 and under 70	70 and under 80	80 and under 90	90 and over.	Age not given	Totals.
Pawtucket	Males	59	56	157	303	213	229	435	324	247	177	109	33	10	4	....	2,356
	Females	53	40	178	278	259	265	523	386	284	206	119	40	9	4	....	2,644
	Totals	112	96	335	581	472	494	958	710	531	383	228	73	19	8	....	5,000
Scituate	Males	23	29	93	186	186	178	271	206	217	168	102	57	19	....	....	1,735
	Females	25	29	100	175	156	182	292	239	208	199	125	45	25	3	....	1,803
	Totals	48	58	193	361	342	360	563	445	425	367	227	102	44	3	....	3,538
Smithfield	Males	121	112	411	662	649	599	1,010	762	673	419	288	100	21	4	4	5,835
	Females	103	122	389	657	635	651	1,282	884	699	524	342	141	36	12	3	6,480
	Totals	224	234	800	1,319	1,284	1,250	2,292	1,646	1,372	943	630	241	57	16	7	12,315
Towns Prov. Co.	Males	763	605	2,302	3,969	3,565	3,200	5,520	4,493	3,717	2,452	1,428	619	141	14	5	32,793
	Females	689	631	2,314	3,846	3,390	3,432	6,476	4,963	3,694	2,558	1,687	717	197	30	10	34,634
	Totals	1,452	1,236	4,616	7,815	6,955	6,632	11,996	9,456	7,411	5,010	3,115	1,336	338	44	15	67,427
Providence City. Wards. I.	Males	104	103	335	605	511	560	900	711	604	346	162	59	7	2	....	5,009
	Females	118	82	308	600	567	642	1,136	859	613	376	239	95	24	...	....	5,659
	Totals	222	185	643	1,205	1,078	1,202	2,036	1,570	1,217	722	401	154	31	2	....	10,668
II.	Males	35	31	93	157	161	220	457	308	232	181	94	42	9	....	....	2,020
	Females	31	29	92	178	162	242	704	448	232	219	140	57	14	....	....	2,598
	Totals	66	60	185	335	323	462	1,161	756	514	400	234	99	23	...	....	4,618

TABLE XXI.—*Continued.* AGE AND SEX.

TOWNS AND DIVISIONS OF THE STATE.		Under 1 year.	1 and under 2	2 and under 5	5 and under 10	10 and under 15	15 and under 20	20 and under 30	30 and under 40	40 and under 50	50 and under 60	60 and under 70	70 and under 80	80 and under 90	90 and over.	Age not given	Totals.
PROVIDENCE CITY. WARDS. III.	Males	94	71	278	441	459	387	613	541	445	269	113	41	9	....	....	3,761
	Females	102	95	287	508	428	369	759	676	449	304	167	84	39	6	....	4,273
	Totals	196	166	565	949	887	756	1,372	1,217	894	573	280	125	48	6	....	8,034
IV.	Males	37	26	122	183	178	175	442	366	262	154	90	41	9	....	....	2,085
	Females	45	39	104	192	190	257	630	444	293	204	123	46	12	3	....	2,582
	Totals	82	65	226	375	368	432	1,072	810	555	358	213	87	21	3	...	4,667
V.	Males	88	72	241	406	293	323	720	655	454	244	119	40	8	....	....	3,663
	Females	88	78	235	403	370	365	798	705	429	293	181	63	22	2	....	4,032
	Totals	176	150	476	809	663	688	1,518	1,360	883	537	300	103	30	2	....	7,695
VI.	Males	97	70	324	537	483	499	833	748	604	379	170	58	8	1	....	4,811
	Females	117	69	292	506	531	550	1,222	972	654	428	229	98	28	6	....	5,702
	Totals	214	139	616	1,043	1,014	1,049	2,055	1,720	1,258	807	399	156	36	7	....	10,513
VII.	Males	100	65	267	512	436	354	625	579	500	267	120	40	5	....	....	3,870
	Females	95	80	271	485	474	445	915	738	497	280	162	69	18	1	....	4,530
	Totals	195	145	538	997	910	799	1,540	1,317	997	547	282	109	23	1	....	8,400
Whole City.	Males	555	438	1,660	2,841	2,521	2,518	4,590	3,908	3,101	1.840	868	321	55	3	....	25,219
	Females	596	472	1,589	2,872	2,722	2,870	6,164	4,842	3,217	2,104	1,241	512	157	18	...	29,376
	Totals	1,151	910	3,249	5,713	5,243	5,388	10,754	8,750	6,318	3,944	2,109	833	212	21	...	54,595

TABLE XXI.—*Continued.* AGE AND SEX.

TOWNS AND DIVISIONS OF THE STATE.		Under 1 year.	1 and under 2	2 and under 5	5 and under 10	10 and under 15	15 and under 20	20 and under 30	30 and under 40	40 and under 50	50 and under 60	60 and under 70	70 and under 80	80 and under 90	90 and over.	Age not given	Totals.
Charlestown.......	Males....	10	13	36	63	63	58	82	60	59	53	38	20	4	1	....	560
	Females..	3	16	37	54	72	70	79	70	71	34	35	24	6	3	....	574
	Totals....	13	29	73	117	135	128	161	130	130	87	73	44	10	4	....	1,134
Exeter............	Males....	7	13	43	77	100	87	116	79	69	79	46	31	10	2	....	759
	Females..	17	14	49	76	71	77	97	88	82	79	45	33	9	2	....	739
	Totals....	24	27	92	153	171	164	213	167	151	158	91	64	19	4	....	1,498
Hopkinton	Males....	33	24	82	138	147	138	177	146	139	97	60	36	12	1	....	1,230
	Females..	27	25	73	118	138	149	195	183	156	100	67	39	12	....	....	1,282
	Totals....	60	49	155	256	285	287	372	329	295	197	127	75	24	1	....	2,512
North Kingstown..	Males....	25	25	72	164	179	174	265	190	142	150	84	42	12	....	2	1,526
	Females..	19	33	92	171	161	183	283	200	170	159	99	53	12	4	1	1,640
	Totals....	44	58	164	335	340	357	548	390	312	309	183	95	24	4	3	3,166
South Kingstown..	Males....	55	41	193	267	238	204	350	264	208	178	124	50	23	1	6	2,202
	Females..	48	48	185	261	237	210	410	297	208	178	127	69	29	2	2	2,311
	Totals....	103	89	378	528	475	414	760	561	416	356	251	119	52	3	8	4,513
Richmond.........	Males....	7	20	68	96	77	69	155	121	102	67	47	20	6	....	2	857
	Females..	28	14	53	116	96	99	172	123	99	76	52	29	8	2	6	973
	Totals....	35	34	121	212	173	168	327	244	201	143	99	49	14	2	8	1,830

TABLE XXI.—*Continued.* AGE AND SEX.

TOWNS AND DIVISIONS OF THE STATE.		Under 1 year.	1 and under 2	2 and under 5	5 and under 10	10 and under 15	15 and under 20	20 and under 30	30 and under 40	40 and under 50	50 and under 60	60 and under 70	70 and under 80	80 and under 90	90 and over.	Age not given	Totals.
Westerly	Males	44	39	138	243	215	183	284	258	219	135	71	36	10	....	1	1,876
	Females	40	33	121	224	197	188	361	287	202	132	98	42	11	2	1	1,939
	Totals	84	72	259	467	412	371	645	545	421	267	169	78	21	2	2	3,815
WASHINGTON CO.	Males	181	175	632	1,048	1,019	913	1,429	1,118	938	759	470	235	77	5	11	9,010
	Females	182	183	610	1,020	972	976	1,597	1,248	988	758	523	289	87	15	10	9,458
	Totals	363	358	1,242	2,068	1,991	1,889	3,026	2,366	1,926	1,517	993	524	164	20	21	18,468
WHOLE STATE	Males	1,930	1,607	5,915	10,143	9,358	9,039	15,004	12,236	10,234	6,776	3,888	1,674	407	32	20	88,263
	Females	1,914	1,668	5,835	10,029	9,258	9,562	18,474	14,324	10,472	7,405	4,762	2,199	696	83	21	96,702
	Totals	3,844	3,275	11,750	20,172	18,616	18,601	33,478	26,560	20,706	14,181	8,650	3,873	1,103	115	41	184,965

TABLE XXII. AGE AND PARENTAGE.—*Showing the number of American, and of Foreign Parentage, in each division of ages, in each Ward of the City of Providence; those of mixed parentage being placed according to the birth place of their fathers:*

CITY OF PROVIDENCE: AGE AND PARENTAGE.

WARDS.	PARENTAGE.	Under 1.	1 and under 2.	2 and under 5.	5 and under 10.	10 and under 15.	15 and under 20.	20 and under 30.	30 and under 40.	40 and under 50.	50 and under 60.	60 and under 70.	70 and under 80.	80 and under 90.	90 and over.	TOTALS.
I	Am..	67	65	225	459	454	586	850	731	637	391	220	97	24	..	4,806
	For..	155	120	418	746	624	616	1,186	839	580	331	181	57	7	2	5,862
	Total	222	185	643	1,205	1,078	1,202	2,036	1,570	1,217	722	401	154	31	2	10,668
II	Am..	37	36	138	248	250	316	659	471	386	325	211	90	19	..	3,186
	For..	29	24	47	87	73	146	502	285	128	75	23	9	4	..	1,432
	Total	66	60	185	335	323	462	1,161	756	514	400	234	99	23	..	4,618
III	Am..	52	53	199	364	404	470	762	574	468	381	198	101	38	3	4,067
	For..	144	113	366	585	483	286	610	643	426	192	82	24	10	3	3,967
	Total	196	166	565	949	887	756	1,372	1,217	894	573	280	125	48	6	8,034
IV	Am..	45	37	134	218	234	280	707	563	381	290	177	78	19	3	3,166
	For..	37	28	92	157	134	152	365	247	174	68	36	9	2	..	1,501
	Total	82	65	226	375	368	432	1,072	810	555	358	213	87	21	3	4,667
V	Am..	71	56	187	339	315	374	839	751	498	332	216	83	22	1	4,084
	For..	105	94	289	470	348	314	679	609	385	205	84	20	8	1	3,611
	Total	176	150	476	809	663	688	1,518	1,360	883	537	300	103	30	2	7,695
VI	Am..	131	77	373	630	675	744	1,421	1,206	941	637	308	132	27	6	7,308
	For..	83	62	243	413	339	305	634	514	317	170	91	24	9	1	3,205
	Total	214	139	616	1,043	1,014	1,049	2,055	1,720	1,258	807	399	156	36	7	10,513
VII	Am..	72	51	222	389	386	398	802	692	498	335	165	60	15	..	4,085
	For..	123	94	316	608	524	401	738	625	499	212	117	49	8	1	4,315
	Total	195	145	538	997	910	799	1,540	1,317	997	547	282	109	23	1	8,400
Whole City.	Am..	475	375	1,478	2,647	2,718	3,168	6,040	4,988	3,809	2,691	1,495	641	164	13	30,702
	For..	676	535	1,771	3,066	2,525	2,220	4,714	3,762	2,509	1,253	614	192	48	8	23,893
	Total	1,151	910	3,249	5,713	5,243	5,388	10,754	8,750	6,318	3,944	2,109	833	212	21	54,595

TABLE XXIII. ATTENDING SCHOOL.—*Showing the population in each town between the ages of* 5 *and* 15, *and the number of all ages who attended Public, Select, or Catholic Schools, in each town, during the year ending June* 1, 1865.

TOWNS AND DIVISIONS OF THE STATE.	POPULATION.			ATTENDING SCHOOL DURING THE YEAR.			
	5 years and under 10	10 years and under 15	Total population 5 to 15 years.	Public Schools.	Select Schools.	Catholic Schools.	Whole No. attending School during the year.
Barrington	85	87	172	167	15	...	182
Bristol	491	446	937	755	138	....	893
Warren	261	308	569	441	57	....	498
BRISTOL COUNTY	837	841	1,678	1,363	210	....	1,573
Coventry	430	408	838	601	22	....	623
East Greenwich	202	248	450	339	49	....	388
West Greenwich	122	138	260	252	..	....	252
Warwick	866	851	1,717	1,013	72	....	1,085
KENT COUNTY	1,620	1,645	3,265	2,205	143	....	2,348
Jamestown	32	47	79	65	2	....	67
Little Compton	103	132	235	266	14	1	281
Middletown	121	102	223	204	23	....	227
Newport	1,259	1,054	2,313	1,248	871	412	2,531
New Shoreham	164	186	350	371	..	....	371
Portsmouth	217	201	418	352	44	....	396
Tiverton	223	219	442	399	10	....	409
NEWPORT COUNTY	2,119	1,941	4,060	2,905	964	413	4,282
Burrillville	580	522	1,102	795	10	1	806
Cranston	1,261	972	2,233	1,557	113	209	1,879
Cumberland	880	841	1,721	1,105	53	268	1,426
East Providence	248	216	464	434	35	....	469
Foster	193	199	392	409	9	....	418
Glocester	241	207	448	407	10	....	417
Johnston	395	314	709	507	34	....	541
North Providence	1,756	1,586	3,342	1,808	97	498	2,403
Pawtucket	581	472	1,053	678	33	152	863
Scituate	361	342	703	642	44	....	686
Smithfield	1,319	1,284	2,603	1,991	71	7	2,069
TOWNS PROV. COUNTY	7,815	6,955	14,770	10,333	509	1,135	11,977
PROVIDENCE CITY	5,713	5,243	10,956	7,401	1,215	1,273	9,889
Charlestown	117	135	252	242	13	...	255
Exeter	153	171	324	346	3	....	349
Hopkinton	256	285	541	480	32	....	512
North Kingstown	335	340	675	463	104	....	567
South Kingstown	528	475	1,003	762	171	...	933
Richmond	212	173	385	326	12	....	338
Westerly	467	412	879	612	139	....	751
WASHINGTON COUNTY	2,068	1,991	4,059	3,231	474	....	3,705
WHOLE STATE	20,172	18,616	38,788	27,438	3,515	2,821	33,774

TABLE XXIV. ATTENDING SCHOOL.—*Being table XXIII for the Cities of Providence and Newport, by Wards.*

CITY OF PROVIDENCE. TABLE XXIII. *By Wards.*

WARDS CITY OF PROVIDENCE.	POPULATION.			ATTENDING SCHOOL DURING THE YEAR.			
	5 years and under 10.	10 years and under 15.	Total population 5 to 15 years.	Public Schools.	Select Schools.	Catholic Schools.	Whole No. attending School during the year.
I.	1,205	1,078	2,283	1,386	248	450	2,084
II.	335	323	658	409	219	17	645
III.	949	887	1,836	1,397	145	1	1,543
IV.	375	368	743	451	158	112	721
V.	809	663	1,472	913	101	238	1,252
VI.	1,043	1,014	2,057	1,621	211	159	1,991
VII.	997	910	1,907	1,224	133	296	1,653
Whole City	5,713	5,243	10,956	7,401	1,215	1,273	9,889

CITY OF NEWPORT. TABLE XXIII. *By Wards.*

WARDS CITY OF NEWPORT.	POPULATION.			ATTENDING SCHOOL DURING THE YEAR.			
	5 years and under 10.	10 years and under 15.	Total population 5 to 15 years.	Public Schools.	Select Schools.	Catholic Schools.	Whole No. attending School during the year.
I.	236	192	428	308	75	29	412
II.	254	207	461	272	85	62	419
III.	149	156	305	169	98	22	289
IV.	188	207	395	228	*509	67	804
V.	432	292	724	271	104	232	607
Whole City	1,259	1,054	2,313	1,248	871	412	2,531

* The pupils of the United States Naval Academy are included in this Ward.

TABLE XXV. *Showing the number of Deaf and Dumb, Blind, Insane, Idiotic, Paupers, and Convicts, in each town in the State.*

TOWNS AND DIVISIONS OF THE STATE.	Deaf and Dumb.	Blind.	Insane.	Idiotic.	Paupers.	Convicts.	Totals.
Barrington	....	1	2	2	3	....	8
Bristol	5	8	2	1	12	1	29
Warren	1	1	....	....	12	....	14
BRISTOL COUNTY	6	10	4	3	27	1	51
Coventry	3	....	8	3	15	....	29
East Greenwich	1	3	4	....	17	....	25
West Greenwich	....	4	6	3	11	1	25
Warwick	2	2	2	3	21	....	30
KENT COUNTY	6	9	20	9	64	1	109
Jamestown	1	1	1	....	1	....	4
Little Compton	1	1	1	1	8	....	12
Middletown	....	1	2	2	1	....	6
Newport	7	17	19	23	27	....	93
New Shoreham	5	4	1	5	14	....	29
Portsmouth	2	1	5	6	11	....	25
Tiverton	1	2	5	6	6	....	20
NEWPORT COUNTY	17	27	34	43	68	....	189
Burrillville	2	1	2	5	21	....	31
Cranston	4	3	7	8	22	....	44
Cumberland	4	5	5	1	30	....	45
East Providence	2	2	1	1	2	....	8
Foster	3	3	9	10	8	....	33
Glocester	5	3	....	2	10	....	20
Johnston	....	2	8	2	12	....	24
North Providence	1	9	6	7	13	....	36
Pawtucket	....	5	2	2	6	....	15
Scituate	1	....	1	1	12	1	16
Smithfield	5	5	11	3	20	3	47
TOWNS PROV. COUNTY	27	38	52	42	156	4	319
PROVIDENCE CITY	20	17	145	15	169	107	473
Charlestown	1	2	1	....	5	....	9
Exeter	3	4	4	10	14	....	35
Hopkinton	2	6	2	5	7	....	22
North Kingstown	1	1	5	....	7	....	14
South Kingstown	5	2	18	8	21	1	55
Richmond	....	3	1	3	5	....	12
Westerly	1	1	1	2	....	....	5
WASHINGTON COUNTY	13	19	32	28	59	1	152
WHOLE STATE	89	120	287	140	543	114	1,293

TABLE XXVI. Want of Education.—*Showing how many persons in each town in the State, of the age of 15 years and over, can neither read nor write, and how many can read but cannot write; the statistics according to parentage.*

TOWNS AND DIVISIONS OF THE STATE.	AMERICAN PARENTAGE.						IRISH PARENTAGE.		ENGLISH SCOTCH & WELSH.	
	WHITES.		BLACKS.		TOTAL AMER.					
	Can neither read nor write.	Can read but cannot write.	Can neither read nor write.	Can read but cannot write.	Can neither read nor write.	Can read but cannot write	Can neither read nor write.	Can read but cannot write.	Can neither read nor write.	Can read but cannot write.
Barrington	......	2	4	4	4	6	17	5	...	....
Bristol	15	13	17	5	32	18	123	63	12	21
Warren	7	...	6	2	13	2	42	4	1	....
Bristol County	22	15	27	11	49	26	182	72	13	21
Coventry	50	18	1	....	51	18	33	19	3	5
East Greenwich	7	1	8	1	15	2	24	1	1	....
West Greenwich	43	40	....	....	43	40	5	2	....	....
Warwick	69	40	9	5	78	45	212	77	28	14
Kent County	169	99	18	6	187	105	274	99	32	19
Jamestown	1	...	4	1	5	1	6	......	....	....
Little Compton	8	2	....	....	8	2	12	14	1	1
Middletown	2	1	1	1	3	2	7	3	....	1
Newport	24	9	92	36	116	45	695	126	12	3
New Shoreham	38	....	4	....	42	....	......	......	1	....
Portsmouth	9	3	2	....	11	3	154	11	....	....
Tiverton	68	38	12	2	80	40	8	2	3	1
Newport County	150	53	115	40	265	93	882	156	17	6
Burrillville	38	32	....	....	38	32	270	91	10	16
Cranston	35	29	44	15	79	44	505	186	28	14
Cumberland	21	18	2	2	23	20	522	247	29	12
East Providence	8	5	1	2	9	7	47	28	....	2
Foster	47	32	....	....	47	32	4	1	....	....
Glocester	11	4	....	...	11	4	14	1	....	....
Johnston	12	9	3	2	15	11	105	67	11	16
North Providence	18	25	14	4	32	29	836	379	116	53
Pawtucket	11	12	1	....	12	12	292	241	26	21
Scituate	51	38	1	1	52	39	28	40	4	....
Smithfield	29	12	1	5	30	17	490	217	27	38
Towns Prov. County	281	216	67	31	348	247	3,113	1,498	251	172
Providence City	26	43	137	90	163	133	2,671	1,458	57	60
Charlestown	21	7	12	8	33	15	2	1	...	....
Exeter	76	32	7	3	83	35	.....	......	....	....
Hopkinton	74	36	4	2	78	38	5	7	1	2
North Kingstown	75	31	33	6	108	37	24	7	4	1
South Kingstown	123	68	40	13	163	81	52	20	1	4
Richmond	52	26	6	....	58	26	15	6	1	....
Westerly	16	....	1	...	17	....	93	2	14	...
Washington County	437	200	103	32	540	232	191	43	21	7
Whole State	1,085	626	467	210	1,552	836	7,313	3,326	391	285

TABLE XXVI.—*Continued.* WANT OF EDUCATION. *Showing how many persons in each town in the State, of the age of 15 years and over, can neither read nor write, and how many can read but cannot write; the statistics according to parentage.*

TOWNS AND DIVISIONS OF THE STATE.	GERMAN.		OTHER FOREIGN.		TOTAL FOREIGN.		TOTAL AMERI'N AND FOREIGN.	
	Can neither read nor write.	Can read but cannot write.	Can neither read nor write.	Can read but cannot write.	Can neither read nor write.	Can read but cannot write.	Can neither read nor write.	Can read but cannot write.
Barrington	......	......	75	......	92	5	96	11
Bristol	5	2	13	1	153	87	185	105
Warren	......	......	6	......	49	4	62	6
BRISTOL COUNTY	5	2	94	1	294	96	343	122
Coventry	2	......	47	2	85	26	136	44
East Greenwich	......	......	......	......	25	1	40	3
West Greenwich	......	......	......	......	5	2	48	42
Warwick	......	......	72	6	312	97	390	142
KENT COUNTY	2	......	119	8	427	126	614	231
Jamestown	......	......	......	......	6	......	11	1
Little Compton	......	......	4	......	17	15	25	17
Middletown	......	......	......	1	7	5	10	7
Newport	......	......	3	5	710	134	826	179
New Shoreham	......	......	......	......	1	......	43	......
Portsmouth	......	......	......	......	154	11	165	14
Tiverton	1	1	5	......	17	4	97	44
NEWPORT COUNTY	1	1	12	6	912	169	1,177	262
Burrillville	......	......	122	10	402	117	440	149
Cranston	1	......	24	3	558	203	637	247
Cumberland	......	......	120	54	671	313	694	333
East Providence	......	......	3	2	50	32	59	39
Foster	......	......	......	......	4	1	51	33
Glocester	......	......	6	......	20	1	31	5
Johnston	......	1	......	......	116	84	131	95
North Providence	25	4	3	1	980	437	1,012	466
Pawtucket	......	......	......	1	318	263	330	275
Scituate	......	......	......	......	32	40	84	79
Smithfield	......	1	283	7	800	263	830	280
TOWNS PROV. COUNTY	26	6	561	78	3,951	1,754	4,299	2,001
PROVIDENCE CITY	9	4	31	14	2,768	1,536	2,931	1,669
Charlestown	......	......	......	......	2	1	35	16
Exeter	......	......	......	......	......	......	83	35
Hopkinton	......	......	10	2	16	11	94	49
North Kingstown	......	......	44	11	72	19	180	56
South Kingstown	......	......	......	......	53	24	216	105
Richmond	1	1	10	1	27	8	85	34
Westerly	......	......	......	......	107	2	124	2
WASHINGTON COUNTY	1	1	64	14	277	65	817	297
WHOLE STATE	44	14	881	121	8,629	3,746	10,181	4,582

TABLE XXVII. Want of Education.—*Being Table XXVI, for the Cities of Providence and Newport, by Wards.*

CITY OF PROVIDENCE. TABLE XXVI. *By Wards.*

WARDS CITY OF PROVIDENCE.	AMERICAN PARENTAGE. Whites. Can neither read nor write.	Whites. Can read but cannot write.	Blacks. Can neither read nor write.	Blacks. Can read but cannot write.	Total American. Can neither read nor write.	Total American. Can read but cannot write.	IRISH PARENTAGE. Can neither read nor write.	Can read but cannot write.	ENGLISH, SCOTCH AND WELSH, Can neither read nor write.	Can read but cannot write.	GERMAN. Can neither read nor write.	Can read but cannot write.	OTHER FOREIGN. Can neither read nor write.	Can read but cannot write.	TOTAL FOREIGN. Can neither read nor write.	Can read but cannot write.	TOTAL AMERICAN & FOREIGN Can neither read nor write.	Can read but cannot write.
I	10	10	35	38	45	48	702	225	12	10	3	1	3	3	720	239	765	287
II	3	2	23	22	26	24	121	115	2	3	..	1	1	2	124	121	150	145
III	2	13	13	5	15	18	491	217	6	6	2	1	9	6	508	230	523	248
IV	1	..	7	6	8	6	141	134	..	4	..	..	4	1	145	139	153	145
V	3	5	6	2	9	7	397	212	10	10	1	..	4	2	412	224	421	231
VI	5	9	49	16	54	25	388	201	7	8	1	..	3	..	399	209	453	234
VII	2	4	4	1	6	5	431	354	20	19	2	1	7	..	460	374	466	379
Whole City	26	43	137	90	163	133	2,671	1,458	57	60	9	4	31	14	2,768	1,536	2,931	1,669

CITY OF NEWPORT. TABLE XXVI. *By Wards.*

WARDS CITY OF NEWPORT.	AMERICAN PARENTAGE. Whites. Can neither read nor write.	Whites. Can read but cannot write.	Blacks. Can neither read nor write.	Blacks. Can read but cannot write.	Total American. Can neither read nor write.	Total American. Can read but cannot write.	IRISH PARENTAGE. Can neither read nor write.	Can read but cannot write.	ENGLISH, SCOTCH AND WELSH. Can neither read nor write.	Can read but cannot write.	GERMAN. Can neither read nor write.	Can read but cannot write.	OTHER FOREIGN, Can neither read nor write.	Can read but cannot write.	TOTAL FOREIGN. Can neither read nor write.	Can read but cannot write.	TOTAL AMERICAN & FOREIGN Can neither read nor write.	Can read but cannot write.
I	14	7	5	4	19	11	52	10	4	1	....	....	2	2	58	13	77	24
II	3	..	25	14	28	14	119	23	2	..	...	....	....	1	121	24	149	38
III	6	2	17	6	23	8	78	22	1	1	....	....	....	....	79	23	102	31
IV	..	..	26	9	26	9	106	26	1	1	....	....	..	....	107	27	133	36
V	1	..	19	3	20	3	340	45	4	..	....	....	1	2	345	47	365	50
Whole City	24	9	92	36	116	45	695	126	12	3	....	....	3	5	710	134	826	179

TABLE XXVIII. NATURALIZED VOTERS. — *Showing how many natives of foreign countries have become voters under the laws of Rhode Island, in each town and county in the State.*

TOWNS AND DIVISIONS OF THE STATE.	NATURALIZED VOTERS. BIRTH PLACE.												
	Ireland.	England.	Scotland and Wales.	Germany.	British America.	France.	Portugal and Western Islands	Norway.	Sweden.	Denmark.	Italy.	Holland and Switzerland.	Totals.
Barrington													
Bristol	3	1	1	1									6
Warren	12	4		1								1	18
BRISTOL COUNTY	15	5	1	2								1	24
Coventry	2		1										3
East Greenwich	2	1											3
West Greenwich	1												1
Warwick	23	12	1										36
KENT COUNTY	28	13	2										43
Jamestown													
Little Compton		1					1						2
Middletown		1											1
Newport	68	12	5	1	3		2						91
New Shoreham		2											2
Portsmouth		2											2
Tiverton											1		1
NEWPORT COUNTY	68	18	5	1	3		3				1		99
Burrillville	27	10								1			38
Cranston	105	32	2	4	3		2	1	3				152
Cumberland	33	12											45
East Providence	11	2								1			14
Foster	2	1			1								4
Glocester	5	1											6
Johnston	17	8	2	2									29
North Providence	89	12	2	5	1						1		110
Pawtucket	112	36	5	2									155
Scituate	2	1											3
Smithfield	28	12	2	2									44
TOWNS PROV. CO.	431	127	13	15	5		2	1	3	2	1		600
PROVIDENCE CITY	349	68	21	17	8	4	6	1	1	1	1	1	478
Charlestown													
Exeter													
Hopkinton		3	2										5
North Kingstown	1												1
South Kingstown	1	3											4
Richmond	1			1									2
Westerly	2	2											4
WASHINGTON CO.	5	8	2	1									16
WHOLE STATE	896	239	44	36	16	4	11	2	4	3	3	2	1,260

TABLE XXIX. Naturalized Voters. *Being Table XXVIII, for the Cities of Providence and Newport, by Wards.*

CITY OF PROVIDENCE. TABLE XXVIII. *By Wards.*

WARDS CITY OF PROVIDENCE.	NATURALIZED VOTERS. BIRTH PLACE.												
	Ireland.	England.	Scotland and Wales.	Germany.	British America.	France.	Portugal and West'n Islands.	Norway.	Sweden.	Denmark.	Italy.	Switzerland.	Ward Totals.
I	106	17	5	6	4	....	....	...	...	...	....	....	138
II	3	3	2	1	....	....	....	...	...	...	....	....	9
III	48	7	1	2	1	2	6	1	1	1	....	....	70
IV	17	7	2	....	....	2	....	...	...	...	....	1	29
V	22	4	3	1	1	....	....	...	...	...	....	....	31
VI	61	20	3	4	2	....	....	...	...	...	1	....	91
VII	92	10	5	3	....	....	....	...	...	...	....	....	110
Whole City	349	68	21	17	8	4	6	1	1	1	1	1	478

CITY OF NEWPORT. TABLE XXVIII. *By Wards.*

WARDS CITY OF NEWPORT.	NATURALIZED VOTERS. BIRTH PLACE.						
	Ireland.	England.	Scotland.	Germany.	British America.	Portugal.	Ward Totals.
I	2	3	......	....	....	2	7
II	16	1	......	....	1	....	18
III	....	1	......	1	....	....	2
IV	9	2	1	....	2	....	14
V	41	5	4	....	....	....	50
Whole City	68	12	5	1	3	2	91

TABLE XXX. MILITARY AND NAVAL SERVICE.—*Showing how many of the inhabitants of each town in the State, who were living on the first day of June, 1865, were at that time, or had been since 1860, in the Military or Naval Service of the United States.*

TOWNS AND DIVISIONS OF THE STATE.	Now in the Army.	Now in the Navy.	Formerly in the Army.	Formerly in the Navy.	Totals in Military Service.	Totals in Naval Service.	Totals in Army and Navy.
Barrington	7	....	15	....	22	....	22
Bristol	67	4	109	27	176	31	207
Warren	41	12	58	6	99	18	117
BRISTOL COUNTY	115	16	182	33	297	49	346
Coventry	76	2	44	2	120	4	124
East Greenwich	26	5	72	3	98	8	106
West Greenwich	28	....	16	....	44	....	44
Warwick	163	3	189	10	352	13	365
KENT COUNTY	293	10	321	15	614	25	639
Jamestown	1	....	4	1	5	1	6
Little Compton	13	1	5	....	18	1	19
Middletown	4	2	16	....	20	2	22
Newport	115	139	155	54	270	193	463
New Shoreham	4	2	9	....	13	2	15
Portsmouth	7	1	19	....	26	1	27
Tiverton	16	2	33	4	49	6	55
NEWPORT COUNTY	160	147	241	59	401	206	607
Burrillville	76	2	49	2	125	4	129
Cranston	120	9	207	15	327	24	351
Cumberland	213	11	123	9	336	20	356
East Providence	31	2	53	10	84	12	96
Foster	27	1	33	2	60	3	63
Glocester	57	1	23	....	80	1	81
Johnston	90	6	95	8	185	14	199
North Providence	47	9	487	14	534	23	557
Pawtucket	123	13	170	13	293	26	319
Scituate	69	6	52	4	121	10	131
Smithfield	238	11	274	24	512	35	547
TOWNS PROV. CO.	1,091	71	1,566	101	2,657	172	2,829
PROVIDENCE CITY	871	112	1,379	137	2,250	249	2,499
Charlestown	24	1	8	2	32	3	35
Exeter	19	1	12	2	31	3	34
Hopkinton	46	3	42	2	88	5	93
North Kingstown	50	1	59	7	109	8	117
South Kingstown	55	5	68	14	123	19	142
Richmond	17	....	35	....	52	....	52
Westerly	41	3	82	2	123	5	128
WASHINGTON CO.	252	14	306	29	558	43	601
WHOLE STATE	2,782	370	3,995	374	6,777	744	7,521

TABLE XXXI. MILITARY AND NAVAL SERVICE.—*Showing how many of the inhabitants of each County in Rhode Island, who were living June* 1, 1865, *were at that time, or had been since* 1860, *in the Military or Naval Service of the United States; and also showing the States in which they enlisted.*

STATE IN WHICH THEY ENLISTED.	MILITARY AND NAVAL SERVICE. COUNTIES OF RHODE ISLAND.						
	Bristol County.	Kent County.	Newport County.	Providence County: Towns.	Providence City.	Wash'gton County.	Whole State.
Arkansas	....	....	....	....	1	....	1
California	2	....	3	4	3	2	14
Connecticut	2	19	3	42	36	31	133
Florida	....	....	1	....	....	....	1
Georgia	....	....	1	....	....	....	1
Illinois	2	3	3	4	2	....	14
Indiana	....	....	1	....	....	....	1
Iowa	....	....	....	2	2	....	4
Kentucky	....	....	2	....	4	....	6
Louisiana	....	....	1	....	....	....	1
Maine	....	1	7	10	6	3	27
Maryland	1	1	4	....	2	....	8
Massachusetts	25	17	50	294	167	23	576
Michigan	....	....	....	1	....	....	1
Mississippi	....	1	....	1	....	....	2
Missouri	....	....	....	1	1	....	2
New Jersey	1	....	....	4	17	....	22
New Hampshire	....	....	....	14	14	4	32
New York	12	15	23	60	103	18	231
Ohio	....	2	....	2	....	....	4
Pennsylvania	2	1	4	3	14	4	28
Rhode Island	298	576	504	2,370	2,102	515	6,365
Tennessee	....	....	....	....	2	....	2
Vermont	....	1	....	5	6	....	12
Wisconsin	....	....	....	....	2	1	3
District of Columbia	1	....	....	....	1	....	2
U. S. Regulars	....	2	....	12	12	....	26
Rebel Service	....	....	....	....	2	....	2
Totals	346	639	607	2,829	2,499	601	7,521

TABLE XXXII. OCCUPATIONS.—*Showing the Occupations of persons of the age of 15 years and over, as reported in the Census of the Population in the whole State.*

Actors	4
Agents	165
Architects	24
Armorers	3
Apprentices	14
Artists	78
Assessors	22
Asylum Keepers	16
Astrologer	1
Auctioneers	9
Authors	4
Baggage Masters	14
Bakers	182
Bankers	12
Bank Officers	99
Barbers	121
Bar Tenders	61
Basket Makers	6
Belt Makers	20
Bill Posters	2
Bird Stuffers	3
Blacksmiths	861
Bleachers	93
Block Makers	9
Block Printer	1
Boat Builders	57
Boat-men	53
Boarding House Keepers	103
Bobbin Makers	26
Boiler Makers	151
Bolt Cutters	3
Book Binders	28
Book-keepers	378
Book Sellers	17
Bottlers	14
Box Makers	68
Braiders	20
Braid Makers	2
Brakemen	36
Brass Finishers	17
Brewers	27
Brick Makers	165
Brokers	13
Bronzers	4
Broom Makers	14
Brush Makers	10
Burnishers	12
Butchers	299
Cabinet Makers	79
Canvassers	4
Car Builders	14
Card Makers	5
Carpenters	2457
Carpet Weavers	4
Carriage Makers	125
Carriage Painters	19
Carriage Trimmers	21
Carvers	4
Caulkers	15
Chain Makers	36
Chair Makers	7
Chasers	43
Chemists	15
Cigar Makers	210
City Officers	7
City Missionaries	2
Civil Engineers	16
Clairvoyants	2
Clergymen	230
Clerks	1927
Cloak Makers	9
Clock Cleaners	6
Clock Makers	15
Cloth Trimmers	18
Cloth Folders	14
Clothing Dealers	24
Coachmen	234
Coal and Wood Dealers	60
Coffee Grinders	2
Collectors	22
Color Mixers	5
Comb Makers	9
Conductors	52
Confectioners	86
Consuls	2
Contractors	5
Cooks	192
Coopers	113
Cork Makers	2
Corset Makers	5
Cotton Dealers	31
Custom House Officers	13
Dentists	61
Designers	11
Die Cutters	5
Die Sinkers	10
Dipper Maker	1
Distillers	7
Draughtsmen	14
Dredgers	2
Dress Makers	692
Drovers	3
Druggists and Apothecaries	123
Dyers	199
Dye Wood Cutter	1
Editors	6
Enamellers	6
Engine Builders	5
Engineers	311
Engine Turners	24
Engravers	141
Envelope Maker	1
Errand Boys	8
Expressmen	111

TABLE XXXII.—*Continued.* OCCUPATIONS.

Occupation	Number
Fancy Workers	44
Farmers	10754
File Makers	97
Finishers	21
Firemen, Steam Boilers	91
Fish Dealers	28
Fishermen	497
Fresco Painters	7
Fruit Dealers	22
Fullers	4
Furniture Dealers	19
Gardeners	271
Gas Fitters	70
Gas Inspectors	5
Gaugers	2
Gold Beaters	5
Grocers	631
Gilders	9
Gun Smiths	330
Hair Cloth Maker	1
Harness Makers	136
Hatters	51
Hoop Skirt Makers	49
Horse Dealers	6
Horse Trainers	2
Hose Maker	1
Hostlers	190
Hotel Keepers	97
House Movers	11
Hunter	1
Ice Cream Makers	2
Ice Dealers	6
Ink Manufacturer	1
Inspectors	20
Insurance Agents	21
Intelligence Office	1
Inventors	4
Iron Fence Makers	4
Jail Keepers	8
Janitors	3
Japanner	1
Jewelers	1215
Junk Dealers	40
Laborers	5440
Lamp Makers	2
Lamp Lighters	6
Lapidaries	20
Lathers	6
Lawyers	124
Librarians	3
Light House Keepers	10
Lime Burners	3
Liquor Dealers	123
Lock Makers	2
Looking Glass Makers	2
Lumber Dealers	47
Machinists	2193
Machine Printers	22
Machine Stitchers	7
Mail Carriers	2
Magician	1
Melodeon Maker	1
Manufacturers	504
Marble Workers	44
Mariners	1070
Market-men	96
Masons	767
Matrons	5
Mattrass Maker	1
Mechanics	73
Merchants	1155
Messenger	1
Milkmen	25
Millers	120
Milliners	301
Millwrights	25
Miners	100
Moulders	441
Music Teachers	69
Musicians	59
Nail Manufacturers	61
News Boys	2
Nurses	183
Nurserymen	2
Nut Maker	1
Oil Refiners	47
Omnibus Drivers	3
Operatives	2950
" Bleachery	323
" Brass Foundry	26
" Chemical Works	24
" Cotton Mills	5755
" Flax Mill	3
" Foundry	111
" Gas Works	16
" Penholder Factory	25
" Print Works	644
" Rolling Mill	78
" Rubber Works	54
" Screw Factory	297
" Woolen Mills	3298
Opticians	3
Organ Builders	2
Overseers	128
Oystermen	71
Packers	11
Painters and Glaziers	696
Paper Box Makers	24
Paper Carriers	6
Paper Hangers	15
Paper Makers	9
Pattern Makers	70
Paymasters	6
Pearl Manufacturers	7
Pedlars	202

TABLE XXXII.—*Continued.* OCCUPATIONS.

Occupation	Number
Peg Manufacturer	1
Penny Posts	4
Photographers	57
Physicians	251
Piano Tuners	2
Picker Makers	27
Picture Frame Maker	1
Pilots	26
Pipers	13
Planing Works	4
Platers	10
Planter	1
Plough Makers	2
Plumbers	58
Policemen and Constables	129
Polishers	31
Pork Packers	16
Porters	69
Post Masters	33
Presidents of Companies	9
Printers	196
Professors	10
Proof Reader	1
Pump Makers	4
Rag Gatherers	4
Rail Road Masters	30
Rail Road Laborers	103
Rake Makers	8
Razor Grinders	2
Reed Makers	17
Refiners	22
Refrigerator Makers	2
Riggers	16
Reporters	3
Roller Coverers	57
Roofers	12
Rope Makers	11
Saddlers	6
Safe Makers	4
Sail Makers	27
Saloon Keepers	204
Sash and Blind Makers	38
Sausage Makers	2
Scroll Sawers	1
Sculptors	2
Scythe Makers	52
Seamstresses	325
Secretaries of Companies	13
Secretary of State	1
Servants	3503
Sewing Machine Manufactories	5
Sextons	21
Sheriffs and Deputies	7
Ship Carpenters	83
Ship Chandlers	6
Shipping Offices	2
Shoe Dealers	56
Shoe Makers	513
Sign Painters	13
Silver Smiths	175
Slaters	2
Soap Makers	49
Spice Grinders	2
Sporting Men	5
Spring Bed Manufacturer	1
Spring Maker	1
Stable Keepers	109
Stair Builders	7
Stevedores	3
Stone Cutters	258
Stove Mounters	7
Stucco Workers	27
Students	312
Straw Workers	141
Sugar Refiners	80
Superintendents	120
Supervisors	2
Surveyors	18
Sutlers	3
Tailors	262
Tailoresses	566
Tanners and Curriers	89
Tax Collectors	4
Teachers	856
Teachers of Dancing	5
Teachers of Drawing	2
Teamsters	692
Telegraph Operators	34
Ticket Masters	2
Time Keepers	10
Tin Smiths	130
Tipper	1
Tobacconists	17
Toll Gate Keeper	1
Tool Makers	16
Town Clerks	21
Town Crier	1
Town Officers	4
Treasurers	12
Tube Makers	15
Turners	69
Umbrella Makers	9
Undertakers	32
Upholsterers	50
Varnishers	12
Wardens of Prison	2
Washerwomen	162
Watch Makers	35
Watchmen	209
Wax Flower Maker	1
Weighers	5
Well Diggers	11
Wheelwrights	154
Wig Makers	3
Willow Worker	1
Wire Makers	13
Wood Sawyers	39
Wool Dealers	18
Worsted Maker	1

REMARKS ON THE TABLE OF OCCUPATIONS.

The number of persons whose occupations are given in the preceding table is, 65,059. In the United States Census of 1860, the number was 62,886. In the present census, housekeepers, including women employed in household duties at home, have not been included in the tables.

The number whose occupation is given, includes a large percentage of the population. We may class the whole population as follows: —

Number, occupations given	65,059
Housekeepers, one to each family	39,208
Persons under 15 years of age	57,657
Persons of 70 years and over	5,091
Deaf and dumb, blind, insane, &c	1,293
Total	168,308

This leaves 16,657 persons in the whole population, not accounted for. The most of these are females, living at home, and persons who are incapacitated for labor.

The table of occupations is the most unsatisfactory of any in the census. It is impossible to obtain any uniformity in the manner of stating the occupations in different towns. In the instructions to the Enumerators, particular directions were given to specify, in connection with Operatives, the kind of work in which they were employed; but we find in the returns, 2,950 operatives without any specification.

Under other general terms, such as Merchants, Laborers, Mechanics, &c., many persons are included who should have been more particularly designated.

For these reasons, and many others, which injure the value of the table, and which will suggest themselves to those who examine it, I have not thought it worth while to give the table of occupations by towns; but have included the returns for the whole State in one table, with the occupations arranged in alphabetical order.

PART II.

AGRICULTURAL STATISTICS.

TABLES.

CENSUS OF RHODE ISLAND,

JUNE 1, 1865.

TABLE XXXIII. Agricultural Statistics *of the State of Rhode Island. Census of June* 1, 1865.

TOWNS AND DIVISIONS OF THE STATE.	ACRES OF LAND.				CASH VALUE.		
	Plowed. 1865	Mowing. 1865	Pasturing. 1865	Unimproved. 1865.	Of Farms including Buildings. 1865.	Of Stock. 1865.	Of Tools and Implements. 1865.
Barrington	716	968	1,481	1,123	$533,750	$38,776	$15,430
Bristol	1,136	1,959	2,273	606	911,560	69,118	27,779
Warren	316	636	521	557	161,820	14,261	5,594
Bristol County	2,168	3,563	4,275	2,286	1,607,130	122,155	48,803
Coventry	1,764	4,907	7,635	16,131	670,205	96,655	27,602
East Greenwich	641	1,792	2,522	4,315	343,435	43,276	11,005
West Greenwich	1,192	3,860	5,414	16,579	319,215	49,917	12,276
Warwick	1,945	3,561	7,880	2,419	1,237,000	125,819	39,594
Kent County	5,542	14,120	23,451	39,444	2,569,855	315,667	90,477
Jamestown	779	1,210	3,238	227	279,100	57,414	7,945
Little Compton	1,406	2,625	4,048	2,863	680,615	109,552	15,695
Middletown	1,223	2,741	2,597	174	1,288,150	118,781	23,099
Newport	242	689	1,291	100	1,026,500	39,500	11,250
New Shoreham	1,012	1,415	1,518	....	295,200	49,059	11,630
Portsmouth	2,044	3,526	4,864	926	1,192,075	136,006	25,812
Tiverton	1,134	2,607	3,070	5,292	674,447	70,541	18,295
Newport County	7,840	14,813	20,626	9,582	5,436,087	580,853	113,726
Burrillville	904	3,928	4,212	15,316	566,600	71,633	28,055
Cranston	1,862	3,764	3,949	6,609	1,455,185	158,214	50,832
Cumberland	1,054	5,229	5,674	5,897	793,300	104,876	22,441
East Providence	902	1,773	1,521	963	562,200	52,595	14,435
Foster	1,315	5,519	7,804	13,965	534,984	102,790	31,140
Glocester	1,008	4,539	5,918	14,678	529,010	83,131	16,572
Johnston	1,084	2,719	2,846	5,704	945,122	77,479	25,853
North Providence	229	1,528	1,674	1,770	1,145,150	61,079	21,858
Pawtucket	183	177	279	260	190,100	9,788	3,247
Scituate	1,901	5,242	7,315	16,328	1,571,500	143,718	73,022
Smithfield	1,754	7,247	8,327	13,351	1,416,550	169,818	48,514
Towns Prov. Co.	12,196	41,665	49,519	94,841	9,709,701	1,035,121	335,969
Providence City	108	231	117	136	1,222,000	12,030	3,985
Charlestown	1,114	2,915	7,105	6,272	286,100	48,795	9,542
Exeter	1,690	5,250	7,838	13,568	407,215	85,731	14,056
Hopkinton	794	2,999	5,209	7,298	314,100	50,296	10,463
North Kingstown	2,101	4,089	10,098	7,436	53,700	145,238	20,395
South Kingstown	2,253	4,789	8,740	7,228	903,275	119,550	29,286
Richmond	735	3,524	8,378	9,210	356,015	69,485	12,192
Westerly	1,245	3,285	7,101	3,789	1,524,064	81,567	28,233
Washington Co.	9,932	26,851	54,469	54,801	3,844,469	600,662	124,167
Whole State	37,786	101,243	152,457	201,090	24,389,242	2,666,488	717,127

TABLE XXXIII.—*Continued.*—Agricultural Statistics.

TOWNS AND DIVISIONS OF THE STATE.	TONS OF HAY.		HAY SEED.		WHEAT.		RYE.		INDIAN CORN.	
	Tons of Hay. 1864.	Tons of Hay. 1865.	Clover Seed, Pounds of. 1864.	Grass Seed, Bushels of. 1864.	Acres Sown. 1864.	Bushels Raised. 1864.	Acres Sown. 1864.	Bushels Raised. 1864.	Acres Planted. 1864.	Bushels Raised. 1864.
Barrington	874	1,015	....	20	....	....	91	881	197	5,040
Bristol	1,770	1,927	....	177	....	30	34	852	367	12,821
Warren	475	528	6	2	....	....	11	126	131	3,388
Bristol County	3,119	3,470	6	199	....	30	136	1,859	695	21,249
Coventry	3,026	3,032	65	95	....	....	108	961	707	15,708
East Greenwich	1,282	1,393	170	....	....	....	59	519	372	9,330
West Greenwich	1,684	1,704	488	170	1	5	52	325	576	9,703
Warwick	3,619	3,423	15	20	15	126	415	4,619	841	24,782
Kent County	9,611	9,552	738	285	16	131	634	6,424	2,496	59,523
Jamestown	741	971	....	128	....	....	59	995	341	10,775
Little Compton	2,080	2,622	8	178	....	....	....	....	721	27,760
Middletown	2,859	3,415	....	....	....	....	1-4	25	569	21,771
Newport	881	990	....	....	....	....	1	30	90	4,200
New Shoreham	1,375	1,540	....	...	....	..	....	....	470	13,037
Portsmouth	2,411	3,244	....	734	4	118	51	1,463	729	24,909
Tiverton	2,006	2,221	....	...	1	24	5 1-4	98	560	18,566
Newport County	12,353	15,003	8	1,040	5	142	116	2,611	3,480	121,018
Burrillville	2,323	2,399	....	....	1	10	111	1,037	382	10,552
Cranston	4,328	4,398	....	....	....	2	235	2,067	587	23,033
Cumberland	4,020	3,934	....	....	2	14	104	1,169	438	14,487
East Providence	1,572	1,641	....	....	....	....	128	1,611	260	8,209
Foster	3,065	3,278	2,635	257	2	12	69	703	711	16,495
Glocester	2,648	2,711	....	....	....	....	127	1,101	444	12,673
Johnston	2,497	2,423	46	4	3-8	8	66	738	311	9,671
North Providence	1,560	1,539	....	....	11	94	30	419	198	7,844
Pawtucket	156	167	164	15	1-4	2	33	282	77	1,950
Scituate	4,092	4,046	50	....	11	245	116	1,796	686	21,229
Smithfield	6,056	5,040	....	15	1-8	3	158	1,798	525	24,816
Towns Prov. Co.	32,317	32,176	2,895	291	28	390	1,177	12,721	4,619	150,959
Providence City.	280	260	....	....	....	....	3	42	16	370
Charlestown	1,135	1,383	80	151	....	....	53	343	537	10,440
Exeter	2,034	2,315	....	41	....	....	102	543	808	15,043
Hopkinton	1,318	1,653	120	48	....	....	52	411	479	9,406
North Kingstown	2,718	3,146	....	35	1-2	5	181	2,632	1,031	24,566
South Kingstown	2,803	3,429	780	107	....	...	14	323	1,060	30,057
Richmond	1,238	1,624	40	207	1-2	3	103	693	573	9,773
Westerly	1,639	1,883	45	...	3	52	63	559	724	14,229
Washington Co.	12,885	15,433	1,065	589	4	60	568	5,504	5,212	113,514
Whole State	70,565	75,894	4,712	2,404	53	753	2,634	29,161	16,518	466,633

TABLE XXXIII.—*Continued.*—AGRICULTURAL STATISTICS.

TOWNS AND DIVISIONS OF THE STATE.	OATS.		IRISH POTATO'S		Sweet Potatoes, Bushels of.	Barley, Bushels of.	Buckwheat, Bush. of.	Horses, June 1.	Asses and Mules, June 1.
	Acres Sown. 1864.	Bushels Raised. 1864.	Acres Planted. 1864.	Bushels Raised. 1864.	1864.	1864.	1864.	1865.	1865.
Barrington	91	1,823	108	10,694	....	374	44	159	....
Bristol	155	5,158	143	16,840	....	1,526	....	223	1
Warren	87	2,822	64	5,465	....	256	....	64	....
BRISTOL COUNTY	333	9,803	315	32,999	....	2,156	44	446	1
Coventry	138	1,712	342	35,965	....	523	153	311	....
East Greenwich	12	183	153	12,308	....	1,974	14	146	....
West Greenwich	211	2,149	262	19.035	....	186	101	181	....
Warwick	118	2,334	522	46,523	20	1,676	330	354	....
KENT COUNTY	479	6,378	1,279	113,831	20	4,359	598	992	...
Jamestown	263	6,981	18	2,162	....	1,835	....	72	....
Little Compton	547	24,270	37	4,609	38	4,357	122	260	5
Middletown	323	15,432	84	12,608	....	5,439	....	282	....
Newport	34	1,015	30	4,850	....	1,340	....	60	....
New Shoreham	326	11,776	90	12,595	....	614	...	108	...
Portsmouth	655	23,828	225	26,652	....	4,507	....	293	2
Tiverton	311	10,191	99	9,828	170	4,029	254	166	40
NEWPORT COUNTY	2,459	93,493	583	73,304	208	22,121	376	1,241	47
Burrillville	59	1,005	265	21,250	....	414	173	267	....
Cranston	31	478	498	49,860	....	1,367	20	908	8
Cumberland	13	306	248	25,757	....	2,571	1	255	2
East Providence	84	2,007	188	22,080	37	532	117	256	1
Foster	174	2,625	362	32,664	15	1,170	440	263	5
Glocester	12	134	298	27,411	....	828	25	288	2
Johnston	1	12	318	31,376	...	862	1	309	....
North Providence	16	225	158	14,327	....	651	26	209	....
Pawtucket	10	....	57	3,340	....	24	....	49	....
Scituate	30	392	661	60,391	....	1,864	9	...	...
Smithfield	55	903	513	50,454	....	4,176	49	527	1
TOWNS PROV. CO.	485	8,087	3,566	338,910	52	14,459	861	3,807	19
PROVIDENCE CITY	1	40	23	2,655	....	85	....	3,021	....
Charlestown	382	9,097	118	9,802	....	188	48	155	....
Exeter	297	4,032	348	21,930	....	411	46	224	....
Hopkinton	220	4,185	107	8,428	...	56	47	153	....
North Kingstown	183	3,072	551	42,300	2	1,981	147	366	....
South Kingstown	841	23,219	279	36,784	...	446	30	311	2
Richmond	281	4,776	239	12,180	1	33	169	188	....
Westerly	347	9,762	194	17,504	1	205	3	229	2
WASHINGTON CO.	2,551	58,143	1,836	148,928	4	3,320	490	1,626	4
WHOLE STATE	6,308	175,944	7,602	710,627	284	46,500	2,369	11,133	71

TABLE XXXIII.—*Continued.*—Agricultural Statistics.

Towns and Divisions of the State.	Sheep, June 1. 1865.	Wool, pounds of 1865.	Swine, June 1. 1865.	Neat Cattle. Milch Cows. 1865.	Working Oxen. 1865.	Other Cattle. 1865.	Value of Cattle killed or sold, year ending June 1 1865.	Butter, Pounds of, year ending June 1. 1865.	Cheese, Pounds of, year ending June 1. 1865.
Barrington	29	88	284	216	56	95	$3,870	11,112	65
Bristol	1,111	2,082	438	391	106	170	10,852	15,624	65
Warren	84	345	161	112	40	34	3,300	4,750	645
Bristol County	1,224	2,515	883	719	202	299	18,022	31,486	775
Coventry	605	1,281	741	762	236	334	19,346	33,366	15,581
East Greenwich	815	1,419	299	354	128	102	17,460	21,255	4,210
West Greenwich	864	1,988	325	411	207	167	2,872	15,847	11,987
Warwick	892	600	799	787	210	224	27,438	39,200	5,609
Kent County	3,176	5,288	2,164	2,314	781	827	67,116	109,668	37,387
Jamestown	1,990	7,210	344	356	80	85	7,105	29,950	1,030
Little Compton	1,988	7,304	541	561	283	448	55,702	37,254	5,850
Middletown	3,547	16,693	483	576	269	256	68,777	30,052	672
Newport	1,165	4,615	128	171	79	57	8,290	2,972	......
New Shoreham	1,889	5,843	419	276	309	351	8,410	15,245	10,875
Portsmouth	3,593	13,423	876	674	346	226	32,284	38,282	325
Tiverton	1,337	4,213	448	448	255	416	28,570	17,143	2,833
Newport County	15,509	59,301	3,239	3,062	1,621	1,839	209,138	170,898	21,585
Burrillville	351	960	392	583	238	226	30,927	23,985	2,300
Cranston	14	......	991	792	157	274	66,805	22,890	700
Cumberland	124	414	623	829	200	501	19,892	44,019	1,840
East Providence	45	174	408	446	50	125	3,690	7,772	500
Foster	1,435	3,518	550	785	257	445	35,346	42,508	24,520
Glocester	486	970	552	758	154	307	24,301	34,427	6,745
Johnston	82	226	486	604	81	184	14,779	16,794	35
North Providence	4	......	380	372	44	87	6,678	2,092	......
Pawtucket	4	13	73	83	2	24	1,090	2,147	......
Scituate	380	1,031	812	979	260	265	45,494	70,285	3,860
Smithfield	130	473	746	1,326	313	409	21,506	54,905	1,170
Towns Prov. Co.	3,061	7,779	6,013	7,557	1,765	2,847	270,508	321,824	41,670
Providence City	......	......	495	324	18	9	1,140	1,850	......
Charlestown	1,856	4,006	245	350	154	340	16,863	23,934	7,100
Exeter	2,557	5,355	368	494	325	380	5,091	28,788	2,083
Hopkinton	1,265	3,210	233	347	138	192	36,646	27,181	6,609
North Kingstown	4,271	9,237	865	733	328	249	76,446	53,135	1,450
South Kingstown	3,863	9,677	883	697	455	443	19,053	38,572	600
Richmond	2,733	5,626	381	375	159	280	23,974	28,466	10,646
Westerly	1,202	2,787	500	546	187	438	14,466	21,664	6,225
Washington Co.	17,747	39,898	3,475	3,542	1,746	2,322	192,539	221,740	34,713
Whole State	40,717	114,781	16,269	17,518	6,133	8,143	758,463	857,466	136,130

TABLE XXXIII.—*Continued.*—Agricultural Statistics.

Towns and Divisions of the State.	Milk, Gallons of, sold, year ending June 1. 1865.	Tobacco, Pounds of. 1864.	Wine, Gallons of. 1864.	Value of Orchard Products. 1864	Value of products of Market Gardens. 1864.	Onions, Bushels of. 1864.	Carrots, Bushels of. 1864.
Barrington	4,072	400	15	$487	$34,112	18,085	16,752
Bristol	42,767	250	22	542	3,337	71,734	47,549
Warren	1,238	680	..	388	1,375	3,320	1,784
Bristol County	48,077	1,330	37	1,417	38,824	93,139	66,085
Coventry	42,994	2,807	90	5,265	12,405	719	208
East Greenwich	16,032	1,745	2,115	2,100	3,632	969	1,060
West Greenwich	34,244	1,054	....	2,705	4,023	437	167
Warwick	118,710	6,698	354	8,325	43,466	4,818	2,295
Kent County	211,980	12,304	2,559	18,395	63,526	6,943	3,730
Jamestown	571	7	8	394	758	763	54
Little Compton	6,600	21	....	183	319	520	104
Middletown	85,123	20	....	663	3,437	6,858	4,159
Newport	54,980	....	....	....	5,100	1,665	330
New Shoreham	40,160	...	...	....	3,564	6,685	910
Portsmouth	22,507	70	....	600	6,102	10,996	2,441
Tiverton	4,370	125	17	4,594	5,475	4,458	394
Newport County	214,311	243	25	6,434	24,755	31,945	8,392
Burrillville	11,850	....	....	5,581	13,956	15	....
Cranston	306,102	....	11	15,065	72,217	947	414
Cumberland	126,062	72	5	13,678	710	58	223
East Providence	102,630	320	30	3,580	14,760	2,154	1,545
Foster	68,393	3,956	5	6,313	9,066	103	6
Glocester	13,850	1,716	63	7,863	4,000	79	152
Johnston	213,959	604	27	11,756	20,242	215	380
North Providence	137,722	75	67	6,704	13,809	445	352
Pawtucket	9,595	....	....	219	475	7	44
Scituate	300,115	2,785	294	18,004	661	543	172
Smithfield	196,558	1,080	16	14,735	9,398	1,583	1,096
Towns Prov. Co.	1,486,836	10,608	518	103,498	159,294	6,149	4,384
Providence City	16,630	....	....	921	4,385	750	225
Charlestown	1,401	1,466	54	626	3,811	294	116
Exeter	114,985	857	10	2,983	7,259	314	298
Hopkinton	842	740	6	1,251	262	73	4
North Kingstown	56,855	385	58	4,468	10,167	7,904	5,093
South Kingstown	1,467	520	....	1,300	9,889	4,409	1,552
Richmond	63,932	1,265	123	1,891	8,813	19	....
Westerly	5,956	3,830	11	401	10,846	664	141
Washington Co.	245,438	9,063	262	12,920	51,047	13,677	7,204
Whole State	2,223,272	33,548	3,401	$143,585	$341,831	152,603	90,020

TABLE XXXIII.—*Continued.*—AGRICULTURAL STATISTICS.

TOWNS AND DIVISIONS OF THE STATE.	Beets, Bushels of. 1864.	French Turnips, Bushels of. 1864.	Flat Turnips, Bushels of. 1864.	Green Peas, Bushels of. 1865.	String Beans, Bushels of. 1865.	Garden Seeds, Value of. 1864.	Strawberries, Quarts of. 1865.
Barrington.........	1,854	4,189	1,759	174	22	$674	1,570
Bristol.............	2,280	11,645	1,340	211	120	7,246	986
Warren............	241	2,533	371	164	79	112	485
BRISTOL COUNTY...	4,825	18,367	3,470	549	221	8,032	3,041
Coventry...........	557	4,105	1,374	834	966	....	1,197
East Greenwich.....	358	1,649	656	221	310	67	395
West Greenwich....	123	2,100	439	13	41	....	178
Warwick...........	2,545	9,788	7,269	3,387	1,351	648	8,675
KENT COUNTY......	3,583	17,642	9,738	4,455	2,668	715	10,445
Jamestown.........	105	2,881	53	....	....	76	132
Little Compton.....	128	14,153	680	....	....	....	800
Middletown	2,188	8,186	4,064	173	130	164	1,595
Newport...........	2,610	1,525	810	100	50	50	......
New Shoreham.....	....	600	....	....	....	....	......
Portsmouth	744	6,044	6,440	741	628	1,999	15,380
Tiverton...........	1,547	8,232	2,948	527	125	401	400
NEWPORT COUNTY..	7,322	41,621	14,995	1,541	933	2,690	18,307
Burrillville.........	....	1,486	713	....	....	....	478
Cranston...........	1,530	6,272	9,355	3,018	804	42	3,377
Cumberland........	59	2,092	1,023	196	70	....	......
East Providence....	1,114	4,945	3,950	320	255	722	1,580
Foster..............	108	3,089	2,615	20	1	....	283
Glocester	213	1,952	1,252	10	420	....	342
Johnston...........	1,841	2,520	2,875	713	288	207	4,959
North Providence...	920	2,635	3,262	1,025	227	....	10,415
Pawtucket..........	5	151	1,234	58	46	....	120
Scituate...........	540	3,814	3,010	783	831	3	194
Smithfield..........	628	4,374	3,304	914	314	55	2,805
TOWNS PROV. CO...	6,958	33,330	32,653	7,057	3,256	1,029	24,553
PROVIDENCE CITY..	950	99	475	62	28	....	700
Charlestown........	299	1,636	142	....	....	....	142
Exeter..............	107	2,163	337	....	....	....	50
Hopkinton.........	43	2,182	609	....	62	4	2,808
North Kingstown...	527	5,632	960	152	....	396	2,234
South Kingstown...	1,282	9,330	101	....	254	41	1,511
Richmond..........	7	2,184	294	....	....	1	747
Westerly...........	197	4,286	234	261	209	9	1,954
WASHINGTON CO...	2,462	27,413	2,677	413	525	451	9,446
WHOLE STATE.....	25,600	138,472	64,008	14,077	7,631	$12,917	66,492

TABLE XXXIII.—*Concluded.*—Agricultural Statistics.

Towns and Divisions of the State.	Eggs and Poultry; Value produced year ending June. 1865. 1865.	Poultry; Value on hand June 1. 1865.	Honey, Pounds of. 1864	Hops, Pounds of. 1864.	Flax, Pounds raised. 1864.	Peat, Cords Dug. 1864.	Fertilizers and Manures, Value bought. 1865.
Barrington.........	$3,052	$1,405	115	....	....	1,192	$3,477
Bristol.............	5,915	2,880	159	18	...	....	13,244
Warren...........	2,278	1,085	515	....	....	...	1,341
Bristol County...	11,245	5,370	789	18	....	1,192	18,062
Coventry...........	11,462	4,870	674	51	15	9	1,512
East Greenwich.....	5,115	4,081	381	28	....	172	246
West Greenwich....	6,538	1,807	318	18	....	2	250
Warwick.	15,368	6,667	963	163	100	1,623	3,527
Kent County......	38,483	17,425	2,336	260	115	1,806	5,535
Jamestown.........	4,955	2,495	....	....	....	....	87
Little Compton.....	19,888	6,944	20	....	....	....	1,155
Middletown........	8,880	4,698	384	...	....	....	8,304
Newport.....	1,540	730	....	....	...	....	1,835
New Shoreham.....	6,643	3,389	.. .	....	....	1,506	....
Portsmouth	13,965	6,877	130	....	....	....	9,201
Tiverton..........	11,075	3,929	498	6	1	....	829
Newport County..	66,946	29,062	1,032	6	1	1,506	21,411
Burrillville.........	5,497	2,708	330	....	....	....	1,047
Cranston...........	20,098	7,134	1,070	....	....	1,535	11,254
Cumberland........	10,448	4,469	692	15	....	246	1,114
East Providence....	4,871	2,551	360	....	....	50	7,718
Foster.............	11,990	7,470	2,665	3	....	....	3,881
Glocester...........	7,248	3,092	1,186	5	....	...	1,333
Johnston...........	9,133	2,314	318	111	100	....	6,035
North Providence...	2,354	1,700	144	12	...	436	5,030
Pawtucket.........	595	820	20	52	....	32	379
Scituate............	21,707	5,516	650	70	....	10	3,735
Smithfield..........	12,459	6,222	910	127	....	232	4,705
Towns Prov. Co...	106,400	43,996	8,345	395	100	2,541	46,231
Providence City..	510	235	25	....	....	....	946
Charlestown........	10,699	2,941	340	....	....	163	1,490
Exeter.............	11,726	3,693	240	....	15	...	636
Hopkinton.........	6,580	1,862	210	....	....	12	1,414
North Kingstown...	20,810	5,579	591	....	....	2,167	3,446
South Kingstown...	19,364	12,629	403	....	....	130	7,054
Richmond..........	7,632	2,441	364	....	....	....	2,212
Westerly..........	11,399	3,954	155	....	14	5	2,782
Washington Co....	88,210	33,099	2,303	....	29	2,477	19,034
Whole State.....	$311,794	$129,187	14,830	679	245	9,522	$111,219

TABLE XXXIV. Agricultural Statistics.—*Showing the number and size of the Farms in each town and county in Rhode Island.*

TOWNS AND DIVISIONS OF THE STATE.	Whole No. of Farms.	1 acre and under 3.	3 and under 10.	10 and under 20.	20 and under 50.	50 and under 100.	100 and under 200.	200 and under 300.	300 and under 400.	400 and under 500.	500 and under 1000.	1000 and over.
Barrington	117	17	19	28	24	22	6	....	...	...	1	..
Bristol	129	10	31	20	24	22	19	2	1	...	...	..
Warren	63	2	6	21	20	13	1	....	...	...	...	..
Bristol County	309	29	56	69	68	57	26	2	1	...	1	..
Coventry	308	1	20	18	61	99	70	27	8	1	2	1
East Greenwich	119	1	3	9	29	42	32	2	1	...	...	..
West Greenwich	207	....	4	5	21	48	91	28	6	3	1	..
Warwick	174	....	7	19	42	56	30	13	6	...	1	..
Kent County	808	2	34	51	153	245	223	70	21	4	4	1
Jamestown	53	4	4	2	10	13	12	5	2	1	...	..
Little Compton	217	4	18	35	82	55	22	....	1	...	...	..
Middletown	140	....	13	24	51	37	13	2	...	...	...	..
Newport	29	1	2	1	10	9	3	....	3	...	...	..
New Shoreham	124	1	10	42	51	13	4	3	...	...	...	..
Portsmouth	183	4	22	22	60	42	23	4	2	1	3	..
Tiverton	452	12	65	81	134	86	57	10	3	...	4	..
Newport County	1,198	26	134	207	398	255	134	24	11	2	7	..
Burrillville	214	...	3	11	41	88	53	9	5	3	...	1
Cranston	204	9	20	23	58	48	34	7	1	1	...	3
Cumberland	246	...	11	20	76	76	56	3	1	2	1	..
East Providence	119	....	16	29	39	26	6	3	...	...	...	..
Foster	311	5	5	5	59	119	100	14	2	2	...	..
Glocester	279	...	13	12	49	111	72	15	4	...	3	..
Johnston	210	....	25	26	70	48	34	5	2	...	...	..
North Providence	179	11	48	31	47	31	10	1	...	...	...	..
Pawtucket	47	2	13	19	9	3	1	...	...	...	...	..
Scituate	385	19	27	32	85	109	81	22	6	2	2	..
Smithfield	392	4	20	41	106	116	83	16	1	1	4	..
Towns Prov. Co.	2,586	50	201	249	639	775	530	95	22	11	10	4
Providence City	15	1	2	4	1	6	1	....	...	...	...	..
Charlestown	143	5	4	9	16	48	46	13	...	...	1	1
Exeter	241	1	5	5	35	70	94	22	6	3	...	..
Hopkinton	150	1	2	6	21	43	66	7	4	...	...	..
North Kingstown	282	4	11	32	63	83	68	16	5	...	...	..
South Kingstown	364	23	50	35	51	69	93	28	6	3	5	1
Richmond	168	19	5	5	20	35	54	18	6	4	2	..
Westerly	222	45	34	24	28	29	41	15	4	2	...	..
Washington Co.	1,570	98	111	116	234	377	462	119	31	12	8	2
Whole State*	6,486	206	538	696	1,493	1,715	1,376	310	86	29	30	7

* See note on next page.

NOTE.— The preceding table shows the number of farms reported in the State. The number and size of the farms of 500 acres and over, included in the table, are as follows:

Barrington, one farm, 505 acres.

Coventry, one farm, 720 acres; one, 990; one, 1,040.

West Greenwich, one farm, 787 acres.

Warwick, one farm, 500 acres.

Portsmouth, one farm, 600 acres; one, 500; one, 541 acres.

Tiverton, two farms, 557 acres each; two, 504 acres each.

Burrillville, one farm, 4,039 acres.

Cranston, one farm, 1,040 acres; one, 1,060; one, 1,500 acres.

Cumberland, one farm, 560 acres.

Glocester, one farm, 595 acres; one, 520; one, 550 acres.

Scituate, one farm, 600 acres; one, 520 acres.

Smithfield, one farm, 940 acres; one, 755; one, 922; one, 602 acres.

Charlestown, one farm, 645 acres; one, 3,275 acres.

South Kingstown, one farm, 545 acres; one, 592; one, 546; one, 515; one, 524; one, 1,922 acres.

Richmond, one farm, 554 acres; one, 506 acres.

Whole number, 37.

ADDITIONAL AGRICULTURAL STATISTICS.

An attempt was made to obtain some items of information connected with the Agricultural interests of the State, in addition to those included in the regular agricultural blanks. The result is the following statistics, which, from the nature of the case, are imperfect. The inquiries were not made in all the towns, and in other towns the statistics were not fully obtained. The items may, however, be of sufficient interest to warrant their publication, and they are given as reported.

DRY BEANS.

The following towns make returns of Dry Beans, for the year 1864, as follows:—

	Bushels.		Bushels.
Barrington	200	Foster	301
Coventry	684	Glocester	231
East Greenwich	96	Johnston	275
West Greenwich	939	Scituate	634
Warwick	830	Smithfield	783
Jamestown	29	Exeter	427
Tiverton	121	North Kingstown	541
Burrillville	394	South Kingstown	672
Cranston	246	Richmond	289
Cumberland	52		
Total			7,244

TIMBER AND WOOD.

Some towns report the number of feet of timber, others only the value; some report the number of cords of wood, others the value only, as follows, for the year ending June, 1865:

TOWNS.	TIMBER.		WOOD.	
	Feet.	Dollars.	Cords.	Dollars.
Barrington	600	......	100	......
Coventry	25,000	......	7,837	......
East Greenwich	9,800	......	2,226	......
West Greenwich	......	......	7,962	......
Warwick	150,000	......	2,005	......
Tiverton	......	......	1,097	......
Burrillville	......	......	20,000	......
Cranston	......	100	......	2,666
Cumberland	......	......	50	......
Foster	......	5,433	......	18,307
Glocester	......	......	2,900	......
Johnston	......	......	3,462	......
Scituate	202,950	......	6,674	......
Charlestown	......	......	......	3,724
Hopkinton	......	100	......	15,348
North Kingstown	......	1,955	......	8,632
South Kingstown	......	2,881	......	3,648
Richmond	......	......	......	13,182
Westerly	......	1,809	......	13,656
Totals	388,350	12,278	54,313	80,808

CRANBERRIES.

The following towns report Cranberries gathered in 1864, as follows:—

	Bushels.		Bushels.
East Greenwich	262	Exeter	145
West Greenwich	337	Hopkinton	26
Burrillville	1000	North Kingstown	75
Glocester	33	Richmond	326
Johnston	323	Westerly	221
Smithfield	537		
Total			3,285

STRAW.

A few towns report Straw in 1864, as follows:—

	Tons.		Dollars.
Jamestown	205	Cranston	855
Tiverton	253	Cumberland	184
Charlestown	217	Foster	1,208
Hopkinton	140	Exeter	2,600
South Kingstown	533	North Kingstown	2,468
Richmond	149	Westerly	517
Total	1,497	Total	7,832

Tiverton reports 500 tons of Husks.

BERRIES.

The following towns report Berries gathered, as follows:—

WHORTLEBERRIES.

	Quarts.		Quarts.
Glocester	33,600	North Kingstown	25,808
Charlestown	15,360	Richmond	5,744
Exeter	19,200	Westerly	544
Hopkinton	2,304		
Total			102,560

Bristol reports Eighteen Dollars worth of Gooseberries.

Jamestown reports 72 bushels of Blackberries.

North Providence reports 221 quarts of Raspberries.

MISCELLANEOUS.

Cabbages.—Bristol reports 350 dollars worth, and Smithfield 1,375 dollars worth.

Hemlock Bark.—Glocester reports 22 cords of hemlock bark..

Grapes.—North Providence reports 5 bushels of grapes, and East Providence 600 pounds Exotic grapes.

Tomatoes.—North Providence reports 1,200 bushels of tomatoes.

Bees.—Foster reports 103 swarms of bees.

Pork.—Johnston reports 104,255 pounds, and Little Compton reports 21,833 dollars worth of Pork.

Lambs.—Little Compton reports 5,962 dollars worth of lambs.

Cream.—Smithfield reports 601 dollars worth of cream.

Peat.—The 1,506 cords of Peat, returned in the tables for New Shoreham, were estimated to be worth 4,134 dollars.

Flax.—In the whole State, there were reported 2 1-4 acres sown, in 1864, and one-twentieth of an acre, in 1865.

PART III.

FISHERIES AND SHORE STATISTICS.

TABLES.

CENSUS OF RHODE ISLAND,

JUNE 1, 1865.

TABLE XXXV. FISHERIES AND SHORE STATISTICS.—*Showing the Statistics in Rhode Island, for the year ending June* 1, 1865.

TOWNS.	Salt Marsh.	SALT HAY.			SEA DRIFT.		
	Acres.	Tons.	Average Value per Ton.	Total Value.	Cords.	Average Value per Cord.	Total Value.
Barrington	271	231	$12.03	$2,785	1,285	$1.58	$2,036
Bristol	157	126	9.14	1,152	1,502	2.01	3,029
Warren	69	28	5.10	143	538	2.50	1,349
East Greenwich	7	13	11.36	142	5	.25	1
Warwick	161	167	11.11	1,856	6,134	1.00	6,134
Jamestown	127	80	3.79	304	2,123	1.22	2,610
Little Compton	130	11	10.00	110	6,775	.49	3,340
Middletown	317	34	10.23	348	1,915	1.81	3,475
Newport	....	....	....	....	1,987	1.74	3,461
New Shoreham	....	....	....	....	3,220	1.03	3,320
Portsmouth	333	232	7.06	1,638	2,157	1.13	2,448
Tiverton	565	224	7.91	1,773	190	1.22	231
Cranston	....	....	....	....	....	....	....
East Providence	32	32	11.12	356	568	1.49	841
PROVIDENCE CITY	4	3	5.00	15	102	3.00	306
Charlestown	315	149	6.15	917	152	2.70	410
North Kingstown	304	276	8.79	2,426	2,702	1.23	3,324
South Kingstown	534	425	9.41	3,999	2,188	.56	1,225
Westerly	205	85	6.83	581	603	.90	543

RECAPITULATION.

COUNTIES AND STATE.	Salt Marsh.	SALT HAY.			SEA DRIFT.		
	Acres.	Tons.	Average value per Ton.	Total Value.	Cords.	Average value per Cord.	Total Value.
BRISTOL COUNTY	497	385	$10.59	$4,080	3,325	$1.92	$6,414
KENT COUNTY	168	180	11.13	1,998	6,139	99	6,135
NEWPORT COUNTY	1,472	581	7.18	4,173	18,367	1.02	18,885
TOWNS PROVIDENCE CO.	32	32	11.12	356	568	1.49	841
PROVIDENCE CITY	4	3	5.00	15	102	3.00	306
WASHINGTON COUNTY	1,358	935	8.47	7,923	5,645	.97	5,502
WHOLE STATE	3,531	2,116	8,76	18,545	34,146	1.11	38,083

TABLE XXXV.—*Continued.* FISHERIES AND SHORE STATISTICS.

TOWNS.	FISH SEINED FOR MANURE.			FISH CAUGHT FOR FOOD.		
	Barrels.	Average value per Barrel.	Total value.	Pounds.	Average value per Pound.	Total value.
Barrington	....	$	$......	7,510	.06 cts.	$475
Bristol	330	.75	248	500	.04	20
Warren	7,200	.53	3,830	2,000	.10	200
East Greenwich	250	.20	50	95,075	.05 71-100	5,435
Warwick	9,640	1.00	9,640	42,590	.05 54-100	2,362
Jamestown	282	.22 8-10	64	10,845	.03 19-20	429
Little Compton	2,283	.60	1,370	309,900	.03 3-100	9,388
Middletown	....	....	....	....	....	....
Newport	....	....	...	627,440	.06 9-25	39,937
New Shoreham	....	....	....	606,000	.04 83-100	29,300
Portsmouth	58,000	.82 8-10	48,000	320,000	.04	12,800
Tiverton	73,916	.83 4-10	61,610	41,300	.03 8-10	1,584
Cranston	....	....	....	5,000	.07	350
East Providence	1,007	.39 7-10	398	10,700	.05 68-100	608
Providence City	1,000	.25	250	26,000	.06 68-100	1,738
Charlestown	230	.50	115	136,250	.05	6,822
North Kingstown	....	....	....	79,000	.01	800
South Kingstown	280	1.46 4-10	410	135,750	.06 22-100	8,452
Westerly	50	1.00	50	6,500	.06 06-100	394

RECAPITULATION.

COUNTIES AND STATE.	FISH SEINED FOR MANURE.			FISH CAUGHT FOR FOOD.		
	Barrels.	Average value per Barrel.	Total value.	Pounds.	Average value per Pound.	Total value.
BRISTOL COUNTY	7,530	cts.54	$ 4,078	10,010	.06 9-10	$ 695
KENT COUNTY	9,890	.98	9,690	137,665	.05 66-100	7,797
NEWPORT COUNTY	134,481	.82 6-10	111,044	1,915,485	.04 88-100	93,438
TOWNS PROVIDENCE CO	1,007	.39 7-10	398	15,700	.06 22-100	958
PROVIDENCE CITY	1,000	.25	250	26,000	.06 68-100	1,738
WASHINGTON COUNTY	560	1.02 6-10	575	357,500	.04 60-100	16,468
WHOLE STATE	154,468	.81 6-10	$126,035	2,462,360	.04 91-100	121,094

TABLE XXXV.—*Continued.* FISHERIES AND SHORE STATISTICS.

TOWNS.	SHELL FISH.				
	Clams.	Quahogs.	Scallops.	Oysters.	Total value of all Shell Fish.
	Bushels.	Bushels.	Bushels.	Bushels.	Dollars.
Barrington	962	457	....	1,001	2,313
Bristol	200	....	...	....	200
Warren	1,215	10	....	....	1,225
East Greenwich	1,415	339	6,635	13	6,313
Warwick	9,127	2,953	1,627	242	13,949
Jamestown	162	6	....	....	98
Little Compton	....	....	....	....	....
Middletown	119	....	...	....	232
Newport*	....	....	....	....	2,200
New Shoreham	....	....	....	4,200	1,680
Portsmouth	7,715	145	500	....	4,331
Tiverton	576	55	...	...	468
Cranston	200	....	....	....	200
East Providence	3,405	830	....	12,100	19,662
Providence City	404	2,966	3	50,450	54,122
Charlestown	200	....	....	1,812	1,515
North Kingstown	5,740	1,480	870	....	6,791
South Kingstown	257	....	18	3,070	3,345
Westerly	....	....	....	7	11

* Newport reports 42,900 pounds of Lobsters, from 5 to 5 1-2 cents per pound; total value. 2,200 dollars.

RECAPITULATION.

COUNTIES AND STATE.	SHELL FISH.				
	Clams.	Quahogs.	Scallops.	Oysters.	Total value of all Shell Fish.
	Bushels.	Bushels.	Bushels.	Bushels.	Dollars.
BRISTOL COUNTY	2,377	467	....	1,001	3,738
KENT COUNTY	10,542	3,292	8,262	255	20,262
NEWPORT COUNTY	8,572	206	500	4,200	9,009
TOWNS PROVIDENCE CO.	3,605	830	....	12,100	19,862
PROVIDENCE CITY	404	2,966	3	50,450	54,122
WASHINGTON COUNTY	6,197	1,480	888	4,889	11,662
WHOLE STATE	31,697	9,241	9,653	72,895	118,655

TABLE XXXV.—*Continued.* FISHERIES AND SHORE STATISTICS.

TOWNS.	RANGE OF PRICES IN EACH TOWN.									
	Salt Hay. Ton.		Sea Drift. Cord.		Fish for Manure. Barrel.		Fish for Food. Pound.		Shell Fish. Bushel.	
	From Dolls.	To Dolls.	From Dolls.	To Dolls.	From Dolls	To Dolls.	From Cts.	To Cts.	From Dolls	To Dolls
Barrington	8.00	16.00	1.00	3.00	....	....	.02	.10	.50	1.00
Bristol	6.00	12.00	2.00	2.50	....	.75	....	.04	....	1.00
Warren	3.00	8.00	1.00	5.00	.40	.75	....	.10	....	1.00
East Greenwich	8.00	15.00	...	.25	....	.20	.04	.10	.34	1.00
Warwick	8.00	12.00	....	1.00	....	1.00	.03	.08	....	1.00
Jamestown	1.50	7.00	.50	4.00	.20	.25	.03	.10	.50	1.00
Little Compton	....	10.00	.19	.50	....	.60	.01	.05	....	..
Middletown	....	....	....	....	....	....	....	....	1.00	2.00
Newport	....	....	1.00	2.00	....	....	.04	.08	....	....
New Shoreham	....	....	1.00	2.00	..	....	.02	.06	....	.40
Portsmouth	4.00	10.00	.25	2.00	.75	1.00	....	.04	.50	1.00
Tiverton	5.00	8.00	.50	4.00	.62	.86	.03	.06	.50	2.00
Cranston	....	....	....	....	....	....	.07	.07	1.00	1.00
East Providence	10.00	12.00	1.50	2.00	.35	.75	.07	.10	1.00	1.50
Providence City	....	5.00	....	3.00	....	.25	.06	.08	1.00	2.00
Charlestown	2.00	10.00	.50	5.00	...	.50	.05	.10	.75	1.25
North Kingstown	8.00	10.00	1.00	2.00	....	....	.01	.10	.75	1.00
South Kingstown	2.00	10.00	.50	2.00	1.00	2.00	.04	.10	.75	1.00
Westerly	2.00	15.00	.50	2.00	1.00	1.00	.05	.08	1.50	1.75

RECAPITULATION.

COUNTIES AND STATE.	RANGE OF PRICES IN EACH COUNTY.									
	Salt Hay. Ton.		Sea Drift. Cord		Fish for Manure. Barrel.		Fish for Food. Pound.		Shell Fish. Bushel.	
	From Dolls.	To Dolls.	From Dolls.	To Dolls.	From Cts.	To Dolls.	From Cts.	To Cts.	From Dolls	To Dolls
BRISTOL COUNTY	3.00	16.00	1.00	5.00	.40	.75	.02	.10	.50	1.00
KENT COUNTY	8.00	15.00	.25	1.00	.20	1.00	.03	.10	.34	1.00
NEWPORT COUNTY	1.50	10.00	.19	4.00	.20	1.00	.01	.10	.40	2.00
TOWNS PROVIDENCE Co	10.00	12.00	1.50	2.00	.35	.75	.07	.10	1.00	1.50
PROVIDENCE CITY	...	5.00	....	3.00	...	.25	.06	.08	1.00	2.00
WASHINGTON COUNTY	2.00	15.00	.50	5.00	.50	2.00	.01	.10	.75	1.75
WHOLE STATE	1.50	16.00	.19	5.00	.20	2.00	.01	.10	.34	2.00

An attempt was made, by the "*Rhode Island Society for the Encouragement of Domestic Industry*," to obtain the statistics of the Fisheries of the State in connection with the United States Census of 1860. Though incomplete, as was expected, sufficient was obtained to show that the fisheries furnish no inconsiderable portion of the resources of the State. In connection with the census of 1865, another attempt was made to obtain these statistics, the result of which is given in the preceding pages. The amounts are much greater than those obtained by the census of 1860; but are still less than the truth.

In the report presented to the General Assembly, (January Session, 1861,) it is said:

"While the continental shore line of Rhode Island is only 45 miles, it has 320 miles of shore washed by the ebbing and flowing tides. Five out of the thirty-two (now thirty-three,) towns that compose the State, are situated on islands. The bays embraced within the State abound with fish, many kinds of which are fitted for food, while others are only used for the manufacture of fish oil and for manures. The shores and shoals of these bays and of the extensive salt ponds near the southern coast, abound with shell-fish. Besides this, every ebbing tide leaves, on almost every portion of these shores, a rich and valuable deposit of sea-weed and drift."

The importance of these statistics is obvious.

The total value of the products of the fisheries and shore statistics, as returned by the census of 1865, was $422,412.

PART IV.

MANUFACTURES.

CENSUS OF RHODE ISLAND,

JUNE 1, 1865.

MANUFACTURES.

In obtaining the statistics of Manufactures for the State census, assurances were given that nothing should be published which would show the private business of any individual or company. But after arranging the tables by counties, it was found that they included more than one hundred single manufactures, the particulars of which would thus be shown.

To avoid this, it has been necessary to abandon the tabular form for the statistics, and to make various combinations, which will be explained hereafter.

The following shows the particulars of the various Manufactures in the whole State, for the year ending June 1, 1865, as obtained by the census.

The number and amounts of the articles manufactured are not always stated in the returns, and *it should be remembered* that, in many cases, the "value of the manufactures" includes many items which are not named among the articles manufactured.

Agricultural Implements.

Number of Manufacturers	6
Capital Stock	$8,500
Value of Raw Materials	$7,160
Plows and Cultivators made	565
Horse Rakes made	200
Hand Rakes made	3,000
Snaths made	1,000
Value of all Manufacturers	$13,200
Hands employed, males	15

Ale and Lager Beer.

Number of Manufacturers	3
Capital Stock	$22,200
Value of Raw Materials	$35,300
Ale and Lager Beer made, barrels	4,250
Value of all Manufactures	$68,700
Hands employed, males	12

ARTIFICIAL TEETH.

Number of Manufacturers	23
Capital Stock	$21,500
Value of Raw Materials	$21,800
Sets of Artificial Teeth manufactured	2,310
Value of Manufactures	$81,000
Hands employed, males	41

BASKETS.

Number of Manufacturers	8
Value of Raw Material	$12
Baskets made	2,660
Value of Manufactures	$928
Hands employed, males	8

BLACKSMITHING.

Number of Manufacturers	100
Capital Stock	$53,715
Coal used, tons	535
Iron used, tons	6,743
Steel used, lbs	7,517
Value of Raw Material	$96,900
Value of Manufactures	$212,220
Hands employed, males	213

BLANK BOOKS.

Number of Manufacturers	2
Capital Stock	$12,500
Value of Raw Materials	$22,000
Value of Manufactures	$35,000
Hands employed, males, 19; females, 12; total	31

BOBBINS AND SPOOLS.

Number of Manufacturers	10
Capital Stock	$62,800
Value of Raw Material	$40,950
Bobbins and Spools made, gross	433,161
Value of Manufactures	$106,530
Hands employed, males, 111; females, 6; total	117

BOOTS AND SHOES.

Number of Manufacturers	120
Capital Stock	$119,785
Leather used, lbs.	32,540
Value of Raw Material	$210,422
Boots and Shoes made, pairs	272,423
Value of Manufactures	$450,404
Hands employed, males, 412; females, 71; total	483

BRASS CASTINGS.

Number of Manufacturers	6
Capital Stock	$26,000
Brass used, lbs	15,000
Copper used, lbs.	64,247
Tin used, lbs.	4,000
Lead used, lbs	12,000
Value of Raw Material	$46,300
Value of Manufactures	$115,900
Hands employed, males	22

BREAD, CRACKERS, &c.

Number of Manufacturers	15
Capital Stock	$77,300
Value of Raw Materials	$358,088
Value of Manufactures	$498,500
Hands employed, males, 146; females, 6; total	152

BRICKS.

Number of Manufacturers	3
Capital Stock	$233,000
Value of Raw Material	$6,000
Bricks made	12,100,000
Value of Manufactures	$120,500
Hands employed, males	205

BRUSHES.

Number of Manufacturers	3
Capital Stock	$10,800
Bristles used, lbs.	6,750
Value of Raw Material	$6,700
Brushes made	14,000
Value of Manufactures	$16,700
Hands employed, males, 7; females, 7; total	14

FANCY GOODS, BOOK CLASPS, &c.

Number of Manufacturers	2
Capital Stock	$7,000
Brass used, lbs	6,000
Gold and Silver	$2,000
Value of Raw Materials	$19,400
Book Clasps made	126,600
Value of Manufactures	$36,000
Hands employed, males, 17; females, 14; total	31

CABINET WARE AND UPHOLSTERY.

Number of Manufacturers	14
Capital Stock	$88,000
Value of Raw Material	$83,670
Value of Manufactures	$238,970
Hands employed, males, 161; females, 19; total	180

CANDLES AND SOAP.

Number of Manufacturers	13
Capital Stock	$188,700
Tallow used, lbs	752,500
Potash used, lbs	81,600
Resin used, lbs	117 500
Caustic Soda used, lbs	22,000
Value of Raw Material	$216,550
Hard Soap made, boxes	90,924
Soft Soap made, bbls	2,358
Candles made, lbs	106,000
Value of Manufactures	$527,770
Hands employed, males, 78; females, 4; total	82

CARRIAGES AND WAGONS.

Number of Manufacturers	56
Capital Stock	$103,400
Value of Raw Materials	$83,100
Value of Manufactures	$208,319
Hands employed, males	211

CARPENTRY.

Number of Manufacturers	59
Capital Stock	$126,900
Lumber used, ft	6,002,000
Shingles used	3,030,000

Value of Raw Materials	$473,650
Buildings erected	148
Value of Manufactures	$939,550
Hands employed, males	534

CIGARS.

Number of Manufacturers	29
Capital Stock,	$52,350
Tobacco used, lbs	189,595
Value of Raw Materials	$90,597
Cigars made	8,844,970
Value of Manufactures	$208,870
Hands employed, males, 85 ; females, 94 ; total	179

COFFINS.

Number of Manufacturers	14
Capital Stock	$20,200
Lumber used, ft	28,750
Value of Raw Materials	$43,338
Coffins made	2,705
Value of Manufactures	$68,233
Hands employed, males	26

CLOTHING.

Number of Manufacturers	51
Capital Stock	$178,315
Cloth used, yds	191,856
Value of Raw Material	$470,158
Coats made	14,314
Pants made, prs	37,094
Vests made	35,533
Shirts made	6,000
Value of Manufactures	$810,357
Hands employed, males, 197 ; females, 469 ; total	666

CONFECTIONERY, ICE CREAM, &c.

Number of Manufacturers	6
Capital Stock	$7,300
Sugar used, lbs	113,000
Value of Raw Materials	$28,080
Candy made, lbs	118,000
Value of Manufactures	$41,000
Hands employed, males, 18 ; females, 6 ; total	24

COFFEE AND SPICES.

Number of Manufacturers	3
Capital Stock	$22,500
Value of Raw Materials	$65,000
Value of Manufactures	$95,000
Hands employed, males, 17 ; females, 1 ; total	18

COPPERSMITHING AND PLUMBING.

Number of Manufacturers	7
Capital Stock	$46,300
Value of Raw Materials	$87,300
Value of Manufactures	$123,600
Hands employed, males	59

COFFIN TRIMMINGS.

Number of Manufacturers	2
Capital Stock	$3,000
Brass used, tons	12
Silver used, oz	154
Acid used, carboys	82
Iron tacks, used, lbs	2,400
Value of Raw Materials	$15,010
Trimmings made, gross	23,200
Value of Manufactures	$23,775
Hands employed, males, 12 ; females, 8 ; total	20

COOPERAGE.

Number of Manufacturers	6
Capital Stock	$34,600
Hoops used	315,000
Staves used	644,189
Heads used	99,106
Value of Raw Materials	$30,000
Barrels and Casks made	64,350
Nail Kegs made	49,553
Pails and Buckets made	1,300
Value of Manufactures	$63,315
Hands employed, males	37

EDGE TOOLS.

Number of Manufacturers	5
Capital Stock	$66,400
Iron used, tons	119
Steel used, tons	52

Value of Raw Materials	$77,650
Scythes made	118,000
Sabres made	13,500
Corn Knives made	8,400
Axes made	200
Value of Manufactures	$222,200
Hands employed, males	99

CHARCOAL.

Number of Manufacturers	47
Charcoal made, bushels	580,800
Value of Manufactures	$48,680
Hands employed, males	115

BLOCKS, PUMPS AND SHIP FITTINGS.

Number of Manufacturers	2
Capital Stock	$2,500
Value of Raw Materials	$3,450
Value of Manufactures	$21,500
Hands employed, males	15

COTTON, WOOL AND FLAX MACHINERY.

Number of Manufacturers	18
Capital Stock	$543,300
Value of Raw Materials	$439,755
Value of Manufactures	$1,183,000
Hands employed, males	1,124

COTTON CLOTH.

Number of Manufacturers	74
Capital Stock	$9,884,000
Spindles used	735,274
Looms used	16,535
Raw Cotton, used, lbs	22,232,626
Value of Raw Materials	$15,347,839
Cotton Cloth made, yds	104,865,978
Value of Manufactures	$24,723,988
Hands employed, males, 4,956; females, 6,870; total	11,826

COTTON WICKING.

Number of Manufacturers	3
Capital Stock	$41,000
Spindles used	2,140

Cotton Waste used, lbs.	204,600
Value of Raw Material	$72,000
Wicking made, lbs.	188,880
Value of Manufactures	$114,300
Hands employed, males, 16; females, 22; total	38

COTTON YARN, TWINE, THREAD, &c.

Number of Manufacturers	45
Capital Stock	$1,645,800
Spindles used	89,481
Cotton used, lbs.	4,886,200
Value of Raw Materials	$4,035,820
Yarn and Twine made, lbs.	2,725,950
Spools of Cotton Thread made, doz.	1,565,000
Cotton warps made, yds.	3,875,000
Value of Manufactures	$5,598,219
Hands employed, males 630; females 874; total	1,504

CALICO PRINTING.

Number of Manufacturers	6
Capital Stock	$3,230,000
Value of Raw Materials	$19,272,973
Cotton Cloth Printed, yds.	95,814,863
Value of Manufactures	$23,551,216
Hands employed, males, 1,617; females, 259; total	1,876

DRESSES AND CLOAKS.

Number of Manufacturers	48
Capital Stock	$10,250
Value of Raw Materials	$141,900
Dresses made	8,780
Cloaks and Mantillas made	4,000
Value of Manufactures,	$196,200
Hands employed, females	181

DRUGS AND CHEMICALS.

Number of Manufacturers	4
Capital Stock	$139,500
Value of Raw Materials	$180,900
Value of Manufactures	$357,000
Hands employed, males, 126; females, 10; total	136

DYEING AND BLEACHING.

Number of Manufacturers	6
Capital Stock	$432,400
Value of Raw Materials	$255,400
Cotton Cloth Bleached and Dyed, yds	30,867,518
Value of Manufactures	$482,387
Hands employed, males, 253; females, 24; total	277

FISH OIL AND GUANO.

Number of Manufacturers	19
Capital Stock	$128,350
Fish used, bbls	124,100
Value of Raw Materials	$105,460
Oil made, bbls	5,118
Guano made, tons	2.825
Soap made, lbs	25,000
Value of Manufactures	$222,150
Hands employed, males	198

FILES.

Number of Manufacturers	3
Capital Stock	$215,000
Coal used, tons	265
Steel used, tons	225
Value of Raw Materials	$78,200
Files made	540,000
Value of Manufactures	$226,500
Hands employed, males, 126; females, 30; total	156

FIRE ARMS.

Number of Manufacturers	3
Capital Stock	$430,000
Value of Raw Materials	$680,000
Rifles and Muskets made	81,000
Cartridges made	15,000,000
Rear Sights for Muskets made	60,000
Musket Bands, sets	15,000
Value of Manufactures	$1,940,000
Hands employed	1,040

JEWELERS' TOOLS.

Number of Manufacturers	5
Capital Stock	$1,000

GAS PIPE, FIXTURES AND BURNERS.

Number of Manufacturers	6
Capital Stock	$118,000
Value of Raw Materials	$145,500
Value of Manufactures	$221,000
Hands employed, males, 84; females, 3; total	87

GAS,—ILLUMINATING.

Number of Manufacturers	5
Capital Stock	$1,067,700
Coal used, tons	10,941
Lime used, casks	1,950
Sulphate of Iron used, lbs	32,084
Value of Raw Materials	$143,864
Gas made, cubic feet	91,222,000
Coal Tar made, bbls	3,222
Coke made, bush	321,900
Value of Manufactures	$349,336
Hands employed, males	131

GRANITE WORK.

Number of Manufacturers	3
Capital Stock	$1,900
Value of Raw Materials	$1,650
Value of Manufactures	$5,000
Hands employed, males	8

GRIST MILLS.

Number of Mills	30
Capital Stock	$341,700
Grain ground, bush	624,400
Dye Woods ground, tons	500
Salt ground, bush	10,000
Hands employed, males	94

GOLD AND SILVER REFINING, AND GOLD PLATING.

Number of Manufacturers	4
Capital Stock	$12,000
Value of Raw Materials	$25,500
Value of Gold and Silver Refined	$516,000
Hands employed, males	14

HARNESSES, TRUNKS AND VALISES.

Number of Manufacturers	36
Capital Stock	$58,950
Value of Raw Materials	$94,010
Harnesses made	1,187
Valises and Travellings Bags made	32,400
Trunks made	2,600
Value of Manufactures	$222,336
Hands employed, males, 111; females, 103; total	214

HAIR CLOTH.

Number of Manufacturers	3
Capital Stock	$185,000
Looms used	585
Hair used, lbs	34,334
Cotton warp used, lbs	4,581
Value of Raw Materials	$429,118
Hair Cloth made, yds	1,271,500
Value of Manufactures	$1,091,666
Hands employed, males, 74; females, 123; total	197

HATS AND CAPS.

Number of Manufacturers	4
Capital Stock	$5,350
Value of Raw Materials	$14,700
Hats and Caps made	6,000
Value of Manufactures	$25,742
Hands employed, males, 10; females, 6; total	16

HORSE SHOES, HORSE SHOE AND CUT NAILS, CHAIN CABLE, &c.

Number of Manufacturers	8
Capital Stock	$801,450
Iron used, tons	11,960
Coal used, tons	18,159
Value of Raw Materials	$761,750
Horse Shoes, made	3,026,000
Horse Shoe Nails made, lbs	407,100
Cut Nails made, casks	80,000
Refined Iron made, tons	5,000
Chain Cable made, tons	1,000
Wire Rod made, tons	1,000
Value of Manufactures	$952,700
Hands employed, males	488

HOOP SKIRTS AND CORSETS.

Number of Manufacturers	5
Capital Stock	$18,300
Steel used, lbs	1,100
Cotton Tape and Lacing, lbs	550
Value of Raw Materials	$27,500
Hoop Skirts made	39,750
Corsets made	600
Value of Manufactures	$41,800
Hands employed, males, 2; females, 79; total	81

IRON CASTINGS.

Number of Manufacturers	12
Capital Stock	$606,000
Iron used, tons	7,780
Coal used, tons	3,959
Value of Raw Materials	$536,360
Castings made, tons	710
Stoves made	5,270
Sinks made	4,000
Butt Hinges made, doz	277,598
Assortments of Hardware made, doz	60
Value of Manufactures	$830,600
Hands employed, males, 655; females, 9; total	664

JEWELRY AND JEWELERS' FINDINGS.

Number of Manufacturers	45
Capital Stock	$261,000
Value of Raw Materials	$576,922
Value of Manufactures	$1,200,025
Hands employed, males, 606; females, 118; total	724

JEWELERS' TOOLS.

Number of Manufacturers	5
Capital Stock	$1,000
Value of Raw Materials	$1,200
Value of Manufactures	$5,000
Hands employed, males	5

LEATHER.

Number of Manufacturers	9
Capital Stock	$85,000
Value of Raw Materials	$244,405

Sheep Skins	64,400
Leather, sides	29,650
Calf Skins	5,100
Value of Manufactures	$409,000
Hands employed, males	85

LOOM PICKERS AND BELTING.

Number of Manufacturers	4
Capital Stock	$129,813
Leather used, lbs	131,000
Hides used	10,000
Rivets and Wire used, lbs	10,183
Value of Raw Materials	$265,400
Loom Pickers made, doz	21,949
Leather Belting made, ft	263,182
Lacing Leather made, doz	250
Value of Manufactures	$354,130
Hands employed, males	74

LUMBER.

Number of Manufacturers	47
Capital Stock	$58,725
Wood used, cords	2,018
Value of Raw Materials	$14,614
Boards made, ft	4,912,742
Staves manufactured	2,269,000
Shingles made	2,636,000
Value of Manufactures	$92,442
Hands employed, males	87

LIME AND CASKS.

Number of Manufacturers	3
Capital Stock	$42,000
Lime Rock used, tons	10,944
Wood used, cords	4,237
Value of Raw Materials	$56,011
Lime made, casks	29,487
Casks made	21,000
Value of Manufactures	$74,133
Hands employed, males	44

LUMBER PLANING AND BOX MAKING.

Number of Manufacturers	13
Capital Stock	$176,500

Value of Raw Materials	$160,300
Lumber planed, ft	1,050,000
Boxes made	197,500
Value of Manufactures	$290,000
Hands employed, males	93

MARBLE.

Number of Manufacturers	14
Capital Stock	$82,650
Value of Raw Material	$72,583
Grave Stones and Monuments made	5,316
Furniture Tops and Mantels made	1,075
Value of Manufactures	$168,206
Hands employed, males	153

MACHINERY.

Number of Manufacturers	22
Capital Stock	$842,000
Iron used, tons	7,624
Steel used, tons	26
Rivets used, lbs	20,000
Castings used, tons	864
Brass used, lbs	14,000
Coal used, tons	3,600
Value of Raw Materials	$604,300
Marine Engines made	14
Stationary and Portable Engines made	104
Fire Engines made	3
Printing Presses made	346
Screw Machines made	105
Sewing Machines made	10,000
Steam Boilers made	157
Value of Manufactures	$1,962,800
Hands employed, males	1,612

MILLINERY.

Number of Manufacturers	26
Capital Stock	$23,250
Value of Raw Materials	$25,200
Bonnets made	13,650
Value of Manufactures	$57,400
Hands employed, females	59

MATTRESSES.

Number of Manufacturers	2
Capital Stock	$3,600
Ticking used, yds	2,500
Palm Leaf used, tons	30
Husks and Straw used, tons	13
Excelsior used, tons	3
Value of Raw Materials	$6,000
Mattresses made	1,500
Value of Manufactures	$11,400
Hands employed, males, 3 ; females, 7 ; total	10

NEWSPAPER, BOOK AND JOB PRINTING.

Number of Manufacturers	10
Capital Stock	$213,000
Value of Raw Materials	$186,000
Newspapers printed	5,410,000
Value of Manufactures,	$421,000
Hands employed, males, 163 ; females, 10 ; total	173

PAPER BOXES, CARDS AND ENVELOPES.

Number of Manufacturers	3
Capital Stock	$11,500
Value of Raw Materials	$38,525
Boxes made	467,711
Cards cut	1,570,790
Envelopes made	500,000
Value of Manufactures	$71,063
Hands employed, males, 25 ; females, 72 ; total	97

OILS—WHALE AND SPERM, PETROLEUM, LUBRICATING AND VEGETABLE.

Number of Manufacturers	5
Capital Stock	$186,500
Crude Sperm Oil used, gals	21,194
Crude Petroleum used, gals	49,000
Value of Raw Materials	$132,000
Sperm Oil made, gals	20,000
Spermaceti made, lbs	20,000
Oil Soap made, lbs	35,000
Lubricating Oils made, bbls	1,350
Value of Manufactures	$182,000
Hands employed, males	47

One company in Providence refused all information.

PLANES.

Number of Manufacturers	2
Capital Stock	$200
Value of Raw Materials	$400
Planes made	200
Value of Manufactures	$2,000
Hands employed, males	2

PATTERNS.

Number of Manufacturers	3
Capital Stock	$900
Value of Raw Material	$1,000
Value of Manufactures	$7,500
Hands employed, males	7

PAPER COP TUBES.

Number of Manufacturers	2
Capital Stock	$300
Paper used, lbs	25,000
Value of Raw Materials	$2,450
Cop Tubes made, lbs	22,500
Value of Manufactures	$8,622
Hands employed, males, 2; females, 11; total	13

PATENT MEDICINES.

Number of Manufacturers	7
Capital Stock	$75,800
Value of Raw Materials	$150,800
Value of Manufactures	$304,600
Hands employed, males, 14; females, 17; total	31

PHOTOGRAPHS.

Number of Manufacturers	20
Capital Stock	$38,900
Value of Raw Materials	$51,300
Photographs taken	16,800
Ambrotypes and Tintypes taken	57,500
Cartes de Visite taken	222,500
Value of Manufactures	$119,000
Hands employed, males, 44; females, 29; total	73

PICTURE FRAMES.

Number of Manufacturers	4
Capital Stock	$10,300
Moulding used, ft	30,900
Glass used, boxes	220
Gold Leaf used, packs	175
Value of Raw Materials	$6,850
Picture Frames made	4,600
Value of Manufactures	$16,500
Hands employed, males	15

PYROLIGNEOUS ACID.

Number of Manufacturers	2
Capital Stock	$8,100
Wood used, cords	1,000
Value of Raw Materials	$4,800
Acid made, gals	95,000
Value of Manufactures	$20,140
Hands employed, males	8

PEARL WORKS AND SHELL COMBS.

Number of Manufacturers	2
Capital Stock,	$8,500
Pearl Shells used, lbs	12,000
Tortoise Shells used, lbs	500
Value of Raw Materials	$7,500
Buttons made, gross	7,000
Articles for Jewelry, gross	50
Handles for Table and Pocket Cutlery, gross	150
Value of Manufactures	$23,000
Hands employed, males, 20; females, 5; total	25

ROPES AND LINES.

Number of Manufacturers	4
Capital Stock	$11,200
Hemp used, tons	12
Linen and Flax used, lbs	400
Linen Yarn used, lbs	1,750
Cotton used, lbs	500
Cotton Yarn used, lbs	13,000
Value of Raw Materials	$20,500
Cotton Rope made, lbs	260
Hemp Rope made, tons	11

Cotton Lines made, doz	13,500
Linen Lines made, doz	662
Flax Picking made, lbs	184
Value of Manufactures	$30,300
Hands employed, males, 15 ; females, 2 ; total	17

RUBBER GOODS.

Number of Manufacturers	2
Capital Stock	$175,000
Value of Raw Materials	$750,000
Value of Manufactures	$944,832
Hands employed, males, 134 ; females, 147 ; total	281

SPIRAL SPRINGS, HARDWARE, &c.

Number of Manufacturers	4
Capital Stock	$254,000
Iron used, tons	2,300
Iron Wire used, tons	340
Steel used, tons	10
Value of Raw Materials	$383,500
Value of Manufactures	$654,672
Hands employed, males	271

SHIPS, YACHTS AND BOATS.

Number of Manufacturers	24
Capital Stock	$93,400
Value of Raw Materials	$102,270
Ships built	3
Boats built	258
Value of Manufactures	$230,760
Hands employed, males	142

SASHES, BLINDS AND DOORS.

Number of Manufacturers	12
Capital Stock	$69,700
Lumber used, ft.	785,000
Value of Raw Materials	$48,140
Sashes, Blinds and Doors made	8,130
Value of Manufactures	$115,500
Hands employed, males	78

SUGAR REFINING.

Number of Manufacturers	2
Capital Stock	$175,000
Molasses used, gals	175,000
Value of Raw Materials	$1,417,000
Sugar made, lbs	4,984 000
Syrup and Molasses made, bbls	13,718
Value of Manufactures	$1,550,000
Hands employed, males	115

SAIL MAKING.

Number of Manufacturers	3
Capital Stock	$1,100
Value of Raw Materials	$4,100
Awnings made	150
Canvas Bags made	200
Value of Manufactures	$10,150
Hands employed, males	8

SHORT AND KINDLING WOOD.

Number of Manufacturers	10
Capital Stock	$2,800
Wood used, cords	2,850
Value of Raw Materials	$22,700
Short and Kindling Wood made, cords	2,850
Value of Manufactures	$29,350
Hands employed, males	23

SILVER WARE.

Number of Manufacturers	3
Capital Stock	$348,000
Silver used, oz	176,000
Value of Raw Materials	$390,000
Value of Manufactures	$725,000
Hands employed, males, 296; females, 8; total	304

SATINETS, FLANNELS AND KENTUCKY JEANS.

Number of Manufacturers	32
Capital Stock	$1,373,000
Wool used, lbs	2,967,613
Shoddy used, lbs	30,000
Cotton used, lbs	1,421,813

Value of Raw Materials	$3,632,170
Machinery used, sets	130
Looms used	1,430
Satinets made, yds	4,173,841
Linseys made, yds	1,900,000
Flannels made, yds	1,954,110
Kentucky Jeans made, yds	1,385,265
Cassimeres made, yds	375,000
Value of Manufactures	$6,048,210
Hands employed, males, 1,011 ; females, 862 ; total	1,873

STUCCO WORK.

Number of Manufacturers	2
Capital Stock	$1,500
Value of Raw Materials	$1,162
Value of Manufactures	$12,100
Hands employed, males	5

SHOE AND CORSET LACINGS, BRAIDS, HOOP SKIRT TAPE, &c.

Number of Manufacturers	6
Capital Stock	$371,700
Looms used	13
Spindles used	12,800
Braiders	601
Twisters	3
Cotton used, lbs	659,700
Brass used, lbs	50,000
Coal used, tons	2,000
Value of Raw Materials	$443,650
Shoe and Corset Lacings made, gross	800,000
Braid made, balls of, doz	200,000
Lamp Wicking made, gross	150,000
Tape made, yds	2,380,400
Hoop Skirt Braid made, lbs	83,200
Value of Manufactures	$787,600
Hands employed, males, 161 ; females, 315 ; total	476

SHODDY.

Number of Manufacturers	4
Capital Stock	$4,300
Value of Raw Materials	$21,060
Shoddy made, lbs	134,000
Value of Manufactures	$33,000
Hands employed, males, 11 ; females, 3 ; total	14

STRAW GOODS.

Number of Manufacturers	2
Capital Stock	$4,000
Straw Braid used, yds	280,000
Value of Raw Materials	$4,200
Straw Hats made	14,000
Value of Manufactures	$8,500
Hands employed, males, 8; females, 40; total	48

TIN AND SHEET IRON WARE.

Number of Manufacturers	46
Capital Stock	$102,650
Tin used, boxes	1,600
Sheet Iron used, tons	58
Copper used, lbs	1,850
Zinc used, lbs	3,000
Wire used, lbs	2,000
Value of Raw Materials	$82,752
Value of Manufactures	$179,854
Hands employed, males	135

TOP ROLL COVERING.

Number of Manufacturers	3
Capital Stock	$1,600
Value of Raw Materials	$4,500
Value of Manufactures	$9,000
Hands employed, males, 4; females, 1; total	5

TOYS AND TOBACCO PIPES.

Number of Manufacturers	4
Capital Stock	$32,400
Value of Raw Materials	$12,800
Toys made, gross	4,000
Toys made, sets	1,200
Block Alphabets made, sets	300
Tobacco Pipes made, gross	12
Value of Manufactures	$38,000
Hands employed, males, 16; females, 44; total	60

WILLOW WARE.

Number of Manufacturers	2
Capital Stock	$3,100

Value of Raw Materials	$2,500
Value of Manufactures	$4,700
Hands employed, males	8

WOOD TURNING.

Number of Manufacturers	4
Capital Stock	$5,700
Value of Manufactures	$11,500
Hands employed, males	19

WOOD SCREWS.

Number of Manufacturers	2
Capital Stock	$1,370,000
Coal used, tons	3,107
Iron used, tons	3,677
Brass Wire used, tons	74
Sulphuric Acid used, carboys	1,234
Value of Raw Materials	$834,782
Wood Screws made, gross	3,652,748
Value of Manufactures	$1,460,870
Hands employed, males, 302; females, 289; total	591

WORSTED BRAID AND LACINGS.

Number of Manufacturers	5
Capital Stock	$141,000
Spindles used	2,433
Braiders used	290
Woolen Yarn used, lbs	156,800
Cotton used, lbs	40,000
Value of Raw Materials	$154,880
Braid and Lacings made, yds	9,747,000
Value of Manufactures	$232,955
Hands employed, males, 41; females, 125; total	176

WOOLEN GOODS.

Number of Manufacturers	32
Capital Stock	$3,415,000
Machinery used, sets	230
Looms used	1,302
Wool used, lbs	8,944,415
Value of Raw Materials	$6,068,177
Balmoral Skirts made	30,000
Blankets made	159,143

Cassimeres made, yds	4,310,070
Doeskins made, yds	270,000
Flannels made, yds	257,191
Shawls made	43,359
Woolen Hoods made, doz	15,000
Hosiery made, prs., doz	10,000
Value of Manufactures	$13,127,086
Hands employed, males, 2,201; females, 1,533; total	3,734

WOOLEN YARN.

Number of Manufacturers	7
Capital Stock	$297,000
Wool used, lbs	1,244,400
Spindles used	4,000
Looms used	24
Braiders and Circular Machines used	289
Machinery used, sets	21
Value of Raw Materials	$912,280
Yarn made, lbs	1,047,600
Value of Manufactures	$1,728,700
Hands employed, males, 253; females, 541; total	794

WOOL CARDING.

Number of Manufacturers	3
Capital Stock	$2,800
Wool carded, lbs	7,100
Value of Manufactures	$2,200
Hands employed, males	4

WADDING AND BATTING.

Number of Manufacturers	2
Capital Stock	$112,000
Cotton used, lbs	976,000
Value of Raw Materials	$146,400
Value of Manufactures	$220,800
Hands employed, males, 43; females, 9; total	52

WEAVERS' HARNESSES AND REEDS.

Number of Manufacturers	5
Capital Stock	$49,000
Value of Raw Material	$36,750
Harnesses made, sets	16,780

Reeds made	7,200
Value of Manufactures	$79,960
Hands employed, males, 30; females, 38; total	68

WINE,—GRAPE.

Number of Manufacturers	2
Capital Stock	$1,800
Value of Raw Materials	$1,450
Wine made, gals	2,400
Value of Manufactures	$4,000
Hands employed, males	2

WASHING AND WRINGING MACHINES AND WATER ELEVATORS.

Number of Manufacturers	2
Capital Stock	$253,000
Lumber used, feet	70,000
Iron used, tons	10
Rubber used, lbs	6,560
Value of Raw Materials	$18,300
Washing and Wringing Machines made	1,644
Water Elevators made	500
Value of Manufactures	$30,000
Hands employed, males	23

WOODEN WARE AND HARNESS HAMES.

Number of Manufacturers	2
Capital Stock	$5,800
Timber used, cords	35
Iron used, tons	6
Lead used, tons	2
Value of Raw Materials	$2,690
Hames made, prs	2,500
Value of Manufactures	$6,849
Hands employed, males	8

In addition to those enumerated in the preceding pages, we have returns of the following *nineteen* manufactures, of which there is only one of each kind reported, viz.: "Brass Lamp burners," "Coal Mining," "Corn Brooms," "Cotton Waste cleaning," "Distillery," "Flaxen Goods," "Gold Plating," "Iron fence," "Iron safes," "Lead pipe, shot, &c.," "Musical Instruments," "Paper," "Patent Blankets for Machine Printers," "Spooling Cotton Thread," "Steel type, stencils and punches," "Umbrellas and Parasols," "Vinegar," "Washing Fluid" and "Wigs."

The aggregate statistics of these nineteen manufactures are as follows:

Number of Manufacturers	19
Capital Stock	$276,000
Value of Raw Materials	$305,995
Value of Manufactures	$758,125
Hands employed, males, 204; females, 61; total	265

A few of the articles made are as follows:

Lamp burners, doz	10,000
Lamps made	2,000
Coal mined, tons	11,338
Cotton waste cleaned, lbs	470,000
Bags made	30,000
Carpeting made, yds	500
Washing fluid made, gals	500
Vinegar made, barrels	400
Lead manufactures, tons	600
Cotton Thread spooled, spools	720,000

The aggregate of the statistics of all the manufactures in the whole State for the year ending June 1, 1865, as obtained by the Census, is as follows;

Whole number of Manufacturers reported	1,459
Capital Stock invested	$32,646,603
Value of Raw Materials used	$63,861,552
Total Value of Products for the year	$103,106,395
Hands employed, males, 23,327; females, 13,666; total	36,993

A table given on the next page shows the general statistics of the manufactures reported in each town and county of the State.

TABLE XXXVI.—MANUFACTURES.—*Showing the Statistics of Manufactures in each town and city in Rhode Island, for the year ending June* 1, 1865.

Towns and Divisions of the State.	Number of Manufacturers Reported.	Capital Stock	Value of Raw Materials.	Total Value of Products.	Hands Employed.		
					Males.	Females	Total.
Barrington..........	9	$236,900	$9,045	$125,300	196	14	210
Bristol....	32	435,200	1,748,517	2,122,694	338	199	537
Warren............	28	386,880	621,529	884,689	251	302	553
BRISTOL COUNTY...	69	1,058,980	2,379,091	3,132,683	785	515	1,300
Coventry.....	28	1,026,410	1,809,862	2,682,045	600	548	1,148
East Greenwich.....	23	203,600	267,792	610,239	188	180	368
West Greenwich....	28	152,865	268,234	406,640	139	94	233
Warwick	32	1,920,800	4,554,530	6,551,128	1,560	1,422	2,982
KENT COUNTY......	111	3,303,675	6,900,418	10,250,052	2,487	2,244	4,731
Jamestown..	1	1,500	....	....	1	......	1
Little Compton.....	11	5,200	2,910	7,650	20	......	20
Middletown	2	1,000	1,250	2,800	3	1	4
Newport	81	724,700	674,950	1,383,377	468	214	682
New Shoreham.	......	....	....	....	......	......	......
Portsmouth	19	146,750	90,700	264,075	226	......	226
Tiverton...........	15	11,350	7,620	17,617	54	......	54
NEWPORT COUNTY..	129	890,500	777,430	1,675,519	772	215	987
Burrillville.........	47	966,600	2,509,317	5,268,855	881	567	1,448
Cranston...........	11	1,089,050	7,072,525	9,215,900	748	215	963
Cumberland........	71	3,078,200	4,312,012	7,449,493	1,793	1,553	3,346
East Providence....	11	61,950	139,000	298,550	95	30	125
Foster.............	14	10,450	12,950	30,000	25	.. ..	25
Glocester..........	41	162,400	225,650	354,618	115	20	135
Johnston..........	14	330,200	568,720	842,600	213	282	495
North Providence...	65	2,980,250	4,787,620	8,500,380	1,677	1,282	2,959
Pawtucket.........	26	1,465,390	2,921,016	3,986,760	538	497	1,035
Scituate...........	40	496,900	1,319,311	2,008,003	317	296	613
Smithfield..	57	3,620,300	5,296,626	9,954,799	1,949	1,778	3,727
PROV. CO. TOWNS..	397	14,261,690	29,164,747	47,909,958	8,351	6,520	14,871
PROVIDENCE CITY..	641	10,761,408	18,991,527	30,628,177	9,393	2,879	12,272
Charlestown	8	2,000	1,500	5,100	11	......	11
Exeter.............	25	75,950	78,314	166,460	55	31	86
Hopkinton	33	727,350	1,366,232	2,196,602	323	182	505
North Kingstown...	19	327,050	704,810	1,251,585	181	250	431
South Kingstown...	9	393,000	1,174,000	2,125,000	328	235	563
Richmond..........	13	415,000	773,483	1,515,259	291	255	546
Westerly	5	430,000	1,550,000	2,250,000	350	340	690
WASHINGTON CO....	112	2,370,350	5,648,339	9,510,006	1,539	1,293	2,832
WHOLE STATE.....	1,459	32,646,603	63,861,552	103,106,395	23,327	13,666	36,993

MANUFACTURES.

In the remarks upon the tables, in the Introduction of the present volume, will be found some other statistics, and comparisons relating to the manufacturing interests of the State, including a table showing the number of steam boilers and engines in the State, and their power. I regret that a more full statement of the manufactures of the State, with more minute particulars relating to them, cannot be presented; but for reasons already given on page 72, I feel compelled to omit them.

The manufacturing interests of the State are of very great importance, and the exhibit given of them in the preceding pages is much more complete than that obtained by any national census of the State. This will be seen by a comparison of a few aggregates obtained by the United States Census for the year ending June, 1860, with those obtained by the present census for the year ending June, 1865, as follows:

	U. S. Census. 1860.	State Census. 1865.
Number of manufacturers	1,191	1,459
Capital stock invested	$24,278,295	$32,646,603
Value of raw materials used	$19,858,515	$63,861,552
Value of products for the year	$40,711,298	$103,106,395
Hands employed	32,490	36,993

APPENDIX.

CENSUS OF RHODE ISLAND.

JUNE 1, 1865.

The following are the Acts of the General Assembly, under which the census of 1865 was taken :

AN ACT TO PROVIDE FOR TAKING A DECENNIAL CENSUS OF THE INHABITANTS AND VOTERS OF THE STATE.

(Passed March 17, 1865.)

It is enacted by the General Assembly as follows :

SECTION 1. There shall be taken in the several cities and towns in the year 1865, and every tenth year thereafter, a census of the inhabitants and voters, as they were on the first day of May of the same year, distinguishing in the enumeration of the inhabitants, the males and females, the color of each, the ages within decennial periods, the natives, the foreigners, naturalized voters, and the country in which the foreigners were born ; and in the enumeration of the voters of cities, the number in each ward.

SEC. 2. The census shall be taken in cities by agents appointed by the board of aldermen, and in towns by the assessors. Such agents and assessors shall be sworn to the faithful discharge of their duties, and shall make out a return of the result of said census and shall sign and make oath to the truth thereof. The board of aldermen and assessors shall, on or before the first day of July of the same year, deposit the returns in the office of the Secretary of State.

SEC. 3. The Secretary of State shall, on or before the first day of May of each year in which the census is to be taken, transmit to the clerks of the several cities and towns, printed forms for the returns required by this act. and shall annex thereto a notice that the returns must be made on or before the first day of July.

SEC. 4. If an agent or assessor wilfully neglects or refuses to perform any duty required of him by this act, he shall forfeit a sum not exceeding five hundred dollars, and if he is guilty of deceit or falsehood in the discharge of his duty, he shall forfeit a sum not exceeding two thousand dollars, or be imprisoned not exceeding one year.

AN ACT IN AMENDMENT OF AND IN ADDITION TO AN ACT TO PROVIDE FOR TAKING A DECENNIAL CENSUS OF THE INHABITANTS AND VOTERS OF THE STATE, PASSED AT THE JANUARY SESSION, 1865.

(Passed June 10, 1865.)

It is enacted by the General Assembly as follows :

SECTION 1. The time for which the census shall be taken shall be the first day of June, 1865, and every tenth year thereafter, and the returns shall be made to the Secretary of State on or before the first day of August of each year in which the census shall be taken.

SEC. 2. After the present year, the census shall be taken by agents appointed in each town by the town council, and in each city by the board of aldermen.

SEC. 3. In addition to the census of the inhabitants, the statistics of the manufactures, business, and agriculture of the State for the year ending the first day of June, 1865, and every tenth year thereafter, shall be taken in the several cities and towns of the State.

SEC. 4. The Secretary of State shall, on or before the first day of June, in each year in which the census is to be taken, transmit to the clerks of the several cities and towns, printed blanks for the returns of the statistics of manufactures, business and agriculture, and providing for such information relating to them as he, acting with the advice of the Governor, shall think necessary to be obtained.

SEC. 5. The Governor, with the Secretary of State, are hereby authorized to fix the amount of compensation to be paid to the agents and other persons employed in taking the census.

SEC. 6. The Secretary of State shall prepare, or cause to be prepared under his direction, an abstract of, and report upon the returns of population, manufactures, business and agriculture received by him, as provided for in the first and third sections of this act, which abstract and report shall be presented to the General Assembly at the next January Session after the census is taken, and he is hereby authorized to employ such assistance as may be necessary for this purpose.

SEC. 7. If any person authorized under the provisions of this act, shall wilfully neglect to make the returns required by the first, second and third sections of this act, he shall forfeit and pay a sum not exceeding one hundred dollars; and if any person shall refuse to give the information required in the first and third sections, he shall forfeit and pay a sum not exceeding one hundred dollars.

SEC. 8. The General Treasurer is hereby authorized and directed to pay, upon the order of the Governor, the compensation of the agents and persons employed in taking the census under the provisions of this act; all other expenses incurred thereunder are to be reported to this General Assembly for allowance.

SEC. 9. This act shall take effect on and after its passage.

BLANKS.

Four blanks were used in taking the census of Rhode Island in 1865 ; one each for the statistics of population, agriculture, fisheries, and manufactures.

In the preparation of the blanks, it was thought to be important to reduce their size as much as possible, without omitting any items of information which it was desirable to obtain.

Thus the blank for statistics of population, which is given on the next page, provides for more information than the similar blank used in the United States census of 1860, or in the census of Massachusetts in 1865, while it is very much smaller in size, and more convenient for use.

The blank, given on the next page, was printed on "fools cap" paper, ruled 35 lines to a page, each sheet containing space for 70 names. Its size, when folded and ready for use, was 8½x14 inches, while the United States census blank was 13x18 inches, and that of the Massachusetts census of 1865, was 15x19 inches.

The blank for agricultural statistics was printed on "fools cap" paper, and ruled for 36 farms on each sheet, with 59 questions to each farm.

The blanks for fisheries and for manufactures were printed on small sheets and bound in volumes.

Copies of all these blanks, so far as they can be represented on pages of this size, are given in the following pages.

Census of District .... *in the Town of* .... *R. I., June* 1, 1865.

1	2	3	..........Street. 4.	5			6	7	8	9	10		11	12	13	14	15			
DWELLING HOUSES.				AGE.							CANNOT Read and Write, 15 years and over.						Employment in Military or Naval Service of U. S., since 1860.			
Number in order of Visitation.	Wood, Brick, or Stone.	Families, numbered in the order of visitation.	THE NAME OF EVERY PERSON, (Man, Woman or Child,) Whose usual place of abode was in the family on the first day of June, 1865. ☞ Include as in the family those absent in the Army or Navy.	One year and over.	UNDER ONE YEAR. Mos.	Days.	SEX.	COLOR. White, Black, or Mulatto.	PLACE OF BIRTH. If in Rhode Island name the town; if elsewhere name the state or country.	PARENTAGE. American, English, German, Irish, &c.	R.	W.	OCCUPATION Of every person, (Male and Female) of 15 years of age and over.	Naturalized Voters.	ATTENDING SCHOOL. Public, Select, or Catholic.	Whether Deaf and Dumb, Blind, Insane, Idiotic, Pauper or Convict.	Now in the Army.	Now in the Navy.	Formerly in the Army.	Formerly in the Navy.

Agricultural Statistics, of the Town of ...., *R. I., Census, June* 1, 1865.

NAME	ACRES OF LAND.				CASH VALUE.			TONS OF HAY.				WHEAT.		RYE.		INDIAN CORN.		OATS.		IRISH POTATOES.									
Of Owner, Agent, or Manager of the Farm.	Plowed. 1865.	Mowing. 1865.	Pasturing. 1865.	Unimproved. 1865.	Of Farms, including Buildings. 1865.	Of Stock. 1865.	Of Tools and Implements. 1865.	1864.	1865.	Clover Seed, Pounds of. 1864.	Grass Seed, Bushels of. 1864.	Acres Sown. 1864.	Bushels Raised. 1864.	Acres Sown. 1864.	Bushels Raised. 1864.	Acres Planted. 1864.	Bushels Raised. 1864.	Acres Sown. 1864.	Bushels Raised. 1864.	Acres Planted. 1864.	Bushels Raised. 1864.	Sweet Potatoes, Bushels of. 1864.	Barley, Bushels of. 1864.	Buckwheat, Bushels of. 1864.	Horses, June 1, 1865.	Asses and Mules, June 1, 1865.	Sheep, June 1. 1865.	Wool, Pounds of. 1865.	Swine, June 1, 1865.
1	2	3	4	5	6	7	8	9	10	11	12	13	14	15	16	17	18	19	20	21	22	23	24	25	26	27	28	29	30

REMARKS,

NEAT CATTLE.																							FLAX. Acres Sown.				
Milch Cows. 1865.	Working Oxen. 1865.	Other Cattle. 1865.	Value of Cattle killed or sold, year ending June, 1865.	Butter, Pounds of. Year ending June 1, 1865.	Cheese, Pounds of. Year ending June 1, 1865.	Milk, Gallons of. Sold yr. end'g June 1, 1865.	Tobacco, Pounds of. 1864.	Wine. Gallons of. 1864.	Value of Orchard Products. 1864.	Value of Products of Market Gardens. 1864.	Onions, Bushels of. 1864.	Carrots, Bushels of. 1864.	Beets, Bushels of. 1864.	French Turnips, Bushels of. 1864.	Flat Turnips, Bushels of. 1865.	Green Peas, Bushels of. 1865.	String Beans, Bushels of. 1865.	Garden Seeds, Value of. 1864.	Strawberries, Quarts of. 1865.	Eggs and Poultry, Value produced year ending June, 1865.	Poultry, Value on hand, June 1, 1865.	Honey, Pounds of. 1864.	Hops, Pounds of. 1864.	1864.	1865.	Flax, Pounds Raised. 1864.	Peat, Cords Dug. 1864.	Fertilizers and Manures. Value bought. 1865.
31	32	33	34	35	36	37	38	39	40	41	42	43	44	45	46	47	48	49	50	51	52	53	54	55	56	57	58	59

REMARKS.—Give the amount of any other unusual crops, or any interesting facts.

CENSUS OF RHODE ISLAND,

YEAR ENDING JUNE 1, 1865.

FISHERIES AND SHORE STATISTICS.

TOWN OF ....

1. Owner of Shore Farm? ....
2. Acres of Salt Marsh? ....
3. Tons of Salt Hay? ....
   Value per ton? ....
4. Sea-drift, cords collected? ....
   Value per cord? ....
5. Fish seined for manure. Barrels? ....
   Value per barrel? ....
6. Fish seined and caught for food. Pounds? ....
   Total value of same? ....
7. Clams. Bushels of? ....
8. Quahogs. Bushels of? ....
9. Scollops. Bushels of? ....
10. Oysters. Bushels of? ....
11. Total value of all Shell Fish? ....

Remarks: ....

STATE OF RHODE ISLAND.

Town of.............................. .. ..

CENSUS JUNE 1, 1865. MANUFACTURES.

---

1. Location? .. ..
2. Kind of Manufacture? ....
3. Name of Owner or Company? ....
4. Amount of Capital Stock? $...............................
5. Kind of Power used? ....

   If Steam Power, number of Steam Engines?....No. of Boilers?....

   Total Horse-power of Engines? ....
6. *In Cotton Mills*, number of Spindles?... .. No. of Looms? ......
7. *In Woolen Mills*, number of sets of Machinery?.... No. of Looms?...
8. Amount of each kind of raw material used? ....
9. Total value of raw materials used? .. ..
10. Number or amount of *each kind* of articles manufactured? ....
11. Total value of all articles manufactured? $ ....
12. Number of Males employed? ..... Of Females? ... . Total? .....

Remarks:......................................

NOTICE.

The facts to be obtained in relation to Manufactures and Agriculture, are *for the year ending June* 1, 1865. The above blank is intended as a general guide in obtaining the facts. Of course all the questions given cannot be answered in relation to every kind of manufacture; but a few of them will be found applicable to every kind, and particular care should be given that all the questions which are applicable should be answered.

The information given is to be considered *strictly confidential*, and should be shown to no person. The statistics are to be used by the State only in the aggregates, and nothing will be published which can give information relating to the private business of any company or individual.

Under the head of "*Remarks*," note any interesting facts relating to the history, improvements, or changes in the manufacture; or any other facts that may be furnished.

CENSUS OF RHODE ISLAND,

JUNE 1, 1865.

INSTRUCTIONS.

To the Assessors of Towns and Agents of Cities:

By the Act of the General Assembly, a copy of which has been sent to you, the assessors in the several towns, and appointed agents in the cities, are required to take the census. The blanks have already been sent to your town.

Double the quantity of blanks necessary to take the census have been sent. Use what is necessary, and on the remainder a complete copy of the whole is to be made, to be returned to the Secretary of State.

In the selection of enumerators to do the work, it is of the highest importance that those persons, only, should be employed who are able to write a plain, legible hand, and who are sufficiently acquainted with the population to spell names correctly. You are requested to use particular care on this point.

☞ In most towns it will be necessary to employ more than one enumerator, and to divide the town into districts. This division should be made so that the boundaries of each district will be clearly understood, and the returns of each district should be kept separate. When a district is begun by any enumerator, let the same individual complete that district before doing anything in any other. It is desirable to ascertain the population of villages separately. In dividing your town into districts, you will therefore make such divisions as will show this fact, marking on the margin or top of the sheet. the name of the village. Where a village lies in more than one town, the agents of each town will take only that portion of the village which lies in their town. The arrangement and combination of the returns in this office, will be made to show the population of whole villages.

☞ The blanks must be filled, in all cases, with ink, and not with a pencil. You will see that good ink is used, and that the blanks are kept neatly and in good order.

☞ The enumerators should be ready to begin on the second day of June, and should keep at work, diligently, until the census is completed. For many reasons, it is desirable that the work should be completed as soon as possible, and have it done well.

☞ After the census for a town is finished, a complete copy of the whole is to be made, to return to the office of the Secretary of State. This copy should be in one hand-writing, and in writing that is particularly neat and *plain to read.* This copy must be certified to be correct, and be returned to the Secretary of State as soon as completed; certainly before the first day of August next.

To the Enumerators:

No person should undertake the duties of taking the census, unless he is able to write a neat, legible hand, and to spell correctly. If you cannot do this, you had better not begin. The writing must be with pen and ink.

☞ Each enumerator will have a single district assigned to him. Before you commence, be sure you understand exactly the boundaries of your district, and when you are done, be sure you have obtained the name and particulars of every man, woman and child who was living in your district, *at noon, on the first day of June,* 1865.

☞ You will fill out the head of each page of the blanks with the number of your district and the name of the town. You will also number each page from the beginning to the end of your district. As the pages are double, the number need be placed only on the left-hand corner of each leaf as it is turned over.

☞ At the top of the fourth column in the blanks, the word " street " is printed with a space. In the country towns there should be written here the name of the road, or village, or other name by which the locality is commonly known, in which the inhabitants live whose names are on the page.

☞ For convenient reference, the columns in the blanks are numbered at the top. The figures at the sides of the pages, and also the darker blue line across the pages, are merely for the purpose of guiding the eye, so as to keep the particulars relating to each person on the same line.

☞ By giving particular attention to the following directions, no difficulty will be found in filling the blanks correctly:

1st Column.—*Dwelling houses numbered in the order of visitation.* Under this head, give the number of the dwelling houses in the order of visitation; the first house visited to be numbered 1; the second one visited, 2; the third, 3; and so on to the last house visited in the district. Each house, having a separate entrance, is considered as one dwelling house, though it may contain one or more families. There may be several houses in a block; but if they are separated by walls, and have separate entrances, each is to be considered as one dwelling house, and numbered as such. If a house is used partly for a shop, store, office, or for other purposes, and partly for a dwelling house; it is to be numbered as a dwelling house; but where used for lodging only, it is not. Hotels, poor-houses, asylums, jails, boarding-schools, and other similar institutions, are each to be numbered as a dwelling house; but should be marked under the number as "hotel," "poor-house," &c. When a dwelling house is found, which is not occupied, put the number in the proper place, and write the word "empty" against the number, leaving the rest of the line across the page, blank.

2.—*Dwelling houses; wood, brick, or stone.* In this column, against the number of each dwelling house, write the letters "W," "B," or "S," indicating the principal material of which the house is built.

☞ The blanks for the cities of Providence and Newport are slightly different. In those cities, place the letters W, B, or S, (for wood, brick, or stone,) directly under the number of the house.

3.—*Families numbered in the order of visitation.* Under this head, give the number of each family as visited, in the same manner as the dwelling houses.

One person, living separately in a house or part of a house, and providing for himself, or herself, is to be numbered as one family; or several persons living together upon one common means of support, are one family.

The *resident* inmates of each hotel, jail, poor-house, boarding-school, &c., should be considered as one family.

4.—*Name of every person, &c.* Be sure and give the name, plainly written, of every individual, from the oldest to the youngest, who was a member of the family on the first day of June, 1865. Include, as in the family, those temporarily absent in the army or navy, at school, or college, at sea, travelling, &c., &c.

All members of the family who were living, at noon, on the first day of June, are to be included, though they may have died *after* that date; but children born *after* that date, are not to be reckoned.

Transient persons at hotels are not to be reckoned; but permanent boarders should be.

In taking the census of a family, write the names in the following order: 1. Master of the family, if any; 2. Mistress of the family, if any; 3. Children, in the order of age, beginning with the oldest; 4. Male and female servants; 5. Boarders and other persons.

5.—*Age.* If the age of the person is one year or over, give the age at the last birthday in years, in the first column under the head of "Age." If less than one year and more than one month, give the age in months, in the second column. If less than one month, give the age in days, in the third column. Take special pains to give the exact age, as nearly as possible, of each individual. Leave no blanks; but if it is impossible to get the exact age, give it as nearly as possible, and write the word "about" against the age given.

6.—*Sex.* In this column, write against the name of every person the letter M or F, meaning male or female. Always write the letter needed.

7.—*Color.* This column may be left blank for white persons; but in all cases of colored persons, write against each name the letter B, or M, or Ind., meaning black, mulatto, or Indian.

8.—*Place of Birth.* If in Rhode Island, give the town or city; if elsewhere in the United States, give the name of the State, as Mass., Conn., Maine, New York, &c.; if in other countries, give the name of the country, as England, Ireland, Scotland, Germany, Canada, Nova Scotia, &c.

9.—*Parentage.* The parentage of each individual depends upon the birthplace of his or her parents. Thus, if both parents of a person were born in the United States, the person is American; if both parents were born in Ireland, the person is Irish, &c. If the father was born in England, and the mother in the United States, the parentage should be given E. & A., &c., &c. Be sure and get the information with reference to every individual.

10.—*Cannot read and write, of* 15 *years and over.* In this column, if the individual *can* read and write, leave it blank; if he or she can read, but cannot write, marke a mark under the "W;" if he or she can neither read nor write, make a mark both under the "R" and under the "W."

11.—*Occupation.* Give the kind of occupation as far as possible, and do not use general terms, like "mechanic," and "laborer," when anything more definite can be given. If an "operative," state the kind of mill, as cotton mill, woolen mill, &c., &c.

12.—*Naturalized Voters.* Make a mark in this column against the name of every person of foreign birth, who has acquired the right to vote, by the laws of this State.

13.—*Attending School.* The object of this column is to ascertain *who have attended school during the year ending June* 1, 1865. The column is to be filled by writing against the name of each individual who has attended school, the letters "Pub.," "Se.," or "Cath.," with figures indicating the number of *months* the individual has attended school during the year. Thus, "Pub. 10," "Se. 6," "Cath. 7," mean public schools 10 months, select schools 6 months, Catholic schools 7 months.

14.—*Whether Deaf and Dumb, Blind, &c.* Whenever a person is found, of either of the classes named in this column, write against the name the words Deaf and Dumb, or Blind, or Insane, &c., as the case may be.

15.—*Employment in the Military or Naval Service of the United States since* 1860. It is expected that the census will show the name, and other particulars, of every inhabitant of the State who is now, or has been, in the army or navy of the United States, since 1860, *if they were living on the first day of June*, 1865. This may be indicated, by placing, in the proper place, in colnmn 15, the initials of the State in which they enlisted, as R. I.. Mass., Conn., N Y., &c., showing what State the person enlisted in.

☞ It is expected that special care will be taken to obtain full information relating to every individual in the State, and that there will be no blanks, or "unknown," where the facts can possibly be ascertained.

In case there are marked errors or deficiencies, which render it necessary to do the work over, no pay will be allowed for the service rendered.

☞ Any further explanations relating to the census, may be obtained by applying to Dr. Edwin M Snow, City Registrar, 27 South Main street, Providence.

JOHN R. BARTLETT,

Secretary of State.

www.ingramcontent.com/pod-product-compliance
Lightning Source LLC
LaVergne TN
LVHW050531100826
845148LV00002B/523

* 9 7 8 1 4 2 5 5 1 9 1 5 5 *